T0323795

SYNCHRONIZED CHRONOLOGY

SYNCHRONIZED CHRONOLOGY

RETHINKING MIDDLE EAST ANTIQUITY
A SIMPLE CORRECTION TO EGYPTIAN CHRONOLOGY RESOLVES THE MAJOR PROBLEMS IN BIBLICAL AND GREEK ARCHAEOLOGY

Roger Henry

Algora Publishing
New York

© 2003 by Algora Publishing.
All Rights Reserved.
www.algora.com

No portion of this book (beyond what is permitted by
Sections 107 or 108 of the United States Copyright Act of 1976)
may be reproduced by any process, stored in a retrieval system,
or transmitted in any form, or by any means, without the
express written permission of the publisher.
ISBN: 0-87586-191-1 (softcover)
ISBN: 0-87586-192-X (hardcover)

Library of Congress Cataloging-in-Publication Data: 2002014693

Henry, Roger, 1949-
    The synchronized chronology : a simple correction to Egyptian chronology resolves the major
problems in biblical and Greek archaeology / Roger Henry.
    p. cm.
    Includes bibliographical references.
    ISBN 0-87586-191-1 (pbk. : alk. paper) — ISBN 0-87586-192-X (hardcover : alk. paper)
1. Egypt—History—To 332 B.C.—Chronology. 2. Middle East—History—To 622—Chronology.
3. Chronology, Egyptian. 4. Bible—Antiquities. 5. Greece—Antiquities. I. Title.

DT83 .H54 2002
932'.002'02—dc21

                                    2002015851

Front Cover: The Pharaoh Akhnaton and Greek Pottery

Printed in the United States

TABLE of CONTENTS

List of Illustrations

Maps

PREFACE

Imagine how distorted our understanding of ancient history would be if the chronological framework around which it was built had several extra centuries added. What if the backbone of Egyptian dynasties contained duplicates? If they were far enough back in time there would be no outside reference for comparison. But if duplicates occurred while Greeks and Hebrews were recording history there would be a very predictable consequence. The archaeological remains of the pharaohs from the duplicated dynasties, those with Greek and Hebrew names, would be missing from Egypt.

At the same time, the dynasties with Greek names would be prefigured further back in time with Egyptian names. Those pharaohs would have left abundant archaeological, even monumental, remains. An entire history would be built around the writings left by these pharaohs. And just as surely the Greeks and Old Testament writers would know nothing of those.

How would the effects of this distorted history manifest on those surrounding cultures whose archaeology is cross-dated to Egypt? Greek pottery placed as funerary gifts in pharaohs' tombs locks two chronologies. But Greek history does not have the kind of rigid dating seen in the Hebrew scriptures. So the two main "victims" of faulty Egyptian chronology would be affected in dramatically different ways.

In the following pages, I assert that this is precisely what has happened. While some details of any review of antiquity are bound to be left open to question, I hope the ideas presented here will challenge those engaged in the study of these civilizations to take a fresh look at some important assumptions.

On the one hand, Greek history has been forced to accommodate a Dark Age following the Trojan War, in contradiction to what the Greeks themselves

1

believed happened. Their history indicates that Dorians moved south two generations after the war and so overcrowded eastern Greece with refugees that they had to send out colonies. Archaeologists have bullied historians into accepting a very different version: that, basically, after the war the culture collapsed and Greece was uninhabited for 500 years. Hypothetical (read "pretend") evidence has been used for so long to minimize this gap that nobody even realizes it is happening. But at least the distorted sequences of Greek history remain intact.

What happens when there is a complete rigid history paralleling Egyptian history? Which history will be trusted? Will the Old Testament Chronicles, with sequentially dated reigns of kings and judges for over 1500 years, be accepted? Or will it be assumed that disagreements with Egyptian archaeology disqualify scripture?

The battle between these two versions of history will be the subject of this work. It spans a great deal of time and territory. It is quite impossible to be an expert in all the disciplines touched by the reconstruction. And a certain amount of seemingly boring (at least to the layman) material must be included to support the theory. Those parts or chapters can be skipped, by the casual reader, without losing the story.

It took fifteen years of research before I felt qualified to undertake the project. It then took five years to write and refine the work. I can only thank my family for their patience, and my long time friend and consummate historian Vern Leming for his editorial efforts.

Table 1: The Synchronized Chronology

	Conventional			Synchronized		
Time BC	Conventional Era	Egypt	Palestine	Synchronized Era	Egypt	Palestine
2300-2000	Middle Bronze I	11th Dynasty	Pastoral & Villages			
		12th Dynasty		Middle Bronze I	11th Dynasty	Patriarchs
2000-1800	Middle Bronze IIA	13th Dynasty	Canaanite City States	Middle Bronze IIA	12th Dynasty	Abraham
						Egyptian Sojurn
1800-1550	Middle Bronze IIB-C	2nd Interm. Period			13th Dynasty	
1550-1400	Late Bronze I	18th Dynasty	Egyptian Dominance	Middle Bronze IIB	Arab (Hyksos) Dynasty	Exodus
						Conquest
1400-1200	Late Bronze IIA-B			Middle Bronze IIC		
		1300 19th Dynasty				Judges
1200-1150	Iron IA	20th Dynasty	Hebrew Conquest and Judges			
1150-1000	Iron IB	1087 21st Dynasty		Late Bronze I	Theban Dynasty	
						United Kingdom
1000-925	Iron IIA		United Monarchy			
		945 22nd Dynasty		Late Bronze II		Divided Kingdom
925-720	Iron IIB	817 23rd Dynasty	Divided Kingdom		830 Libyan Dynasty	
		720-715 24th Dynasty		Late Bronze III		
720-586	Iron IIC	751-663 25th Dynasty	Assyrian Conquest	Iron Age	Ethiopian Dynasty	Assyrian Conquest
586-525	Chaldean Empire	663-525 26th Dynasty	Babylonian Captivity		663 Tanitic Dynasty	Babylonian Captivity
		525-404 27th Dynasty		Priest Kings		
525-332	Persian Empire	404-399 28th Dynasty	2nd Common-wealth	^	525 Persian Dynasty	2nd Common-wealth
		399-380 29th Dynasty		^		
		380-343 30th Dynasty		^	2nd Tantic Dynasty	

1. WHAT'S WRONG WITH THIS CHRONOLOGY?

Biblical history is colliding with archaeology. In spite of a common belief that archaeology has supported the history of the Old Testament, there is a profound conflict between the picture of the ancient world understood by modern scholars and the early history of the Hebrews as presented in the Bible. This is not just a disagreement over when an event occurred, such as the walls of Jericho falling. The entire time of bondage in Egypt through the Exodus and Conquest is now considered just "biblical mythology." It even extends to the entire social image of Old Testament life. Instead of the Hebrews replacing the lowly Canaanites with a mature and artistic culture, archaeology understands the reverse to have occurred.

Thus, the Bible's depiction of the origin and development of the Hebrews now can only be accepted as a matter of faith, and biblical scholars are reeling in a state of denial. It is understandable that the moral authority that descends from the "historical" chronicles of the Old Testament would be of more than a minor concern to many people. This erosion of authority has been proceeding since at least the beginning of the last century. In the middle to later decades of the 19th century, the first archaeological expeditions to the Middle East exposed very early Mesopotamian cities mentioned in the Old Testament. A flush of confidence surrounded biblical history. But then the results from Egypt began to fill out a time line of history that had little in common with the Bible.

At first the response from the archaeological community was to suspend judgment until some of the more difficult conflicts could be clarified by further digging. At the same time the Bible was coming under attack on another front as a result of Darwin's studies. The most glaring form of double standard began to be applied to biblical texts. While cuneiform tablets from Mesopotamia or hieroglyphic papyri from Egypt were treated with reverential courtesy, the Old Testament was being deconstructed. Magical events in Egyptian stories, such as Ramses' changing winter into summer for a Hittite bride's wedding trip, does not create doubt in scholars that a royal wedding occurred. The same type of magical event in a biblical tale makes the entire event suspect.

THE OBJECTIVE

This work will present an alternative to the current archaeological picture. It will compare the history and chronology presented in the Bible, which will be referred to as the Synchronized Chronology, with that developed by modern archaeology, which will be referred to as the Conventional Chronology. This alternate system will cover the time from Abraham to the end of the Persian Empire. Dates BC, unless they are the same for both systems, will be shown as BCC for Conventional, and BCS for Synchronized.

The Synchronized Chronology will address a whole family of archaeological problems that cover this long stretch of time. Instead of existing independently from each other, they will be seen as emerging from a common source. Taken individually, the synchronisms examined in this work would not be strong enough to overturn accepted datings. But as an integrated whole, the reconstruction demonstrates a version of history with compelling authenticity.

The Conventional Chronology is based on Egyptian dating, which is considered reliable within a decade or so to well before the traditional time of the Exodus (1450 BCS). Although there are independent *relative* dating systems for many areas in the ancient Near East and Mediterranean (because of local variations in archaeological sequences), they are all ultimately fixed by Egyptian dates. This fact cannot be overemphasized. When Greek pottery is found in Italy, the "Helladic" dating system can date the Italian site. Helladic dates are, of course, set by Egypt since Greek pottery was found in Egyptian tombs. There may also be pottery from Crete, which would allow cross-dating to the "Minoan" scale. But it is all a circular proof since both dating systems defer to Egyptian chronology.

This book will focus on the problems in Egyptian dating, from the Exodus until the Persian Era, with some additional synchronisms further back into earlier parts of the Middle Bronze Age. It may seem a little late to start questioning something that is so pervasive in impact. But the alternative is to accept, without full examination, that biblical history is fiction.

We have immense quantities of textual material from Egypt, Assyria and Babylon, mostly in the form of disconnected chronicles or inscriptions, but nothing comparable to the Bible survived. The Old Testament is an unprecedented survival from ancient times. Technically, the Old Testament books were transcriptions of older records. They were presumably composed in very ancient times. This carries no weight with modern archaeology. Scholarship requires supporting evidence, and Conventional Chronology leaves little to contradict the conclusion that the early history of the Hebrew people was "composed" (read *invented*) during the Babylonian captivity.

Disciplines of biblical study have evolved in which the most severe deconstruction has been applied to the texts. Little respect is paid to the obvious care with which the documents were actually treated in ancient times. Errors are constantly pointed out as evidence that the texts cannot be trusted, as if the ancient copyist were not even more keenly aware of those problems — the errors were allowed to survive, due to an unwillingness to tamper with them.

In much of the Egyptian material, especially on monuments, names have been erased and written over, king lists fabricated to delete undesirable entries, and accomplishments of previous pharaohs shamelessly re-assigned. Old Testament texts, in contrast, go almost too far in self-criticism by holding Hebrew kings to unrealistic standards. The less flattering elements are included along with major events. That in itself would indicate that perhaps biblical history should be given much greater weight than mainstream archaeological works.

I see biblical history as occupying a transitional stage not unlike Greek history at the time of the discovery of Troy. At the time, Homer was considered by the scholarly world as a writer of fiction. Now there are few who would resist the idea of a war much like that which Homer described, even if the dating of that war remains uncertain.

Since other regions, with histories of their own, are dated by Egyptian chronology, any problems with Egyptian chronology would create difficulties for other peoples, and indeed they do! Many of the archaeological sites in Palestine have "equivocal" evidence for the dating of occupational strata. That term is a way of saying that the remains can sometimes be dated to alternate eras, often hundreds of years in conflict (there is an almost complete absence of textual material to provide direct references).

Anatolia, Greece, the Aegean and even Italy have a different, but related problem. Their chronologies have been forced to accommodate a "Dark Age," a lack of archaeological remains so profound (for approximately 1250 BCC to 700 BCC), that a sort of "pseudo history" has been created to cover it.

7

The Egyptian chronology on which it is based is never questioned. In fact, even Egyptian history has a "Dark Age" although I have never seen it acknowledged. The 26th Dynasty, with rulers such as Psammatichus, Necko II and Apries, made famous by Greek and Hebrew writers, presents an archaeo-logical vacuum in which the supposed ruling capital city, *Sais,* left almost nothing for the archaeologist, and certainly nothing to verify the Greek and Hebrew writers. More will be presented on that later.

This study must take us far from the hill country of Judea. As mentioned above, over a millennium and a half in the histories of many countries are involved. It is hoped that scholars in the field of archaeology will take this work seriously. I have in no sense mastered any of the fields involved in this study, and undoubtedly details of this reconstruction will be proven wrong. But that should not detract from the big picture. This book is particularly directed at the educated layman or student, in hopes that it may provide the reader with reason to more closely follow archaeological developments.

This work will draw heavily from the *Ages in Chaos* series by Immanuel Velikovsky. That series (which he considered his *magnum opus*) was never taken seriously by the scholarly world, due to the controversy that attended the earlier publication of his *Worlds in Collision.* Too bad. His "Synchronized Chronology," presented in *Ages in Chaos,* was generally overlooked. Outsiders often have a hard time breaking the barriers that academic circles use to protect scholarly protocol. Velikovsky may have had a chance if he had published *Ages in Chaos* first (it is a work of consummate scholarship); instead, it was completely ignored. There will be no attempt here to defend *Worlds in Collision,* and it is hoped that the reader will suspend whatever feelings are attached to that work. And although there is a monolithic aspect to Velikovsky's work, the unique issues related to chronology can be examined separately.

THE SOLUTION

The entire reconstruction of ancient history is based on two simple corrections to Egyptian history. The accepted sequence of dynasties of Egyptian pharaohs contains two duplications and one parallel dynasty. The list of dynasties upon which Egyptian chronology is structured has been fashioned from several incomplete (and frequently contradictory) versions of a work credited to an Egyptian named Manetho. Later chapters will examine in greater detail the evidence for a reevaluation of Manetho's list. It will be shown that the 19th and 20th Dynasties of the New Kingdom are Egyptian versions of the 26th and 30th known to historians from Hebrew and Greek sources. (And the 21st Dynasty of "Priest Kings" ran parallel with the Persian "Pharaohs.")

For reasons that seem mysterious now, Velikovsky chose to introduce only a portion of his reconstruction with the first volume of *Ages in Chaos* in 1951. It had to stand alone *without explaining the source of the chronological error.* It was not until 1973 that the next volume of the series, *Peoples of the Sea,* was published. By then two generations of mainstream scholars had so thoroughly discredited Velikovsky that the work explaining the source of the whole problem was ignored.

In years of research, I have come across only a very few references to the *Ages in Chaos* series. Little more than a sentence is wasted on what is usually a contemptuous dismissal. The authors will then go on to demonstrate that they are actually ignorant of most or all of the work, which extends through four volumes (and was intended for perhaps six). Almost fifty years have passed since the first volume of the series came out, and countless works on history and archaeology continue to be published using the Conventional Chronology. Whole libraries could be filled with these books doomed by the true line of history.

In the pages ahead, we will present a summary of the Synchronized Chronology in a single volume. Since the reconstruction affects the chronological heart of the New Kingdom, some truly dramatic synchronisms will be presented. Those who are familiar with Velikovsky's work will recognize that many of his arguments are duplicated and condensed here. My own research has demonstrated the soundness of the basic reconstruction. A whole new dimension opens when looking at familiar topics of Egyptian history.

An effort will be made to allow this work to be accessible to the non-specialist. My own exposure to the world of archaeology meant the learning of an entire new language by which specialists communicate. This language is not intentionally esoteric; every advanced discipline evolves along with new terms specific to the field. The terms are actually quite explicit and easily understood in context. To avoid weighing us down on this expedition, I have kept the footnotes to a minimum, preferring to provide a full bibliography at the end. Citations of the works on which I relied most heavily will be abbreviated, as noted in the Bibliography.

Each archaeological site is a unique assemblage of the remains of a community, or a succession of communities over time. This uniqueness is accommodated by referring to a single level as a "stratum" within a sequence of levels each deposited on top of (and after) the one below. These strata are recorded as a dig progresses. Sometimes the remains within a defined stratum will immediately indicate the time frame for that level. For example, written documents may name the king during whose reign the writing was made (this is one extreme). Other times there is a succession of strata with no written remains and it is left to experts in pottery, art or architecture to equate *relative* strata from one site with that from another in a widening matrix of interdependent sequences.

The archaeologists number the strata in successive order and keep the relative order constant as they attempt to assign absolute dates to individual levels. For this reason, each site retains the numbering system developed during excavation. Just remember that level 4 at one site, such as Megiddo, has nothing whatever to do with level 4 at another site. Sometimes the order is from the bottom up, other times from the top down.

Our examination of the Synchronized Chronology will follow the time line of the Bible from before 1800 BCS to Alexander the Great (332 BC). It will be impossible to present the revised history without comparing it to the Conventional Chronology. This is best done with charts. An overall chart is placed before Chapter 1, and more detailed charts will precede blocks of chapters pertaining to particular eras. In addition, reference will constantly be made to the Conventional Chronology where individuals and events are compared within the revised, synchronized time line.

THE KEY TO THE SYNCHRONISMS

The actual mechanism for resolving the chronological problems is to recognize that two dynasties (the 19th and 20th) are duplicated — they are listed twice by Manetho, first with Egyptian names and then with Greek names. And a third dynasty, the 21st, is actually concurrent with the Persian Era. Support for this solution will be presented, era-by-era, throughout this book.

A recently published work, *Centuries in Darkness* by Peter James, is one of those that dismiss Velikovsky with a single line. He only mentions the first of the four volumes, and never hints of an awareness of the arguments or evidence that author presented. It seems to be just a passing reference along with several others who have raised doubts concerning accepted dating. James then discusses the problems in Egyptian chronology that have created "Dark Ages" in the archaeological histories of every culture from Europe to Babylon. His arguments clearly focus the extent of the problem, and he offers a solution that (by abandoning the astronomical dating for Egypt) closes the gaps forced by the Conventional Chronology. But the solution offered by James is minimal. Two centuries, plus or minus, will bring together the end of the Bronze Age and the beginning of the Iron Age. It does provide an elegant solution to a family of problems that have divided scholars for a century, but it is really only a pseudo-solution. James is closing a 200-year gap in a chronology that has already been "fudged" at both ends. Scholars have been engaged in acts of accommodation for so long that a span of 500-600 years has been shortened to 200-250 years.

For example, the end of the Mycenaean Age in Greece marks the end of the Bronze Age. (Historians use the terms "Stone Age," "Copper Age," "Bronze Age" and "Iron Age" to compare cultures within broad eras, which are further subdivided into early, middle and late). The last Greek pottery of the Mycenaean Age is usually associated with the time of Ramses II of the 19th Egyptian Dynasty. This corresponds to about 1250 BCC. The next clearly identifiable class of pottery in Greece is called *Geometric*. It is identified with what is known as *Archaic* Greece and begins about 700 BC. In between lies a hiatus in occupational evidence for all of the Aegean called the Dark Age.

In order to minimize the problem, the beginning and end are brought together by "evidence" — evidence that does not actually exist, but is necessary to narrow the gap. The time of the Trojan War is one of the casualties of this process.

The Trojan War has come to be identified with the closing of the Mycenaean Age. The Greek warriors returned after the war to a changing world. Invading Dorians forced the relocation of Greeks living in the Peloponnese and several generations of colonization followed. Archaeologists studying Egypt have identified this with the time of Ramses III (1182-1151 BCC). He fought an army of invasion employing Aegean mercenaries, presumably the refugees of the collapsing palace economy of Mycenae. (In the final chapters of this work, Ramses III will be placed in his correct time, almost 800 years later, fighting an invasion of Persians allied with Greek mercenaries.)

The "fudging" of the length of the Dark Age is accomplished by extending the Bronze Age to cover the 20th Egyptian Dynasty of Ramses III, down to 1100 BCC, even though there is *no actual evidence for this*. At the other end of the Dark Age, Geometric pottery has been pushed back by about 200 years to 900 BCC (out of necessity rather than evidence), leaving only a 200-year void to be filled with "Protogeometric" potteries.

Since occupational remains in the form of archaeological strata have never been found for any of this (imaginary) period, no one has ever been very comfortable with this solution. Peter James goes only half way in closing the gap. In doing so he has further accommodated the problem. He brings the 20th Dynasty down to overlap with the time of Solomon, thereby offering biblical historians a chance to see the United Kingdom as a true Bronze Age reality. This may satisfy the historian, but the archaeologist knows there are still gaps in occupational strata all the way into the Persian Era.

The histories of two neighbors, Egypt and Israel, have almost no point of identifiable contact for 1000 years in the Conventional Chronology. The identification of the biblical "Shishak" with the Libyan pharaoh "Shoshenq" is the only commonly agreed upon link between the Bible and Egypt in the early Hebrew Kingdoms, and it is a link (rightly) forced to be broken by James. He proposes that Ramses III be identified with Shishak, an identity with little in the way of support. Ramses III never claimed any activity that could be identified with Shishak's conquering of territory and the sacking of Solomon's Temple. We have many duplicate inscriptions of all of Ramses' claimed exploits, and none of them fits the deeds of the biblical "Shishak."

We will see instead that there is an alternative to the Conventional Chronology that does not ignore half the problem. There is a pharaoh who fits the role played by Shishak. He not only prominently displayed the booty he sacked from Solomon's Temple, but his family's dynasty, for generations in both directions, played out roles clearly identifiable from the Bible.

We will see the Exodus, Wandering and Conquest not as a group of events impossible to fit anywhere within Egyptian history but rather as a complementary series, enriching our understanding of both cultures. We will see the entry of the Hebrews into the land of Canaan not as a drop in the cultural level throughout Palestine (the situation forced by the Conventional Chronology) but as the entry of a new and artistically forceful people. And we will see the United Kingdom of David and Solomon fitting perfectly into the mainstream of the Late Bronze Age.

When the United Kingdom divided into the kingdoms of Judah and Israel, a group of surrounding kingdoms and vassal states engaged in a unique series of interactions reflecting the changing political situation in Palestine. Assyria replaced Egypt as the dominant neighbor. According to the Conventional Chronology, Egypt remains silent through all this.

The Synchronized Chronology will bring Egypt into the mainstream of history by comparing one of the most famous collections of letters ever found by archaeologists with events described in biblical scripture. A whole diplomatic library from Tell el Amarna (the pharaoh Ahknaton's capital) will provide a powerful counterpart to the story told in Chronicles and Kings. There are some identities so compelling that even the most skeptical will be forced to weigh them against the current standard.

And finally, the last great native pharaohs of Egypt will have their histories reattached to their correct times. A richly interwoven sequence will align with the written histories of Greece and Israel.

2. FOUNDATIONS OF CONVENTIONAL CHRONOLOGY

In order to set the stage for a challenge to what is commonly accepted as Egyptian chronology, it is essential to understand how that chronology was formed. The Egyptians themselves recorded events by the reignal year of the current monarch. Although we group pharaohs into dynasties, the Egyptians did not. And while we have several fragmentary "king lists," they do not identify parallel dynasties and are inadequate to determine lengths of reigns. For that we have to hope that the inscriptions that have been unearthed cover their full reigns. This is seldom the case.

The dynastic list compiled by Manetho, an Egyptian scribe of the 2nd century BC, survives in the works of Josephus, Africanus and Eusebius. The numbered dynasties and their occupants vary between versions of the lists and in many cases contradict each other (and clear successions written on monuments). Archaeological remains have not been found for some of the dynasties. An entire dynasty from the late kingdom, the 26th, is known only from the Greek and Hebrew sources. The 31st and last dynasty is of the Ptolomies, founded by one of Alexander's generals.

The succession of dynasties has been clustered into Old, Middle and New Kingdoms (separated by "Intermediate" periods of uncertain length), which roughly correspond to the Early, Middle and Late Bronze Ages.

MANETHO

The unreliability of the Manetho dynastic record is fully acknowledged by those who used it to construct Conventional Chronology. The historians and archaeologists who contrived the version of Egyptian dating that is accepted today make almost humorous comments on the veracity of the list, and then proceed to use it anyway, linking certain astronomic observations to points in the Chronology. You might think that the data on which the astronomical calculations are based refer clearly and unambiguously to a particular pharaoh. But, for example, the actual reference (for the early 19th Dynasty) is a name that doesn't appear on any of the three versions of Manetho's lists or any archaeo-logical remains!

Scholars have constructed an Egyptian chronology built around "Sothic" cycles which provide recurring fixed reference points based on the rising of the star Sirius. A Sothic Age is a 1461-year cycle during which the calendar loses 1/4 day per year (the difference between the 365 day Egyptian calendar and the actual year of 365 1/4 days) and then the civil calendar once again agrees with the solar calendar. A Sothic Age is reckoned to have begun in the "Era of Menophre." Never mind that the Egyptians knew nothing of a "Sothic Age" or that the pharaoh Menophre cannot be positively identified; a suitable pharaoh was selected, and the rest is history.

In the 2nd century AD, Censorinus, a Roman, wrote that a Sothic Age began in 139 AD and thus the previous cycle began in 1321 BC. The year 1321 BC is the accepted date for the beginning of the reign of Ramses I, founder of the 19th Dynasty. There have been some who would prefer to place the date in the reign of his successor Seti I (the Great), Ramses II, or even Merneptah. This last pharaoh at least has a name similar to "Menophre," but if that were accepted then the dating would become difficult to reconcile with the accepted date for Ramses III of the 20th Dynasty (Ramses III had been placed at 1150 BC prior to the deciphering of the Rosetta Stone). In fact, his place in Manetho's lists is based on a vacancy in the 20th Dynasty and no other name elsewhere on the lists could be identified with his (Ramses III left his name on a great number of monuments).

Another problem with the "Era of Menophre" is that several experts insist that "Menophre" is the city of Memphis, and that the "Era" refers particularly to the city and not a pharaoh. This would render any assignment to a particular reign meaningless. One other astronomical date has been proposed for a point in the Middle Kingdom, beyond the range of this study, but it is troubled by its own set of difficulties.

Here is a summary of the process by which the timetable of the ancient world is supported:

- A Sothic period began in AD 139 (this was during the life of Claudius Ptolomy, AD 100-178, who is remembered for major astronomical and geographical works plus four volumes on astrology, yet who makes no mention of a Sothic age beginning during his reign).

• If the Egyptians used Sothic dating (and there is no evidence that they did), then the previous cycle began in 1320 BC.

• The "Era of Menophre" began a Sothic cycle.

• Menophre must be Ramses I, otherwise preconceived dating for Ramses III will not work.

• Ramses III is placed in the 20th Dynasty by vacancy.

This could go on, but the real point is that Egyptian astronomical chronology is a house of cards indeed. We will be examining the placement of Ramses III in the 19th Dynasty and even the sequence of Dynasties as currently accepted.

BIBLICAL CHRONOLOGY

When Biblical dates are first capable of cross-referencing from other reliable sources, such as the annals of the Assyrian kings, they are found to be so accurate that the exact year is often verified. Sometimes even the time of year can be identified. For the purposes of this study, biblical dating will be relied upon much further back and will be the framework for *reconstructing Egyptian chronology*. This will not be a tortured distortion of Egyptian history; in fact, that history will become far richer as familiar events and people from Egypt are found to interact with equally familiar people from the Bible. The only real damage done to the Conventional Chronology is to rid the sequence of duplicate and misplaced dynasties.

The duplicated dynasties badly corrupt the chronology. Some of these duplicates occur in the archaeological context of other countries, giving rise to conflicting dates for major historical movements. Egyptian dating *always* prevails. By matching up biblical dates with events in Egypt, we can resolve some of the following problems:

• The dates for migrations of people in Asia Minor and Europe, which are as confused as the time of the Exodus and Conquest.

• The deities of the Hindus and Persians arrive 600 years ahead of schedule with the "Mittanni" in the northern Euphrates Valley.

• The "Hittite" culture and hieroglyphic writing disappear in central Anatolia, only to reappear 300 years later in northern Syria.

• Greek migrations (forced by the Dorian invasion following the Trojan War) can only be identified by archaeological remains several hundred years later than the conventionally accepted date for the war.

- The traditional date for the foundation of Rome falls several hundred years after Aeneas must have left Troy, and Etruscan dates are similarly troubled.

Many more examples could be added. As was mentioned earlier, once the nature of the problem is noted, the evidence that highlights it becomes much easier to recognize, even predictable. When we look into the legends for an Aegean colony, it can be anticipated that the name of the founder will not be more than a few generations removed from a character in Homer; he would have to be some hero of the Trojan War in Mycenaean times.

Archaeologists have found no evidence for colonization prior to the seventh or eighth centuries BC. Some sites have been claimed to show evidence for contact in the twelfth or thirteenth century BC, based on Mycenaean pottery, but nothing in between. These sites never show even a sterile intermediate layer deposited by erosion. (Typically, such a scenario would call for, say, mud-brick houses to dissolve and cover any artifacts, until the ground is later worn away by further erosion.) Time itself seems to have stopped during the "Dark Age" that fills the occupational void. This may pass for an acceptable state of affairs occasionally, but for Italy, Greece, the Aegean and Anatolia it is the rule. The pattern is so common that one wonders why it is not questioned. Perhaps the predictability is a source of security in itself.

The Synchronized Chronology reveals a more logical progression of history. As the Middle Bronze Age gives way to the Late Bronze Age, a unique type of city-state kingdom arises. Diplomatic relationships and even the idioms of expression are shared (Conventional Chronology would repeat this order again in the Iron Age, confusing the evolutionary sequence). David and Solomon ruled in a world very much like that of the kings of Mycenaea or the pharaohs of the 18th Dynasty. In fact, it was alike because it was the same time.

The mighty 18th Dynasty, beginning the New Kingdom of Egypt, arose alongside the Judean Kingdom, and began with the same event. The end of that dynasty is experienced in Judea as the mystically preoccupied Pharaoh Akhnaton allows Israel to be swallowed by Assyria. A royal diplomatic library, the Tell El Amarna Tablets, lays the history bare. As Judea struggles with divided loyalties, Egypt and Chaldea fight over the spoils. Some of the most famous events in Egyptian history take their proper place in history, filled out with additional material from the Bible.

Egypt was never conquered by the Chaldaean Empire, but both fell to Persia. Egypt was to briefly emerge from Persian rule with the final native pharaohs of the 30th Dynasty, a short-lived reprieve before falling again. The Greeks under Alexander were hailed as liberators in 332 BC and established the last dynasty, the Ptolomies, founded by one of Alexander's generals.

THE STARTING POINT

The Book of Genesis brings the Hebrew people to Egypt for a considerable length of time. Then the actions of an oppressive pharaoh force an end to the sojourn. The revised timeline starts with the events leading up to and culminating with the Exodus. As described in the Bible, the plagues are God's punishment against the pharaoh for not allowing Moses and his people to go free. A sequence of natural disasters fails to change the pharaoh's mind until the crushing finale when pharaoh drowns in a whirlpool of water that had just allowed the Hebrews to escape.

It is little wonder that Egyptologists can find no place in accepted history for this combination of events. If the Exodus occurred anytime close to the stated 400 years before Solomon's Temple was built, it would have to be placed squarely in the middle of the powerful 18th Dynasty. Efforts to find a more suitable placement have forced a shortening of the time of the Judges, from the 400 years of the Bible to perhaps 200, allowing the Exodus to occur under the 19th Dynasty, maybe under Ramses II.

Unfortunately, the interactions with Egypt's eastern neighbors as depicted on Ramses' inscriptions are no help. And for slaves in any number to escape from the mighty Ramses seems improbable. Perhaps there was not a single large migration but rather a few families at a time in several waves, meeting up with some families that never left Palestine for Egypt in the first place.

A recently published book, which exhaustively covers the current state of archaeology in Egypt and Palestine, is forced to ask:

> Under what conditions and to what purpose did the ancestor traditions of Israel take shape? Where and when did the Exodus theme originate? Of what nature and how reliable is our evidence for the premonarchical history of the component elements of the Iron Age "Israel"? And in all our efforts to formulate the right questions, we should be wise to reject the application of the adjective "Biblical" to "history" and "archaeology."[1]

Examples of opinions similar to Redford's, if not as outspoken, can be found in many modern scholarly works. Even the *Anchor Bible* volume on archaeology is depressingly blunt. Biblical history is not taken seriously as a discipline of study.

But this is not the only opinion emerging from the academic community. J. J. Bimson (*Redating the Exodus and Conquest*) has presented a theory that the

---

1. Redford 263

Conquest occurred at the end of the Middle Bronze Age rather than the end of the Late Bronze Age. This would mean that evidence for the Hebrew occupation of Palestine is not being looked for within the proper sequence of archaeological strata. He suggests that the strongly walled cities of the hill country of Palestine were destroyed during the Middle Bronze Age. Some (like Jericho) were not reoccupied for many centuries. All of the cities of the Conquest (except Ai, and there is some question over its identity) show destructions at this time. Bimson presents a reasonable scenario for considering the Middle Bronze Age to be the time of entry for the Hebrews into Palestine, and that seems reasonable — except that it is far too early for Conventional Chronology.

Bimson did not follow his identification to its logical conclusion (he was correct in the Middle Bronze placement), and failed to challenge the accepted order. Like Peter James, he tried to squeeze a date into the full sequence, in reducing the duration of the Middle Bronze age somewhat; at least the Conquest could be read in the archaeological record. But the accepted time of the Middle Bronze could not be moved enough (the transition from MB I to MB II is the apparent point of destruction of Palestinian cities with a replacement with a more artistic and sophisticated population), and the time span of the Judges simply cannot be pushed back to the end of the Middle Bronze, much less MB I/II.

The problems in Conventional Chronology cannot be solved without challenging some of the basic assumptions. The numbered dynastic lists inspired by Manetho should be replaced. The numbers themselves are a problem, implying divisions where there are none, and family continuity where it does not exist.

The following replacement list is proposed:

PROPOSED	CURRENT	DATES
Middle Kingdom	11th & 12th Dynasty	1800 - 1450 BC
Arab	13th to 17th Dynasty	1450 - 1020 BC
Theban	18th Dynasty	1020 - 830 BC
Libyan	22nd & 23rd Dynasty	830 - 720 BC
Ethiopian	25th Dynasty	720 - 665 BC
Tanitic	19th/26th Dynasty	663 - 525 BC
Persian	27th Dynasty	525 - 391 BC
2nd Tanitic	20th/29th & 30th Dynasty	391 - 342 BC
2nd Persian	31st Dynasty	342 - 332 BC

Except for a brief overview and look at one Palestinian city in Chapter 3, the Middle Kingdom is beyond the scope of this study. Only the ending date will be fixed with any accuracy; the beginning is approximate.

This dynastic sequence can be supported by historic, artistic, linguistic and archaeological evidence. The earlier dates should be considered as best estimates; those after 1000 BC are more secure. There will be instances of famous individuals interacting with equally famous people from supposedly remote ages. Well-known battles from Egyptian inscriptions will be found in surprising historic contexts with vivid written descriptions by Greek and Hebrew sources. The evolution of alphabetic writing will be freed from the troubling duplication of stylistic changes. The entry of Indo-Aryan names and languages into the Middle East will occur only once instead of twice. And Hittite/Chaldean art will progress from provincial stages to a final monumental stage instead of the reverse.

A good theory is one that provides a "fit" to the data it is meant to explain. If, in the process, identities are forced by a timeline, then further tests are placed before the theory. Such is the case with the Synchronized Chronology. The further a connection is examined, the more possibilities are created. Placing the 18th (Theban) Dynasty of Egypt alongside the age of the Hebrew Kingdoms means that some of the letters from Akhnaton's royal library (the Tell el Amarna letters) must be from Jerusalem and Samaria. This is one of the most rewarding synchronisms, shedding light on important interactions between the Kings of Judea and Israel with surrounding rulers. The weakening of Egypt under Akhnaton occurs just as Assyria begins to assert itself. Egypt had played a stabilizing role in the region but could no longer be counted on. Divided loyalties pushed former allies into rivalries that played into the Assyrians hands.

This placement of the 18th (Theban) Dynasty provides the most compelling identities, generation after generation, and compels us to reevaluate the succeeding dynasties. The weakness at the end of the 18th Dynasty was not followed by the glorious 19th Dynasty, with mighty pharaohs such as Seti the Great and Ramses the Great. Rather, Egypt was taken over by Libyans. This doesn't mean that Ramses II has been removed from history — just returned to his proper time, as Necho II of the Tanitic Dynasty. The Libyans were replaced by the Ethiopian kings who had some support from Thebes but could not keep the Assyrians away. The pharaohs of the Tanitic Dynasty began as vassals under Assyria but asserted themselves as soon as that hold weakened. Following his father Seti (Psammetich) who had a stronghold at Riblah on the Orontes River of Syria, Ramses (Necho) attempted to consolidate the region of Carchemish (Kadesh) before the Chaldaean (Hittite) rulers could control the area formerly held by Assyria.

Egypt suffered a crushing defeat at the Battle of Carchemish (Kadesh), and Ramses' description of the event will be compared to Greek and biblical versions. The Chaldaean (Hittite) commander was to become king, as

Nebuchadnezzar. The two enemies signed a peace treaty, copies of which have been found by archaeologists in both countries. Ramses conceded Palestine to Nebuchadnezzar, and with it, ultimately, Jerusalem. Ramses, identified as the Pharaoh of the Oppression and Exodus, is instead found to be the Pharaoh of the Captivity in Babylon. By what black magic could this state of affairs have come to be?

Cambyses of Persia began a new age in history, conquering both the Chaldeans and Egyptians and creating the largest empire ever. The Persian kings even went through the formal ceremonies in both Upper and Lower Egypt to become Pharaohs, including a pretended blood link to an Egyptian royal family. The Hebrews were released from Babylon by Persia and allowed to return to Jerusalem and rebuild.

This work will conclude with the time of the Persians, an age that would seem to hold few surprises. An enormous amount of literature relating to this era survives from ancient writers. Herodotus alone wrote a history of the world to make sure that posterity knew why the Persian War took place. Yet during a last brief reign of native rule, Egypt shook off Persian dominance and gloried in the pharaoh's victory over the combined Persian forces with Greek mercenaries attempting to retake Egypt. Like Necho II, the victorious Pharaoh Nectanebo II left no glories to himself in Egypt that have been found. But Necho II turned out to be Ramses II, who left countless monumental remains. Similarly, the revised chronology proposes that Nectanebo I is the alter ego of Ramses III, who likewise left monumental remains. But Ramses III, instead of fighting P-l-s-tt "Philistines," was fighting P-r-s-tt "Persians." (In ancient Egyptian writing, no distinction is made between what we consider "r" and "l," but we have customarily adopted certain pronunciations, such as Ramses, not Lamses). The ancient writer Diodorus describes for the Pharaoh Nectanebo the battles depicted on the monuments of Ramses III.

At this point the discrepancy in chronology reached 800 years, all the way from Ramses III, who is placed at 1182-1151 BC, to Nectanebo I, who ruled from 380-363 BC.

3. The Exodus and the End of the Middle Kingdom of Egypt

The Israelites prospered during their time in Egypt, but the changing winds of politics, which meant a new pharaoh, pushed history toward a moment of destiny. The Exodus from bondage in Egypt is such a focal point for the people of Israel that it looms above all other events in their history. The sequence of "plagues" leading up to the finale has the character of natural disasters strung together in ever-increasing intensity. The story line involves a battle of endurance between Moses and the Pharaoh. Moses threatens to up the ante, and Pharaoh bows his neck, indicating continued resistance. Then Pharaoh finally gives in, but then changes his mind, again and again.

The story incorporates many common elements found in the mythology of peoples around the world — what psychologist Carl Jung termed "archetypes" latent in the "collective unconscious" of man and liable to surface in any culture.

Man has lived with natural disasters throughout all time. That volcanic explosions, tidal waves, and other cataclysmic events should have left a profound impression on man's psyche no longer seems surprising. The images of our mythology and dreams live independently of our individual life experience, as if tapping that reservoir of collective experience. The story of the Exodus employs themes common to others; how could it be otherwise? Stripped of their human (or rather divine) components, the plagues resemble disasters common to all eras. And Earth's most recent mass extinction, at the close of the last geologic age, the Pleistocene, was a mere 10,000 years ago. It was witnessed and survived by humans. And the humans of that time were hardly "primitive." Their ancestors had made the magnificent cave paintings of Europe 10,000-20,000 years earlier.

Chronology to Chapters 3 & 4						
DATE BC	**EGYPT**			**PALESTINE**		
2200			MB I			
				PASTORAL & VILLAGES		ABRAHAM
2000	MIDDLE KINGDOM	11TH DYNASTY				
		12TH DYNASTY	MB IIA	GROWTH OF CITY-STATES		JACOB AND JOSEPH
1800		13TH DYNASTY				
1600	HYKSOS INVASION	ARAB DYNASTY	MB IIB	EXODUS	FORTIFI-CATIONS WITH GLASIS SLOPES	MOSES
1400			MB IIC	CONQUEST		JUDGES
1200		UPPER EGYPT 17TH DYN.				ABIMELECH & GIDEON
1040	THEBAN CONQUEST	THEBAN DYNASTY	LB I	UNITED KINGDOM		SAUL

Mass extinctions are enormously arbitrary. Indeed, the very fabric of evolution is punctured with episodes that make a mockery of effective adaptation. Survival of the fittest is replaced with survival of whoever survives. Our ancestors can be excused if they saw divine intervention at work when they alone emerged from disasters that overwhelmed others.

The Bible is filled with the passionate struggle of a people with their faith. Their God demanded belief in the face of obstacle after obstacle. The strength of character an individual acquires in meeting adversity with grace is a microcosm of the challenge made by the God of Israel. Being only human, they failed again and again, and as their own severest critic, they recorded it all.

At what point does the Bible pass from mythology (meant to be symbolic) to the historic? Probably not at the Garden of Eden. The "Tree of the Knowledge of Good and Evil" in the garden (as forbidden fruit) seems to be well over on the symbolic side. How about Noah's Ark? While clearly overstepping the range of the totally believable, it nonetheless reflects a theme so common in myth and legend that it is difficult to find a culture without some version of it. But, while major floods occur in many parts of the Earth, the mythical-biblical flood is a memory of something entirely out of the ordinary. And though we may choose to dismiss particulars within the overall legend, there probably was a real event somewhere behind this story. And by the time we get to the Book of Exodus, history has largely replaced the symbolic.

Egyptian and Sumerian mythology are clearly distinguishable from their other writings, even if those are also embellished with superhuman events. That a pharaoh is credited with unbelievable exploits during battle in no way suggests that the battle itself did not take place. We should grant the Bible at least as much credulity as we grant writings from other ancient sources.

THE MOST IMPORTANT SYNCHRONISM

The choice of the Exodus as a starting point allows the possibility that the natural disaster recorded by the Israelites was also noted elsewhere. This includes, of course, the other party involved. Historians have had a very hard time identifying the sequence of events described in Exodus within Egyptian history. More than any other single element, the Exodus defies placement anywhere near the chronological time given in biblical scripture. Rather than examining possible Egyptian chronological problems, the trend has been to dismiss the whole episode as fiction.

There are in fact several texts from Egypt that describe a combination of events remarkably similar to the natural disasters described in biblical scripture as "Plagues." These texts have been known for a very long time to scholars; but until Velikovsky they were never aligned with their Old Testament counterparts. Obviously documents from the end of the Middle Kingdom of Egypt could not be referring to the same events as a biblical story occurring several hundred years later; or could they?

The Synchronized Chronology places the Exodus at the end of the Middle Kingdom of Egypt, a time of great turmoil in Egypt and throughout the rest of the ancient world. The Minoan, Hellenic, Anatolian, Levantine, Mesopotamian and Egyptian civilizations all record changes in occupation.

The documentation from Egypt, placed alongside biblical scripture, actually enriches our understanding of the times leading up to and following the Exodus. Egypt was particularly vulnerable as a result of natural disasters and succumbed to foreign invaders. The Bible helps understand these invaders.

The plagues leading up to the Exodus are separated in time from one another, giving Pharaoh, as the story goes, several chances to change his mind and release the Israelites. The drama is heightened by these repeating incidents (repeating themes are a common element in ancient literature). But therein also lies the seed of doubt. Skeptics see this structuring of the incidents as too supernatural, or more correctly, unnatural. Critics who choose to pick apart

23

biblical epics are missing the point. The heroic elements are just the human embellishments of real events.

The Plagues build in intensity (and terror) from one to the next. They progress from water turned red (blood) (by volcanic dust?), vermin multiplying, and then hail (not ice, but rocks) driven by ferocious winds, followed by zero visibility that went on for days. Volcanism can account for most of these occurrences (except for perhaps the vermin), and undersea earthquakes can cause the sea to retreat, only to come crashing back in tidal waves. Volcanic activity is suggested for Mount Sinai, which had smoke rising "like a furnace."

Egypt has a similar story of natural disasters overwhelming the country, only to be followed by an invasion by foreigners who easily took over and caused further suffering for the people. Three Egyptian sources describe the fall of the Middle Kingdom and the invasion of the Hyksos who ruled the country in the following dynasty: the *Papyrus Ipuwer*, the *El Arish Shrine* and the *Ermitage Papyrus*. Each of them will be quoted and compared with the Book of Exodus.

THE PAPYRUS IPUWER

The Papyrus Ipuwer, a seventeen-page document known as the "Admonitions of an Egyptian Sage," was a New Kingdom transcription of an older source whose grammatical style is that of the Middle Kingdom. Although some authorities place the events described in the papyrus during the First Intermediate Period, others prefer the Second Intermediate Period because they seem to describe the Hyksos invasion. If it was written shortly after the event, a Middle-Kingdom style would make sense (the Second Intermediate Period follows the Middle Kingdom). Several of the middle portions are missing completely, and parts of almost every page and the beginning are fragmentary. Nonetheless, the story appears to be a series of lamentations or admonitions directed at a god for allowing the events to happen.

As the translator says,[1] "It is no merely local disturbance that is here described, but a great and overwhelming national disaster." Here are some excerpts from the papyrus and from the story of the plagues in Exodus, showing the similarity:

---

1. The translation shown here is from A. H. Gardiner in 1909. A more recent translation by R. O. Faulkner is available in *The Literature of Ancient Egypt*. The translations agree essentially, but Gardiner's language more closely resembles Exodus.

- Papyrus 2:5-6 Plague is throughout the land. Blood is everywhere
- **Exodus** 7:20 . . . all the waters that were in the river were turned to blood.
- Papyrus 2:10 The river is blood. Men shrink from tasting- human beings, and thirst after water. Forsooth, gates columns and walls are consumed by fire.
- **Exodus** 7:24 And all the Egyptians digged round about the river for water to drink; for they could not drink of the water of the river.
- **Exodus** 9:23 ..and fire run along upon the ground.
- Papyrus 2:11 The towns are all destroyed.
- Papyrus 2:13 He who places his brother in the ground is everywhere
- **Exodus** 12:30 And Pharaoh rose up in the night, he, and all his servants, and all the Egyptians; and there was a great cry in Egypt; for there was not a house where there was not one dead
- Papyrus 3:13 All is ruin.
- Papyrus 4:2 Years of noise. There is no end to noise
- Papyrus 4:3 Forsooth, the children of princes are dashed against the walls.
- Papyrus 3:14 It is groaning that is throughout the land, mingled with lamentations.
- Papyrus 4:2 Great and small say, I wish I might die.
- Papyrus 3:1 Forsooth, the Desert is throughout the land. The nomes are laid waste. A foreign tribe from abroad has come to Egypt
- Papyrus 4:14 Trees are destroyed
- **Exodus** 10:15 . . . and there remained not any green thing in the trees, or in the herbs of the field, through all the land of Egypt.
- Papyrus 5:5 All animals, their hearts weep. Cattle moan.
- Papyrus 5:12 Forsooth, that has perished which yesterday was seen. The land is left over to its weariness like the cutting of flax.
- **Exodus** 9:31 And the flax and the barley was smitten: for the barley was in the ear, and the flax was boiled.
- Papyrus 6:1 No fruit nor herbs are found.
- Papyrus 6:3 Forsooth, grain has perished on every side.
- Papyrus 7:1 Behold the fire has mounted up on high. Its burning goes forth against the enemies of the land.
- **Exodus** 13:21 And the LORD went before them by day in a pillar of a cloud, to lead them the way; and by night in a pillar of fire, to give them light; to go by day and night.
- Papyrus 9:11 The land is not light (it's dark)
- **Exodus** 10:22-23 . . . and there was a thick darkness in all the land of Egypt for three days: They saw not one another, neither rose any from his place for three days.

25

- Papyrus 6:9 Forsooth, the laws of the judgment hall are cast forth. Men walk upon them in the public places.
- Papyrus 7:1-2 [the pharaoh was lost under unusual circumstances] that have never happened before.
- Papyrus 9:2-3 Behold, cattle are left to stray, and there is none to gather them together. Each man fetches for himself those that are branded with his name.
- **Exodus** 9:3 Behold, the hand of the LORD is upon thy cattle which is in the field, upon the horses, upon the asses, upon the camels, upon the oxen, and upon the sheep: there shall be a very grievous murrain.
- **Exodus** 9:24 So there was hail, and fire mingled with the hail, very grievous, such as there was none like it in all the land of Egypt since it became a nation.
- Papyrus 10:2 Men flee . . . tents are what they make like the dwellers of the hills.
- Papyrus 12:6 Today fear---more than a million of people. Not seen--- enemies---enter into the temples---weep.
- Papyrus 14:11 Men---They have come to an end for themselves. There are none found to stand and protect themselves.
- Papyrus 15:1 What has happened? --through this to cause the Asiatics to know the condition of the land.

THE EL ARISH SHRINE

A black granite shrine found at the Wadi El Arish (between Egypt and Israel) in the 1860s, making itself useful as a cattle trough, is covered with hieroglyphs and drawings inscribed during the Ptolemaic Period. F. L. Griffith, in *The Mound of the Jew and the City of Onias*, describes the shrine and its condition. Only one side and the back are in good enough condition to be confidently read. The translation tells of a time of great distress for Egypt.

King Thom (the name is written in a royal cartouche, reserved for pharaohs) assembles his troops to battle the evil-doers. "Confusion seized the eyes (?) he made his chapel . . . evil fell upon the land, a great disturbance in the palace, disturbed . . . Then the majesty he found her in this (?) place which is called *Pekharti*(?) . . . .there was no exit from the palace by the space of nine days. Now these nine days were in violence and tempest; none whether god or man could see the face of his fellow" (italics added). In the fight at the pool "in At Neves is a pool upon the East of Hat Nebes in which the majesty of Ra proceeds." He departs to heaven. "Now when the majesty of Ra Harmachis [fought] with the evil-doers in this pool, the Place of the Whirlpool, the evil-doers prevailed not over his majesty. His majesty leapt into the so-called Place of the Whirlpool."

26

"The children of the dragon Apep (a Hyksos royal name), the evil-doers and of the red country came upon the road of At Nebes, invading Egypt at nightfall . . . now these evil-doers came from the eastern hills [upon] all the roads At Nebes, invading Egypt." Exodus 14:9 But the Egyptians pursued after them, all the horses and chariots of Pharaoh, and his horsemen, and his army, and overtook them encamping by the sea, beside Pi-hakhiroth, before Bal-zephon. Exodus 14:28 "And the waters returned, and covered the chariots, and the horsemen, and all the host of Pharaoh that came into the sea after them; there remained not so much as one of them."

The El Arish shrine (in very confused language) describes the time of the invasion of the Hyksos. The palace is in distress and the violence of the tempest is such that visibility is zero for nine days. In Exodus 10:22-23, a time of similar affliction is described: "and there was a thick darkness in all the land of Egypt for three days: They saw not one another, neither rose any from his place for three days." Both describe a place with a similar name, Pehkarti on the shrine, and Pi-hakhiroth in Exodus. And both have the pharaoh entering the whirlpool.

THE ERMITAGE PAPYRUS

The third source, the Ermitage Papyrus, tells the same story, but framed as a prophesy and revealing how the event came to characterize a time of doom. "The land is utterly perished and naught remains . . . The sun is veiled and shines not in the sight of men . . . The river is dry . . . The earth is fallen into misery . . . foes are in the East and Asiatics shall descend into Egypt."

THE INVASION

These three sources describe the state of Egypt in the transition from the Middle Kingdom, the mighty 12th Dynasty, to the Hyksos Dynasty or Second Intermediate Period. Except for the invasion of the Amu (Hyksos), this is the story familiar to us from Exodus. But then, having left Egypt, the Israelites were not around to witness the invasion.

Josephus, quoting the Egyptian historian Manetho,[2] tells us of the invasion of the Hyksos: "There was a king of ours, Tutimaeus. Under him it came to pass, I know not how, that God was averse to us, and there came, after a surprising manner, men of ignoble birth out of the eastern parts, and had boldness to make an expedition into our country, and with ease subdued it by force, yet without our hazarding a battle with them." Who were these invaders?

---

2. This is quoted in V.1, 55 as St. Thackeray's translation of *Against Apion, I, 74-75*.

Although even in his time their identity was unclear, Manetho says, "Some say they were Arabians." Almost every culture in Western Asia has been proposed as being the Amu/Hyksos. Perhaps the placement of the Exodus at this same time will provide a clue to their identity.

THE AMALEKITES

Before the Israelites had gotten very far from Egypt they encountered the Amalek, Arab warriors. A battle at Meriba ensued, and the Israelites were hard pressed (Ex 17:13). The Amalekites harassed the Israelites with skirmishes and raids not only in the desert but also as they attempted to enter Canaan from the south, where the Amalekites were in power. A second major battle went against the Israelites and sent them back to the Sinai Desert for a generation of wandering.

Arab historians tell us that the Amalekites were a powerful tribe that ruled in ancient times from Mecca and even had kings who ruled Egypt.[3] The Amalekites also ruled southern Canaan from the time of the wandering to the time of Saul. Saul's victory over the Amalekites is so understated in the Bible that the plain language is overlooked. Their domain stretched from some part of Arabia (Havilah) to Egypt. "And Saul smote the Amalekites from Havilah until thou comest to Shur, that is over against Egypt. And he took Agag the king of the Amalekites alive, and utterly destroyed all the people with the edge of the sword."[4]

The name of the Amalekite king was "Agag"; the Hyksos king was "Apep." It is worth noting that the early Hebrew letters *p* and *g* look very similar; both are written like our numeral 7 with only a slight difference in the angle of the descender.

The length of the Amu/Hyksos rule in Egypt has been a matter of some dispute. The Sothic dating allows only 200 years at the most (1786-1575 BCC). But because of the great cultural changes between the Middle and Late Kingdoms, some scholars insisted on a longer interval. Flinders Petrie proposed that an additional Sothic period be inserted within the Hyksos reign (over a hundred Hyksos kings were listed by Manetho), giving 1660 years (200+1460) for the dynasties. That seems a bit much. Manetho says the Hyksos ruled 511 years. And H.R. Hall says, "Were the sothic date unknown, our evidence would not require more than 400 or at most 500 years between the Two — the 12th and

---

3. See Maçoudi (d. about 956) *Les Prairies d'Or*. Also Al-Samhudi (844-911), Tabari (838-923) and Abulfeda (1273-1331) all quoted in V.1, 61-65.
4. I Samuel 15:7-8

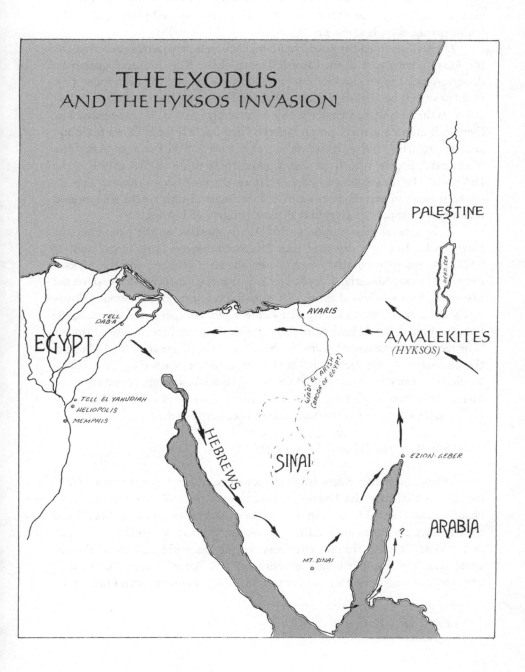

THE EXODUS
AND THE HYKSOS INVASION

PALESTINE

DEAD SEA

EGYPT

TELL DAB'A

AVARIS

AMALEKITES
(HYKSOS)

TELL EL YAHUDIAH
HELIOPOLIS
MEMPHIS

HEBREWS

WADI EL ARISH
(BROOK OF EGYPT)

SINAI

EZION-GEBER

ARABIA

?

MT. SINAI

18th dynasties."[5] If the Synchronized Chronology proposes that the Hyksos period lasted somewhat over 400 years, rather than the 200 years required by Sothic dating, there is ample precedent.

The Hyksos ruled Egypt and southern Canaan from a fortress called Avaris (or Auaris), lying east of the easterly mouth of the Nile. Archaeologists have disagreed over the precise location of this fortress; no site has been found that could positively be identified. Although several sites have been suggested, Tel el-Dab'a on the easterly branch of the Nile is currently favored. Recent excavations there indicate that it was a portal into the Egyptian Nile for both sea trade and land travel (the "Horus Road" heads east from Tel el-Dab'a to Asia. The "Canaanite" people who lived and worked there prior to the arrival of the Hyksos will be the subject of Chapter 4. It *was* a major Hyksos city, but then its strategic location near the Pelusiac mouth (the most easterly) of the Nile assured that it was an important city through most of Egyptian history.

The general presumption is that Auaris must be on the Nile, since the battle took place in a dry river bed. The Synchronized Chronology looks at additional information that suggests an alternate location for the Hyksos fortress. Quoting Manetho, Josephus records that the Auaris was located "on the east of the Bubastis arm of the river."[6] Bubastis was a major city about halfway up the delta on the most easterly edge (allowing for changes in the channels, the Bubastis branch would have coincided with the Pelusiac branch at most times). "The meaning of the name 'Auaris' is 'the town of the desert strip.'"[7] And one of the pharaoh's officers recorded that the city could be reached by land, which would be unusual for a port city of the Nile. The Book of Samuel points to a site east of the delta mouths. Thus, we have three sources that place Arish/Auaris *east* of the easterly branches of the Nile and not necessarily *on* the Nile.

THE DEFEAT OF THE HYKSOS/AMALEKITES

When the native rulers from Thebes in southern Egypt became strong enough to challenge the Hyksos, the victory battle took place in the river channel near Avaris. The assumption has been that the river was the Nile. When Saul defeated the Amalekites at their city on the "Nakkal," we can locate the city on the Wadi El Arish, the only river between the Nile and Israel. (Nakkal is the usual term for that Wadi in the scriptures.) El Arish is then Auaris. It is something of a mystery why this connection of Avaris/Auaris with El Arish has

---

5. CAH I, 169.
6. *Against Apion I,* 78.
7. V. 1, 88

not been made (except by Velikovsky). Hyksos occupation is known to have extended into southern Palestine and a centralized capital at El Arish is certainly not unlikely. The later pharaoh Haremhab punished law offenders by cutting off their noses and banishing them to a place east of Egypt on the way to Syria. Manetho tells of these unclean exiles: "The king . . . assigned them for habitation and protection the abandoned city of the shepherds, called Auaris."[8] The Greeks called this city "Rhinocolura" (cut-off nose) and the Septuagint translation of biblical scripture uses that same name for El Arish!

The Egyptian tale of the defeat of the Hyksos credits an ally with the major role. An inscription on the tomb of an officer in the battle says, "I followed the king on foot when he rode abroad in his chariot. *One* besieged the city of Avaris. I showed valor on foot before His Majesty . . . *One* fought on the water in the canal (riverbed) of Avaris . . . *One* captured Avaris . . . *One* besieged Sharuhen for three years (and) His Majesty took it" (italics added).

Sharuhen is another Hyksos stronghold near Gaza; survivors of Avaris fled there. The Egyptian record does not identify the foreign ally (referred to simply as the *One*) who actually captured the capital Avaris; it would be out of character to do so. But we can suppose that it was none other than the Israelites under Saul who defeated the Amalekites and took their king Agag captive.

Saul was directed to kill them all:

> Thus saith the LORD of hosts, I remember that which Amalek did to Israel, how he laid wait for him in the way, when he came up from Egypt. Now go and smite Amalek, and utterly destroy all that they have, and spare them not; but slay both man and woman, infant and suckling, ox and sheep, camel and ass.[9]

For sparing the life of the king, he was cursed by Samuel, and would lose his kingdom in a later battle against the Philistines, when he was killed by an Amalekite fighting on the side of the Philistines.

The Egyptians, freed from Hyksos rule, consolidated their land and extended their borders to the south into Nubia. The rise of the 18th (Theban) Dynasty marks a great high point in the long history of the country. Likewise the Israelites, now under David, spread their kingdom to its largest extent. Respect for the Israelites was great; they had defeated the kingdom of the Amalekites. The importance of this is largely overlooked in assessing important events of biblical history, but then, "the LORD said unto Moses, 'Write this for a memorial

8. *Against Apion I, 237*
9. I Samuel 15:2-3.

in a book, and rehearse it in the ears of Joshua: for I will utterly put out the remembrance of Amalek from under heaven."[10]

Having placed the Exodus at the fall of the Middle Kingdom of Egypt, we then followed the conquerors, the Amu/Hyksos/Amalekites, to their end. This was done for a purpose. This brackets the time frame of the Hyksos Dynasties within biblical history between the Exodus to the end of Judges. Sandwiched within these limits is another very important era for the Israelites, the Conquest of Canaan. This is a sequence of destructions and re-occupations that should be easily detected in the archaeological record of Palestine. The Israelites may have been related to the Canaanites racially, but culturally they were separated by hundreds of years.

The Synchronized Chronology places the Conquest in the middle of the Middle Bronze Age. Conventional Chronology placed it far later, near the end of the Late Bronze Age. This has been one of the real disasters for biblical history. Unlike the emasculated version of the Israelite takeover of the hill country of Palestine that now prevails in Conventional Chronology, the true course of events can fit the biblical version to the archaeological record.

---

10. Ex 17:14.

4. The Conquest and the Time of the Judges

The Israelites began their conquest of the hill country of Palestine after a generation spent in the (mostly eastern) Sinai. (The current theory that Mt. Sinai was actually in Arabia is supported by the fact that the traditional Mt. Sinai was *not* volcanic at this or any other time.) The campaign proceeded from a start at the Gulf of Aqaba and went into Edom, then north through Jordan to Bashan, land of the Amorites. The Israelites then returned to the east bank of the Jordan River near Jericho, a staging area for preparations to enter the Promised Land.

A few tribes were granted their request to remain in the newly conquered lands east of the Jordan. The tribes of Reuben and Gad and the half tribe of Manasseh were allowed to settle these lands on the condition that their men first help in the military campaign west of the Jordan.

The real conquest of the Promised Land began at Jericho. Here the destruction was complete, almost ritualistic, in "a kind of 'first fruits' offering in which everything was devoted to the Lord."[1] This successful battle was followed by a doomed attack on Ai. The disobedience of one Israelite soldier required this defeat as a punishment; but after that there was victory.

These successes alarmed the other city-states of Palestine into forming a military alliance. They directed their forces to Gibeon, the city that had made a treaty with Joshua. After hearing of the attack on Gibeon, Joshua made a night march to lower Beth Horom and routed the combined forces of the kings of Jerusalem, Hebron, Jarmuth, Lachish and Eglon. Then Joshua chased and killed these five kings in Makkedah, north of Lachish. He captured Libnah, Lachish,

---

1. Pfeiffer, 88.

33

Eglon, Hebron and Debir. With southern Palestine conquered, the city-states of northern Palestine united under the leadership of Jabin, king of Hazor. "Hazor had been the head of all these kingdoms."[2]

The battle of northern Palestine occurred at the Waters of Merom, southwest of Hazor (today called Meron). The decisive victory by Joshua was followed by the destruction of Hazor. "Yet Israel did not burn any of the cities built on their mounds — except Hazor, which Joshua burned."[3] And, "Hazor was indeed the largest Canaanite city throughout the Middle and Late Bronze Ages."[4]

These two campaigns, in southern and northern Palestine, encompassed most of what we think of as Israel. It will come as no surprise to those familiar with the books of Joshua and Judges that these territories did not stay conquered. There were pockets of resistance and there were cities that were retaken by their former inhabitants. There was never a time when the Israelites had unchallenged rule of all Palestine.

What must be emphasized, though, is the overall nature of the conquest as a distinct segment of history. The largest cities of Palestine, in alliance with each other, were defeated by the newcomers. Conventional Chronology has tested many different theories of how the biblical tale could integrate with the archaeological record. None has been successful. "How the 'Israelites' acquired their territories in the hill country of Canaan during Iron Age I continues to be the *most important problem* in Old Testament history."[5]

There is no question that the Israelites took possession of Palestine. Assyrian and other contemporary written records substantiate their later history. The difficulty lies in the archaeological data, and Callaway's quote focuses the problem. The assumption, of course, is that the time frame is Iron Age I (1200-1000 BCC). Typical of that period are small villages and weak cities. Since it is never mooted that the chronology might be wrong, the Conquest is recast into a form compatible with this evidence. "Instead of taking the highlands in mass military campaigns, the settlers claimed unoccupied ruins of ancient cities, or barren hilltops that had never before supported permanent settlements."[6]

This contrast between the archaeological picture and the biblical version could not be greater. There is no middle ground. And since the time of this

---

2. " (Joshua 11:10).
3. Joshua 11:13
4. Mazar 332
5. Callaway, in Tubb 31, italics added.
6. Callaway, in Tubb, 43.

"infiltration" is only 200-250 years before David, the rest of the time of the Judges is even more difficult to pin down archaeologically.

We could examine in detail the steps that have been taken over the last century leading to this version. It would only demonstrate how unavoidable this position had become. The archaeology of Palestine in Iron Age I is placed by Conventional Chronology into the 1200-1000 BCC time frame and displays a low material culture that contrasts with the grandeur of the preceding Bronze Age.

The Synchronized Chronology relocates the beginning of the Iron Age to the time of King Sargon of Assyria (722-704 BC). He was the first king to use iron weapons. But the relocation of alien populations into Palestine had already begun under previous Assyrian kings. The foreign policy of Assyria involved moving conquered people away from their homelands to hinder the formation of alliances.

Now, imagine the problem this has created for scholars. The archeological remains of these poor peoples, crushed and decimated by Assyria, are transformed by faulty chronology into the supposed relics of the Israelite occupation of Canaan! The Synchronized Chronology proposes instead that the Conquest took place in the Middle Bronze Age, where the archaeological picture supports and enhances the image given in the Bible.

THE MIDDLE BRONZE AGE

The Middle Bronze Age is usually divided into MB I and MB II, with the latter subdivided into A, B and C. Some have tried to revise this designation by making MB I into EB IV (Early Bronze IV), and there are some arguments in favor of that, but we will stay with the majority. As long as everyone knows what is meant, it doesn't really matter. The dividing line between MB I and MB II is the beginning of the 12th Egyptian Dynasty. This was a dynasty of powerful pharaohs who left great monuments throughout Egypt.

Sometime during late 12th Dynasty, non-Egyptian immigrants were moving into the eastern Delta. These were a northwestern Semitic people who occupied at least two large sites, Tell el-Dab'a and Tell el-Yahudiyeh. As was described in the last chapter, the former is now believed to have been the site of Avaris, the city that later (in MB IIB) became the Hyksos capital. During MB IIA (2000-1800 BCC, Tell el-Dab'a levels G & H), the settlements grew into large, dense urban centers. Excavations at Tell el-Dab'a tell us about the people who built there.

> The houses of this settlement reveal that the settlers were not Egyptian but people from the Levant. According to Eigner, the layout of the houses

resembles closely both the "Mittelhsaalhous" and the "Breitraumhaus" — ancient architectural types which occur in northern Syria in the second half of the fourth millennium BC.[7]

It is unclear how the building style reached Egypt after such a long interval, but the important point is that northern Syria (*Ur of the Chaldeas*) was the homeland of the biblical Patriarchs.

Meanwhile, MB IIA in Palestine sees the growth of cities and the first fortifications. MB IIB increases the number and size of fortifications substantially, being best known for the steep slopes on which defensive walls were constructed. Presumably the slopes made undermining and siege engines less effective, but they would also put more distance against projectiles and reduced the threat of huge fires built against the walls. Such fires are known to have transferred enough heat through the walls to ignite structures inside.

Virtually all the large cities throughout Palestine, including Jericho, employed these new slopes (sometimes referred to as "glacis") whose packed or plastered surfaces are exceedingly hard to climb. All remaining sites are fortified by the end of MB IIB (1800-1700 BCC) and are then repaired and augmented in MB IIC (1700-1550 BCC), reaching a zenith prior to their destruction at the end. "This was a time of great local prosperity; the number of settlements and tombs increased steadily, and luxurious funerary appointments of Middle Bronze II B-C exceed anything else known in the history of the country."[8]

The southerly and southwesterly portions of Palestine show remains of Hyksos during MB IIB and C. These are sometimes seen as evidence of a "Hyksos Empire." "The ease with which the survivors of the war of liberation (Hyksos expulsion) could hold out against Ahmose (the conquering pharaoh who initiated the Theban 18th Dynasty) at Sharuhen near Gaza has suggested to some the existence of a Hyksos dependency centered in that city, and controlling most of the Philistine plain north to about Joppa."[9]

Scriptural testimony would extend that "dependency" along southern Palestine at least to "Havilah," the easterly limit of the Amalekite region conquered by the Israelites under Saul.

---

7. Bietak, 10.
8. Albright, 87.
9. Redford, 121, parentheses added.

THE BIBLICAL MIDDLE BRONZE AGE

Placed against the contemporary record of the Old Testament, the Middle Bronze Age can be analyzed with rich results. The two Egyptian sites of Tell el-Yahudiyeh and Tell el-Dab'a, occupied by "western Semites" throughout MB IIA, were in peaceful coexistence with the 12th and 13th Dynasties of Egypt. Tell el-Yahudiyeh is located in the eastern Delta (north of Heliopolis), where Ramses III of the 20th dynasty had a royal pavilion. There is a large Jewish cemetery there that dates to the fourth or third centuries BC and probably gave the site its name, "Mound of the Jew."

Tell el-Dab'a is about 11 miles south of Tanis near the Pelusiac mouth of the Nile. Occupation there grew fastest during the 13th Dynasty (late MB IIA). It became a very large Hyksos site through MB IIB and C. It was later known as Per-Ramses and had a large number of remains of Ramses II, one of the reasons he has often been regarded as the pharaoh of the oppression (the epithet "Ramses" means "Son of the Sun," and was applied to many other pharaohs also). The eastern Delta region between these cities would fit the role of the Israelites' "Land of Goshen."

The duration of MB II in the Conventional Chronology is from 2000-1550 BCC. In the Synchronized Chronology, MB II would last from 1900-1040 BCS. This is a substantially longer time than currently recognized. However, Conventional Chronology is fixed by an astronomically-dated point in the Middle Kingdom that causes chronological problems similar to those created for the Late Kingdom.

> "Bietak and other Middle Bronze Age specialists have all commented that the archaeology of MBA appears to require a longer chronology than is currently permissible within the Sothic-based orthodox scheme."[10]

In *Pharaohs and Kings*, David Rohl's "New Chronology" agrees substantially with the Synchronized Chronology for the Middle Bronze Age. Indeed, he credits Velikovsky for the synchronism of the Exodus and Hyksos invasion. But since Rohl does not recognize the duplication of the 19th and 20th Dynasties as the 26th and 30th, respectively, his remaining reconstruction conflicts with that presented here. On the other hand, Rohl extends the Exodus synchronism further back into Egyptian history and presents an interesting story of Israelite

---

10. Rohl, 310.

interaction with Middle Kingdom pharaohs (but beyond the limits of this work).

The Exodus occurs at the transition from MB IIA to IIB (1450 BCS). The archaeological record from the last stages of MB IIA in Tell el-Dab'a reveal a human tragedy.

"Over the course of this period," Bietak observes, "the settlement expanded considerably but suffered a crisis near its end. Tombs found in excavation areas F/1 and A/II, areas which are more than 500m apart from each other, were obviously emergency graves. Some of them are merely pits into which bodies were thrown; most were without offerings. To me, and others, the evidence suggests that an epidemic swept through the town."[11] Bietak admits that there is no actual evidence for an "epidemic" other than the fact of the graves. Rohl is not so reticent. He sees in them the Israelite side of the biblical "Plagues." The survivors abandoned the city, which was then reoccupied by the Hyksos.

The question begs to be asked, are Tell el-Dab'a and Tell el-Yahudiyeh not the cities of the workers who built Pi-Ramses and Pi-Thom (House of Ramses, House of Thom), of Exodus — the cities built by the Israelites? Tell el-Yahudiyeh might be associated with the workers who helped build nearby Heliopolis (which may be Pi-Thom, the city of the pharaoh Tutimaeus, under whom Josephus says the Hyksos invasion took place).

THE CONQUEST OF CANAAN

The Hyksos controlled at least the western part of southern Palestine. The Israelites' first attempt to enter Canaan after the Exodus resulted in a defeat by the Amalekites/Hyksos and a retreat into the Sinai. A generation later, a huge detour around the Amalekites brought Joshua into Palestine from the east. No attempt was made to challenge the Amalekites until the time of Saul, almost 400 years later, although there may have been some involvement between the Amalekites and the Philistines. Saul was killed by an Amalekite fighting with the Philistines after the Amalekites themselves had been defeated, and the Philistines and Hyksos probably had much friendlier relations than the Philistines and Israelites.

In a later chapter, the popular version of the entry of the Philistines into Palestine at the time of Ramses III will be challenged. Scripture tells us that Philistines were already present in the Negev (extreme southerly Palestine) in the time of Abraham. The so-called "Philistine" pottery, seen popularly as an index for Philistine occupation, has nothing whatever to do with Philistines in

---

11. Bietak, 35.

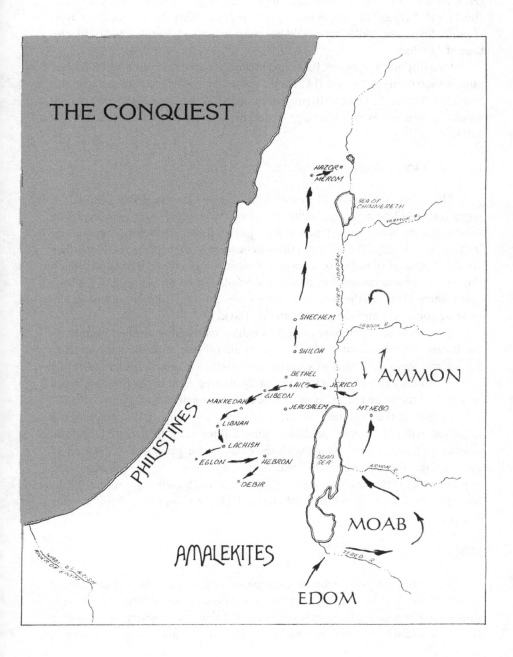

THE CONQUEST

HAZOR
MEROM
SEA OF CHINNERETH
YARMUK R.
RIVER JORDAN
SHECHEM
JABBOK R.
SHILOH
BETHEL
AI(?)
GIBEON
JERICO
AMMON
MAKKEDAH
JERUSALEM
MT. NEBO
LIBNAH
LACHISH
DEAD SEA
EGLON
HEBRON
ARNON R.
PHILISTINES
DEBIR
MOAB
AMALEKITES
ZERED R.
WADI EL ARISH
RIVER OF EGYPT
EDOM

the time of Saul or David. "Philistine Pottery" is easily identified by the characteristic backwards-facing birds, and appears to be just a variety of East Greek "Bird Bowls," typical of Aegean trade after the 7th century BC. Any pottery to be identified with real Philistines could be found as far back as at least MB IIA, the time of Abraham.

Virtually all the cities of Palestine, including those that must be Philistine, built up fortifications in MB IIB. There was a new threat to their security: the Israelites. As Middle Bronze IIB progresses, many of the cities of the hill country would be Israelite. Fortifications grew and became more sophisticated through MB IIC.

ISRAELITE OCCUPATION OF PALESTINE

The tribal subdivision of Palestine by the Israelites probably worked on paper (or would it be papyrus?), but in reality encountered many problems. The tribe of Simeon was assigned the southern part of Judah, Amalekite country, and it disappeared early. The tribe of Dan was never able to displace the Philistines on the coast west of Judah, so a portion of them migrated north to Laish, which they occupied and renamed Dan. Manassah failed to secure a group of fortified cities lining their northern border, Beth-shan, Ibleam, Tanaach and Miggido. That was only accomplished much later by David.

Nonetheless, the number of major fortified cities taken in the Conquest is significant. The MB IIB cities of Palestine should provide evidence of the Israelite arrival, and they do. With the exception of Ai (which may have been the site of a battle with the army of Bethel, inexplicably missing from the list of conquered cities) all of the known sites show new or enlarged fortifications in the early MB IIB, the time of the Conquest. A full review of the various cities named in the Conquest will not be attempted here. John J. Bimson in *Redating the Exodus and Conquest* provides a good summary of the evidence for placing the Conquest in the Middle Bronze Age. The Synchronized Chronology emphasizes the importance of seeing the new population of MB IIB Palestine as *Israelites*. What has been assumed by generations of archaeologists as *Canaanite* culture is really *Hebrew*.

JERICHO

Jerico is perhaps as good an example as any of the difficulty in pinning down the exact date of a destruction or fortification level. The city (or tell) slopes steeply and has been so severely eroded that the majority of the higher surface is an Early Bronze exposure, the later strata having mostly disappeared.

Excavations in the 1920s by Garstang hinted at the great antiquity of occupation at Jerico. Garstang found a pair of fortification walls that he believed were, in fact, the famous walls that fell before the army of Joshua (he dated them toward the end of the Late Bronze Age). This was one of the most publicized archaeological finds of all time.

Unfortunately, excavations by Kathleen Kenyon in the 1950s, performed with much greater care and with reference to other archaeologists' more recent work, showed the walls to be from separate eras, both in the Early Bronze Age.

The defensive walls of Jericho were rebuilt several times within each identifiable age. Sometimes the walls fell outward, sometimes inward; at other times they were undermined and crumbled in place. Earthquakes, erosion and conquests all contributed to the jigsaw puzzle that is Jericho's walls. As mentioned earlier, the job of sorting out the exact levels associated with the Conquest is far beyond the scope of this study; rather, it would be illuminating to examine a site that offers a specific event with unmistakable remains.

SHECHEM

"And Abram (Abraham) passed through the land to the sacred area of Shechem, to the Oak of More, and the Lord appeared to Abram and said 'To thy seed I will give this land.' And he erected an altar there to the Lord, who had appeared to him."[12] Returning from Haran many years later, "Jacob came peaceably to the city of Shechem which was in the land of Canaan when he came from Paddan-Aram. And he encamped before the city, and he purchased the portion of field on which he had pitched his tent from the hands of the sons of Hamor, father of Shechem, for a hundred qesitsas. And he set up an altar there and named it 'El, God of God of Israel'."[13]

Shechem played a special role in the religious tradition of the Israelites. Excavations there show that in the early Middle Bronze IIA a "temenos" or sacred area was built outside the city walls. It might be presumptuous to identify this with the altar of Jacob, but the time and the place both fit. Throughout MB IIB and early IIC the temenos was rebuilt and enlarged, with a courtyard temple being enclosed by the more massive MB IIB&C walls.

In the later MB IIC the small temple was replaced with a massive "Migdol" or tower temple with 16-foot thick walls to support two or three stories. This temple was destroyed in a massive conflagration and the area lay uninhabited for

12. Genesis 12:6-7
13. Genesis 33:18-20

perhaps 100 years. When rebuilt in the Late Bronze Age, a modest temple with 5-foot thick walls was constructed over the same spot.

In about 1150 BCS (MB IIC), Abimelech (the name must be generic), the illegitimate son of Gideon, returned to his native city of Shechem and killed the 70 sons of Gideon, stirred up the people and convinced them to make him king. The Israelites had never had a king before, although they attempted to convince Gideon to take that role. After three years, the people of Shechem revolted but Abimelech defeated them. Since the whole city was involved, he not only destroyed it, but also salted it. And the people who tried to escape the destruction in the "Migdol" (actually a small fortress) were burned alive when Abimelech piled mounds of brush around it and set it afire.

The excavator of Shechem, G. Ernest Wright, could see in the MB IIC temple the sort of "Migdol" structure described in Judges 9:46. It was destroyed by fire and lay unoccupied for a period, just as scripture relates. The Late Bronze temple (that would have been there, according to Conventional Chronology) just did not measure up to the multi-storied building apparently described in the Bible — when Abimelech then attacked the nearby village of Thebez, he was killed by a millstone thrown by a woman from the upper floor of a tower that was probably of similar design.[14]

There is an air of resignation or disappointment in Wright's description of the archaeological story told at Shechem. On the one hand, the Middle Bronze Age temple fits the description in scripture. Unfortunately, the dating is incompatible with Conventional Chronology and the Late Bronze Age temple is just too small to match the story. There is probably no other site in Palestine that offers a clearer argument for the Synchronized Chronology in the Middle Bronze Age. There could hardly be a better match of archaeology with the written record from the era of Abraham and Jacob right through to the time of Abimelech. There is even a vacancy at Shechem following the Midgol's destruction, corresponding to the "salting" of the site.

It would be impossible to do justice to an era as long as the Middle Bronze Age in the present work. With the MB II A to B transition identified with the Exodus (1500 BC), and the time of the Judges lasting through B and C, 400 years are required. MB IIA involves many successive strata at sites in both Egypt and Palestine. Although the length of this period has almost as many estimates as experts who have expressed an opinion, 200 years would be the upper limit for most. However, recent excavations at Tell el-Dab'a have given this period a much longer span, both for the number of occupation levels and to reconcile with the

---

14. Joshua 9:50-53

new lower chronology for Mesopotamia. All current dating systems use an astronomical date for the 12th Dynasty in Egypt, which fixes the related period in Palestine, MB I.

Based on the dependability of the biblical dates so far, there is probably reason to see MB IIA as reflecting the 400 years of Israelite occupation in Egypt. The beginning of the period has only light archaeological remains compared to the end. Abraham's arrival in Shechem fits the beginning of MB IIA better than any other time. Excavations such as those by Kenyon at Jericho have shed more interesting light on this period.

ABRAHAM AND THE AMORITE MIGRATION

The Middle Bronze Age of inland Palestine represented a complete break with the Early Bronze Age; the pottery and even the type of brick changes. Building activity was suspiciously light, compared to the number of burial tombs found. Several feet of erosional sediment had built up before substantial construction occurred, yet the mounds were clearly inhabited. The newcomers were evidently semi-nomadic (living in tents), and an examination of their burials revealed that contemporary groups had several different burial customs simultaneously. Apparently, related tribes coexisted peacefully there.

Egyptian sources, the Execration texts, depict a tribal organization with more than one chief per community (with Amorite names) for inland Palestine in MB I. Cities did not become common until well into MB IIA. The pottery suggests an origin in northern Syria, an area with both cities and semi-nomadic peoples. At this same time in the area east of northern Syria, the Assyrian King List begins with "seventeen kings living in tents."[15] It takes no straining of the evidence to see this as compatible with the time of Abraham. His family occupied Haran in northern Syria and "Ur of the Chaldeas." This "Ur" is not the ancient southern Mesopotamian city, but rather "of the Chaldeas," (considered an anachronism since the Chaldaean era of Babylon dates from so much later, the 7th and 6th centuries BC).

This Ur must be in the land of the Urartians of Armenia. They were the people of the god "Chaldae" and their homeland included Mt. Ararat ("R-R-T" in early Hebrew, and probably more correctly pronounced Mt. Urartu). Much more will be said about Chaldeans occupying this area when we discuss the Kingdom of the Hittites, but that is much later in time. For now, it is useful to recall that when Jacob returned to the "land of his fathers," it was to Haran, not southern Mesopotamia.

---

15. Saggs, 24.

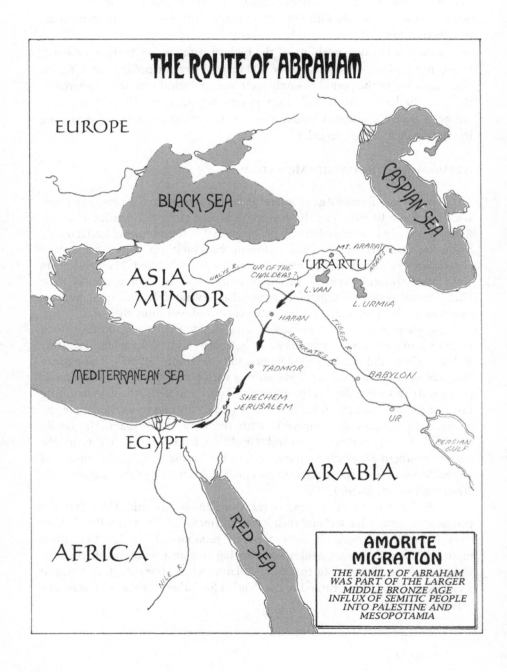

THE ROUTE OF ABRAHAM

EUROPE

BLACK SEA

CASPIAN SEA

ASIA MINOR

HALYS R.

UR OF THE CHALDEAS ?

URARTU

MT. ARARAT

ARAXES R.

L. VAN

L. URMIA

HARAN

EUPHRATES R.

TIGRIS R.

MEDITERRANEAN SEA

TADMOR

BABYLON

SHECHEM JERUSALEM

UR

EGYPT

ARABIA

PERSIAN GULF

AFRICA

RED SEA

NILE R.

AMORITE MIGRATION

THE FAMILY OF ABRAHAM WAS PART OF THE LARGER MIDDLE BRONZE AGE INFLUX OF SEMITIC PEOPLE INTO PALESTINE AND MESOPOTAMIA

So the Middle Bronze Age began with semi-nomadic tribal people moving into Palestine from the north. A long period of occupation by western Semitic people in Palestine and the Egyptian Delta proceeded through the MB IIA as cities grew and then, with MB IIB and C, defenses. The sequence is entirely in agreement with the Bible.

THE ORIGIN OF THE ALPHABET

Archaeologists lament the lack of written sources in Palestinian sites. Egypt and Mesopotamia abound in written artifacts; in Palestine they are almost non-existent (even into the Late Bronze Age). Writing is mentioned from very early times in the Bible. And the earliest Hebrew writing is *alphabetic*. Egypt had a proto-alphabetic writing derived from hieroglyphics, and written in script on papyrus. Mesopotamia used a form of writing called cuneiform, made by pressing a wedge-shaped stylus into wet clay in arrangements designating words or sounds. The Hebrews undoubtedly created their writing from the proto-alphabetic mode of the Egyptians, and likewise used a script adapted for papyrus or perhaps skins (none of which has survived the Palestinian climate).

Experts have determined that true alphabetic writing was the invention of Semitic-speaking people in the Middle Bronze Age. The earliest forms are referred to as proto-Canaanite and proto-Sinaitic (found near the turquoise mines of el Khadem in the Sinai). The available inscriptions are too brief to draw many conclusions, but the presence of proto-alphabetic writing in the early Middle Bronze Age Sinai would again fit the Israelites.

In fact, do we not have a wealth of writing from Palestine in the Middle Bronze Age, in the Books of Genesis, Exodus, Leviticus, Numbers, Deuteronomy, Joshua, Judges, Ruth and Samuel (and probably Job)? We accept early Egyptian writings based on transcriptions made hundreds of years later. The same is true of Mesopotamia. Why should Palestine be any different? Why have we reached the point where, as Redford put it, biblical archaeology should be narrowly defined as recovering early manuscripts of biblical texts? The problem is in the chronology. Forced to use the Egyptian scale, the events of the Bible do not fit *anywhere*. This cannot be overemphasized. But placed in their correct ages, they provide a rich panorama of life in Middle Bronze Age Palestine.

5. The 18th Dynasty and the United Kingdom

Chapter 4 covered the two ends of the Hyksos era, from their invasion of Egypt to their final defeat by the first pharaoh of the 18th Dynasty together with Saul and the Israelites. Identifying the Hyksos with the Amalekites served to synchronize Egyptian chronology with biblical history at two significant points. Those two points also bracket the time of the Judges in Hebrew history (1450-1040 BCS).

The present chapter begins a multi-part study of the Theban (18th) Dynasty. This important era has several important synchronisms that cover over 200 years of history. In biblical terms, this is from Saul to Jehosaphat. The Theban Dynasty left extensive records for many famous pharaohs; it was a high point in the long history of Egypt. Likewise, the United Kingdom of Israel is chronicled with some of the most comprehensive and concise records surviving from the ancient world. Either the chronology under discussion is correct in this era, or it will flounder when tested for synchronisms. The reader is invited to compare any modern text on biblical archaeology for the United Kingdom against the version of history presented here.

The United Kingdom

Saul's victory over the Amalekites led to his becoming the first real king of the Israelites. At that time of his life, "the Lord was with him" and he played his important role in the destiny of the people. His later obsessive jealousy of David and fall from grace fulfilled Samuel's prophecy that he would lose his kingdom for failing to kill the Amalekite king Agog.

	Chronology to Chapters 5-8		
	RULERS		
DATE	EGYPT	PALESTINE	GREECE
	THEBAN DYNASTY	JUDAH ISRAEL	
1040-1020	AHMOSE	SAUL	LM I
1000	AMENOPHIS I	DAVID	
980	THUTMOSE I	965 SOLOMON	
960	THUTMOSE II		
940	HATSHEPSUT	REHOBOAM JEROBOAM	
920	THUTMOSE III	ABIJAM NADAB	LM II
900	AMENOPHIS II THUTMOSE IV	ASA BAASHA	LM III A
880	AMENOPHIS III	AHAB	
860	JEHOSEPHAT AMENOPHIS IV		
840	(AKHENATEN)	JEHORAM JEHORAM (?) AHAZIAH/ ATHALIA JEHU	
820		JOASH	

When Saul died, David became king in the city of Hebron. All of Israel recognized him as ruler and the United Kingdom was born. David's success in battle was clear evidence that "the Lord was with him." He expanded the territory to its greatest extent and passed on to Solomon a powerful empire.

Except for the coastal strip, the kingdom extended inland across the Jordan from Edom in the south to the Euphrates in the north.

The United Kingdom lasted from c. 1004 BC to 928 BC, almost 80 years, enough time to leave considerable occupational remains for archaeologists. Certainly there *should* be clear stratified deposits over this large area showing a relatively uniform culture. But Conventional Chronology insures that the archaeological deposits customarily associated with the time of the United Kingdom are misplaced by hundreds of years. This makes the comparison of those remains with their biblical description a tortured exercise.

Historians are inclined to accept the gist of the biblical texts of this era. "Although the historical evaluations of the biblical sources relating to the United Kingdom vary, historians treat it in general with credibility, believing it to be rooted in the Jerusalem royal 'court history.'" But archaeologists are not so confident; they must rely on hard evidence. "Unfortunately, the archaeological evidence for the period of the United Monarchy is sparse, often controversial, and it does not provide unequivocal answers. . . . The time of Saul hardly finds any expression in the archaeological record . . . The archaeological evidence concerning David's reign is also poor and ambiguous."[1]

We can guess why this is so. Since contemporary events in Egypt are conventionally dated to the 15th and 16th centuries BC, the true remains of the United Kingdom (littered with Theban Dynasty remains) are misplaced in time.

Precisely the same problem plagues Greek archaeology, although it is treated somewhat differently. Greeks did not have the kind of sequentially dated history that we have in the Old Testament, so the problem was solved by inserting a "Dark Age" in between the Mycenaean Age of Trojan Warriors described by Homer (ending 1200 BCC) and the historical Greece of 750 BC and later. Were it not for the Assyrian records of the ninth century BC and later, which give strong credibility to the biblical events leading up to that time, we would probably have a Dark Age in Palestine also. The Greek Dark Age will be examined in more detail in Chapters 9 and 10.

THE THEBAN DYNASTY

When the Pharaoh Amose freed Egypt from the Hyksos, other important matters needed to be dealt with. Some archaeologists believe that the destruction of many cities in southern Palestine at this time was an act of vengeance by the Egyptians against the remaining Hyksos. But this is pure

---

1. Mazar 369, 371, 374.

speculation, since the Egyptians themselves made no such claims. (According to another view, the destructions were actually the work of the Israelites!)

Egypt was busy regaining Nubia, a primary source of its traditional wealth. The records of the first four pharaohs of the 18th dynasty are largely glorifications of their success in extending and consolidating the southern territories. The word "Nubia" does not refer so much to the people or land of the south, but rather to gold (the Egyptian word for gold is NUB). Egypt was absolutely exuberant in its display of wealth in gold. Huge obelisks were plated with gold, coffins were made from solid gold, and correspondence from foreign rulers makes it clear that they expected large gifts of gold from Egypt. As Egypt focused on restoring its control over Nubia, Palestine was seen not an object of territorial conquest but rather as a respected ally from the Hyksos/Amalekite wars and a trading partner.

Evidently, Egypt did mount occasional military actions across the Sinai against the Philistines, but few records remain. Thutmose I, the third pharaoh of the 18th Dynasty, subdued Nubia and then "overthrew the Asiatic." "After these things" he "journeyed to Retenu to wash his heart among the foreign countries."[2] (Retenu is the Egyptian word for the hill country of Palestine.) Perhaps this was a celebration with his ally David (or more likely Solomon). They shared the same Philistine enemy.

Thutmose still ruled when Solomon took the throne, and among Solomon's wives was a pharaoh's daughter. That pharaoh had conquered the Philistine city of Gezer and gave it to his daughter as a dowry. This may be the "heart washing" event described by Thutmose I above.

QUEEN SHEBA

During his reign, Solomon's kingdom is described in terms of building projects, military strength and artistic wealth in a manner that we associate with the great contemporary powers of Egypt, Babylon and Crete. He entertained the most important rulers of his time. Interestingly, the visitor featured most prominently in the parallel records in Kings and Chronicles is a certain "Queen of Sheba." Scholars have long tried to reconcile the presumed power and stature of Solomon with the exaggerated importance of this visit from the obscure southern Arabian district of Saba. This identification of Sheba with Saba is based solely on the similarity of names and ignores an ancient writer who specifies the actual homeland of the queen.

---

2. ARE II 81.

Josephus begins his description of the queen's visit with the following words:

> Now the woman who at that time ruled as queen of Egypt and Ethiopia was thoroughly trained in wisdom and remarkable in other ways, and, when she heard of Solomon's virtue and understanding, was led to him by a strong desire to see him which arose from the things told daily about his country.[3]

Conventional Chronology places the weak 21st-Dynasty pharaohs on the Egyptian throne in Solomon's time, and none of them was a woman. But the Synchronized Chronology places the daughter of Thutmose I, Hatshepsut, in power at this time. Could Hatshepsut (pronounced ha-sheep-soo) be the Queen of Sheba? Of the few women rulers of Egypt, hers was the longest and most impressive reign.

Following the normal Egyptian practice of shortening names, she would be the (Pharaoh) Queen "Shepsu." It is also possible that Hebrew copyists may have interpreted the HA in Hatshepsut as the definite article, and therefore translated it as "of the," resulting in the reference to the "Queen *of* Sheba.")

This might seem to be a bit of a stretch, unless the potential link between Egyptian and Israelite history could be strengthened by the queen having recorded a visit to Solomon. And, indeed, featured as one of the two most important events in Hatshepsut's life (the other is her divine birth) is her visit to Punt (also called "God's Land"). On her beautiful temple (known as "Deir el Bahari") are symmetrical walls inscribed with reliefs illustrating these two events.

Nothing else in her life warranted such treatment. That Hatshepsut considered that expedition so remarkable gives us further grounds to compare the event with the Queen (of) Sheba's visit to Solomon's Jerusalem.

It must be noted first that most Egyptian scholars have attempted to identify Punt (God's Land) by analyzing the goods depicted on Hatshepsut's ships. A great variety of exotic items are shown, but most prominent are the incense trees, native to southern Arabia and Somalia. This hint has led to Punt being identified with either and even both of these regions. Yet inscriptions from the time of Hatshepsut's successors Thutmose IV and Amenhotep III specifically place Punt in Retenu (Palestine). We will not be without precedent in accepting the latter identity.

Solomon allied himself with the Phoenician king of Tyre, Hiram. This gave Hiram access to a port on the Arabian Gulf at Aqaba and widened Solomon's

---

3. AJ 8, VI, 5.

trading contacts through Hiram's navies. A few lines after describing his visit to Ezion Geber and Eloth on the Gulf of Aqaba (Chron. 8:17), Solomon describes the visit by Sheba:

> And when the Queen of Sheba heard of the fame of Solomon, she came to prove Solomon with hard questions at Jerusalem, with a very great company, and camels that bare spices, and gold in abundance, and precious stones: and when she was come to Solomon, she communed with him of all that was in her heart.
>
> And Solomon told her all her questions: and there was nothing hid from Solomon which he told her not. And when the queen of Sheba had seen the wisdom of Solomon, and the house that he had built, and the meat of his table, and the sitting of his servants, and the attendance of his ministers, and their apparel; and his cupbearers also, and their apparel; and his ascent by which he went up into the house of the Lord; there was no more spirit in her.
>
> And she said to the king, It was a true report which I heard in mine own land of thine acts and of thy wisdom: Howbeit I believed not their words, until I came, and mine eyes had seen it: and behold, the one half of the greatness of thy wisdom was not told me: for thou exceedest the fame that I heard.
>
> Happy are thy men, and happy are these thy servants which stand continually before thee, and hear thy wisdom.
>
> Blessed be the Lord thy God, which delighted in thee to set thee on his throne, to be king for the Lord thy God: because thy God loved Israel, to establish them for ever, therefore made he thee king over them, to do judgment and justice.
>
> And the servants also of Hiram and the servants of Solomon, which brought gold from Ophir, brought algum (incense) trees and precious stones. And the king made of the algum trees terraces to the house of the Lord, and to the king's palace, and harps and psalteries for singers: and there were none such seen before in the land of Judah.
>
> And King Solomon gave to the queen of Sheba all her desire, whatsoever she asked, beside that which she had brought unto the king. So she turned, and went away to her own land, she and her servants.[4]

This entire passage has been quoted in order to emphasize several elements that will be compared with Queen Hatshepsut's visit to God's Land, in particular:

- "his ascent by which he went up into the house of the Lord" (9:4)
- "the king made of the algum (incense) trees terraces to the house of the Lord" (9:11)
- "the servants also of Hiram" (9:10).

---

4. II Chron. 9:1-12

The texts accompanying Queen Hatshepsut's reliefs tell that:

> A command was heard from the great throne, an oracle of the god himself, that the ways to punt should be searched out, that the *highways to the myrrh-terraces* should be penetrated: I will lead the army on water and land, to bring marvels from God's Land for the god, for the fashioning of her beauty . . . I have led them on water and on land . . . and I have reached the myrrh-terraces."[5]

The Deir el Bahari relief of the landing in Punt depicts the chief of Punt 'P-'r-'hw (Perehu or Paruah) greeting the expedition. This would be Solomon's governor of Eloth (which is the district of the port on the Gulf of Aqaba) whose name in scripture is "Paruah." Northern Semitic or Caucasian people inhabit Punt, but a few Negroes are also depicted along with a variety of exotic plants and animals, including apes. Among the officials are the "chiefs of Irem," who look similar to the Egyptians. These would be the "servants of Hiram" who provided the exotic trade goods for Solomon: "once in three years came the navy of Tarshish (Hiram's) bringing gold, and silver, ivory, and apes, and peacocks."[6] And according to Josephus, also Negroes (Ethiopians).[7]

The queen's trip apparently served to show off her two fleets of ships, on the Arabian and Mediterranean coasts, similar to Solomon's presence on both. After leaving the Gulf of Aqaba she traveled by land to Jerusalem. From there she returned by way of the Mediterranean so that her ships could sail all the way to Thebes for the triumphant arrival.

Hatshepsut was so impressed with traveling the highway to the myrrh-terraces of Punt that she later established a "Punt" for her god Amon, her beautiful temple "Deir el Bahari," "to establish for him Punt in his house, to plant the trees of God's Land beside her temple in his garden."[8] "Thus the splendid temple was made a terraced myrrh-garden for the god."[9]

We recall that Solomon "made of the algum (incense) trees terraces to the house of the Lord." The ascent through Jerusalem to the temple was lined with terraces planted with exotic trees, especially algum trees. The architecture of Hatshepsut's temple is unique in Egypt and has been called the most beautiful building in all of Egypt. The long ramp ascending to the temple rises through terraces stepped with pillared colonnades. These terraces were probably planted

---

5. ARE II 285, 288 (italics added).
6. II Chronicles 9:21.
7. JA VIII vii 2.
8. ARE II 295.
9. Gardner 277

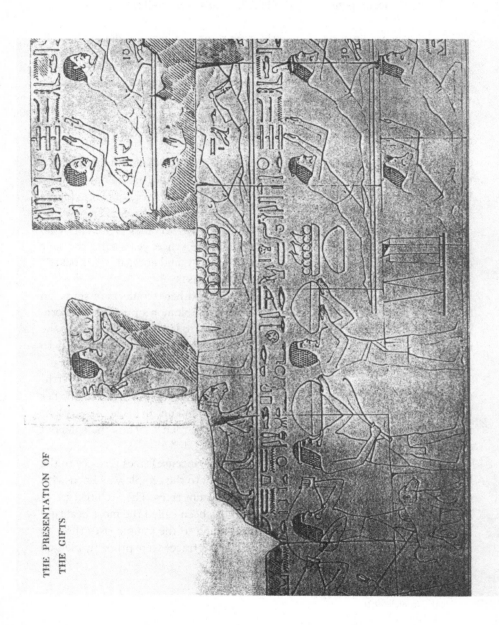

THE PRESENTATION OF
THE GIFTS

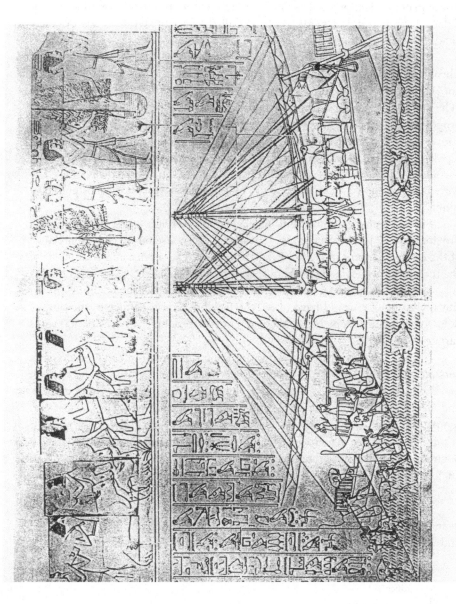

LOADING EGYPTIAN BOATS

with the precious myrrh trees, just as in Jerusalem. "The myrrh of Punt has been brought to me . . . all the luxurious marvels of this country were brought to my palace in one collection. . . . They have brought to me the choicest products . . . of cedar, of juniper and of meru-wood; . . . all the goodly sweet woods of God's Land."[10]

With nothing remaining of Solomon's temple, the description in II Chronicles 3 and I Kings 6 can only give us hints of its actual appearance. Does not Hatshepsut's temple offer a tantalizing hint of at least the style of Solomon's? (The site requires a 90 degree rotation on the long axis; then the similarity in proportions is clear. Solomon's temple is deeper than it is wide, the Egyptian temple is wider than it is deep, accommodating the topography.) The "Punt" in "God's Land" specifically inspired her temple. The approach to her temple is particularly impressive, with incense trees planted on the terraces along the way. But she copied even more than the physical attributes of the temple in "Punt."

She even made innovations to the temple service based on the model provided by the Jerusalem temple: "The queen was conscious of the resemblance of the temple-gardens in Deir el Bahari and Punt. The service and equipment of the temple receive some light from the mention of its High Priest, with twelve subordinate priests in four orders."[11] I have never seen it mentioned, but Conventional Chronology would have to see the Israelite temple service in the time of Solomon as being a copy of Hatshepsut's Egyptian temple services of 500 years earlier.

Consider the irony involved in comparing the Synchronized Chronology's version of the direction of influence at the time of Solomon with the opinion based on Conventional Chronology. "Solomon . . . wanted palaces and gardens and a temple, which might rival, even if only in a small way, the palaces and temples of Egypt and Chaldea, of which he had heard such glowing accounts."[12] "Compared with the magnificent monuments of Egypt and Chaldea, the work of Solomon was what the Hebrew kingdom appears to us among the empires of the ancient world — a little temple suited to a little people."[13]

It is a shame that we don't have the kind of diplomatic correspondence from these early rulers of the 18th Dynasty that we have from those closer to the end. The Tell el-Amarna tablets from the royal city of Akhnaton reveal the kind

---

10. Gardner 280.
11. ARE II, note to Sec. 291.
12. Maspero b 741.
13. Ibid., 747.

of detailed interaction among the foreign kingdoms and vassal states of Egypt that must have existed in Hatshepsut's time. But even the records she did leave were substantially defaced by her jealous successor and rival Thutmose III.

Hatshepsut was the only surviving *royal* child of Thutmose I. However, two sons from minor wives (or concubines) each wanted the throne, and were frustrated by Hatshepsut's claim. We know these two sons as Thutmose II and III, and both of them contributed to the defacing of her inscriptions and reliefs. One relief depicts a large image of Hatshepsut facing an image that has been completely hacked away. Egyptian artistic conventions were no doubt offended by a non-Egyptian being shown the same size as the pharaoh (or a god), and Hatshepsut certainly claimed the title of pharaoh (as opposed to simply Queen): she even wore the artificial beard that was the exclusive province of the pharaoh. If only the defaced image could be restored, might we have an actual portrait of Solomon?

From the time of Saul until early in the reign of Thutmose II, well over 100 years, Egypt and Israel enjoyed the best of relations. The visit of a pharaoh to the court of a foreign ruler (except in combat) is an event unprecedented in Egyptian history. Jerusalem held a unique status among the cities of the ancient world, not just to the Egyptians but over a very long period to all surrounding people. In the time of Abraham, "Melkizedek king of Salem (Jerusalem) brought forth bread and wine: and he was the priest of the Most High God."[14] The city was referred to by the Egyptians as "God's Land," in the Middle and even the Old Kingdom.

After Hatshepsut's reign, Jerusalem is often called by a different term. For the next part of the Theban Dynasty, the city is referred to as Kadesh, a name used for it in many places in the Old Testament, and the very word by which Jerusalem is known in Arabic to this day, "el Kuds" (*the Holy* or *the Holiness*).

One problem with the word is that it is a generic term for a holy city. There are at least three "Kadesh" cities in Palestine alone, Kadesh-Barnea, Kadesh-Naphtali and Kadesh (Jerusalem). In later times, the Egyptians knew at least one other Kadesh north of Palestine. Scholars identify that Kadesh with a city on the Orontes River. But in a later chapter, that city on the Orontes will be shown to be Riblah, and the northerly Kadesh to be Carchemish, Car (city) of Chemosh (sun god).

The same Semitic word for *Holy* (Kadesh) is even seen in the name of an Egyptian deity *Kudsu*, who scholars believe to be *Asherah*, the pagan goddess so hated by the Hebrew prophets. For now, suffice it to say that when the word

---

14. Genesis 14:18.

57

Kadesh is used, at least in the rule of Thutmose III, Jerusalem is meant (more on that in the next chapter).

With the end of Hatshepsut's reign, an era of peace comes to an end. She was the last of the old royal family of Ahmose that founded the 18th Dynasty. This international era of peace even gave a name to the Hebrew king who ruled at this time. We do not know the actual name (or names) by which the king we know as Solomon was called. That word is the same as "shalom" and means "peace," a reference to the character of his reign. Such epithets are common for ancient royalty, not just in Israel, and it creates problems when we search written records of various countries for mention of kings' names.

In the next chapter, the Synchronized Chronology will be tested by the generations that follow Solomon and Hatshepsut. The House of David suffers a rift when one of Solomon's sons begins to show signs of rebellion against the chosen successor to the throne. The rebel takes refuge in Egypt with a similar rebellious claimant, Thutmose III, who was after Hatshepsut's throne.

Before we pass on to this next period of history, we should introduce another player in the developing world of this "Late Bronze Age," the Greeks. The Aegean is one more source of rich historical records that will bear an important role in restructuring the order of ancient history. The corresponding designation for this time in the "Helladic" time scale is either Late Helladic I, or more commonly, Mycenaean I.

At about the same time as the rise of the Theban Dynasty, a new ruling class begins using "shaft graves" in Greece. The corpses are of a conspicuously larger physique than seen up to that time. Many scholars identify this as the coming of the Greeks into Greece. By the end of Hatshepsut's reign, the well-known Mycenaean sites on Greece had grown and started on a course of international trade.

As Mycenaean I transitions into II (at about the time of Thutmose III), the first palace is built in Mycenaea (still well before the date of the Trojan War). So we meet again that familiar irony in comparing Conventional Chronology to Synchronized Chronology.

Whereas David and Solomon have long been thought to have created their kingdom in the power vacuum following the collapse of the great Late Bronze Age kingdoms, we now see that they arose at the same time. In fact, Solomon's kingdom was already faltering before the first palace was built at Mycenaea!

6. THE WARS OF EGYPT AND ISRAEL

When Josephus described Solomon's guest as the Queen of Egypt and Ethiopia, he was revealing an important connection that is only now becoming widely recognized. The Theban Dynasty had more than just cultural roots in Black Africa; a major element of the royal bloodline was black. Southern Egypt has a very long archaeological link with Nubia, extending well back into the Neolithic era.

The very nature of Egyptian kingship (with Matrilineal descent) is on the Black African model, and there was probably a greater involvement by blacks in the ethnic mix of Egypt than has traditionally been acknowledged. Bernal observes that "It is generally, and reasonably, agreed today that if the members of the royal family of the 18th Dynasty were foreign, they were Nubian. It is equally probable, however that they were Upper Egyptian, and from their portraits they would seem to have been Blacks."[1]

There is still some uncertainty in the early lineage of the Theban Dynasty, but the Black element must have been there virtually from the start. Not only was Amenhotep I depicted as Black, but his mother (Ahmose-Neferteroi, wife of the first pharaoh of the 18th Dynasty, Amosis) was also so depicted. The community of workers at Dier el-Medina, whose duties centered around constructing burial chambers and all the related artifacts, was not far from the Valley of the Kings.

> The entire dynastic family beginning with the two Taos (parents of Kamose) were worshiped as the Lords of the West; and many princely

---

1. Bernal, 384.

59

names...are found on the tomb-walls of these humble folk . . . Special prominence was here given to Queen Ahmose-Neferteroi, depicted for some unaccountable reason with a black countenance...An even more important role in the necropolis came to be played by Amenophis I (Amenhotep I), to whom several chapels were dedicated.[2]

The new title *King's son of Kush* was introduced during the Theban Dynasty. "Kush" was the usual Egyptian term for Nubia, just as "Ethiopia" was the word used by Hebrew and Greek writers. Speculation over the meaning of this title routinely overlooks the obvious: that it means exactly what it says. This was a son of the pharaoh who was "of Kush." The role of the bearer of this title became a sort of junior pharaoh, in training for the job he was to assume some day.

This detour into the Ethiopian connection will have an important bearing on the way that history has been misunderstood. Egypt and Israel will continue to interact after the time of Solomon, but the chronicles on both sides have left incomplete histories. Many of the kings of Israel and Judah, whose reigns span decades of important activities, are chronicled by just a few paragraphs in the Old Testament which monotonously conclude with "and the rest of the acts of (king's name) are written in the chronicles of the kings of Judah." The compilers who left us those records were more concerned with moral lessons than with worrying that future historians would lament their editing. The records left by Egypt had even less noble motives.

One of the more interesting sidelights to the Ethiopian connection survives in the ancient holy book of Abyssinia, the "Kebra Nagast" or "The Book of the Glory of Kings." The presence of Christian elements indicates the book's origin to be from the first few centuries AD at earliest, but some of the legends are survivals of much earlier times. The first king of Ethiopia, Menelik, is said to be the son of Solomon and the "Queen of the South" (Sheba). Her name in the book is "Makeda." Coincidentally, Hatshepsut's royal name in the Punt reliefs is "Makera." In the legend, Menelik returned to Jerusalem to rob the temple, taking the ark with him while Solomon pursued him as far as Egypt. Ethiopians to this day insist that the ark is housed in a small church in the capital city of Axum. This legend preserves the idea of the Queen's successor going back to Jerusalem and robbing the temple.

The Synchronized Chronology suggests that the Hebrew chroniclers understood Thebes to be Ethiopian. Indeed the character of Upper Egypt was alien to the Hebrew's experience in the Delta. In at least one other case (in the

---

2. Gardiner, 175.

time of Asa, King of Jerusalem 908-866 BC), an invading pharaoh is referred to as "Zerah the Ethiopian." This is much too early for the "Ethiopian Dynasty" (ca 700 BC), so it is usually dismissed as sloppy recording on the part of the Israelites. Later in this chapter, Zerah will be identified with a pharaoh of the 18th Dynasty.

SOLOMON'S PUNISHMENT

In the scriptures, Solomon angered the Lord by not only marrying "many strange women" forbidden to Israelites, but they also "turned away his heart after other gods." Solomon would keep his kingdom as long as he lived, but his son Rehoboam would only inherit the tribes and the regions of Judah and Benjamin with Jerusalem, the rest being taken away for Solomon's unfaithfulness.

The course of events that led to the division of Israel began as a result of the oppressive forced labor under Solomon. One of the leaders of the laborers, Jeroboam, was encouraged by the prophet Ahijah to organize a workers' revolt. When the revolt failed, Jeroboam took refuge in Egypt with the pharaoh "Shishak." — He remained there until he heard that Solomon was dead.

On his return to Israel, Jeroboam (still regarded as an important leader) and the people of Israel gathered at Shechem to confront Rehoboam with an ultimatum: either lift the heavy yoke of service and taxation, or they would reject him as king. After pondering an answer for three days, Rehoboam disregarded his wise counselors and said, "My father made your yoke heavy, and I will add to your yoke; my father also chastised you with whips, but I will chastise you with scorpions."[3] If this were Greek tragedy, we would look back in sympathy at Rehoboam; after all, he was fulfilling a predetermined fate. It was his father's doing, wasn't it?

With that decision, Israel split off from Judah with 10 tribes. Rehoboam was left with a shrunken kingdom and a new enemy. And Jeroboam was not his only enemy. In the time of David, Edom was conquered and all the males were killed, except for the infant Hadad, who was taken to Egypt. He found such favor with the pharaoh that he was given a wife who was the sister of Tahpenes, the Queen.[4] This would have been in the time of Ahmose, whose queen was named *Tanthap* (actually, since the hieroglyphics in a cartouche can sometimes be arranged in unpredictable ways, for esthetic reasons, the syllables may have been arranged differently so that her name could indeed have been *Tahpenes*).

---

3. I Kings 12:14.
4. I Kings 11:19.

The pharaoh reluctantly allowed Hadad to return to Edom after David's death. "And he was an adversary to Israel all the days of Solomon, beside the mischief that Hadad did: and he abhorred Israel, and reigned over Syria."[5] The sons of Hadad, "Ben Hadad," ruled from Damascus for so long that the name became the generic title for the king.

Jerusalem was now surrounded by enemies. Even the friendship and alliance with Egypt was to end. The rule of Hatshepsut (the only royal child of Thutmose) gave way to that of a concubine's son. Thutmose III had been kept in the background during his older half-sister's reign. In the Punt reliefs, he is seen offering incense to the god, and it is almost certain that he went on the trip, seeing firsthand the riches of Jerusalem. His later resentment of Hatshepsut for delaying his rise to the throne led him to deface many of her monuments (and add her years of rule to his own). Egypt had also been at peace throughout the time of Hatshepsut. Now Thutmose III was determined to be a real pharaoh. It was time to flex his muscles.

Rehoboam must have become king just a few years before Thutmose III. He immediately began making preparations for war with Jeroboam. But the war was not to be, for the Lord told them not to fight against their brethren, but to return to their homes. They obeyed this order and for three years Rehoboam dealt wisely with his people and strengthened the cities of Judah. But Rehoboam had already proven that he could display shockingly bad judgment.

> And it came to pass, when Rehoboam had established the kingdom, and had strengthened himself, he forsook the law of the Lord, and all Israel with him. And it came to pass that in the fifth year of Rehoboam, Shishak, king of Egypt came up against Jerusalem, because they had transgressed against the Lord. With twelve thousand chariots and threescore thousand horsemen: and the people were without number that came with him out of Egypt; the Lubim, the Sukkims, and the Ethiopians. And he took the fenced cities which pertain to Judah, and came to Jerusalem.[6]

The King and the princes of Judah humbled themselves before the Lord. Mercy was taken on them. The Lord would not allow Shishak to destroy Jerusalem, but they would become servants of the pharaoh. "So Shishak king of Egypt came up against Jerusalem, and took away the treasures of the house of the Lord, and the treasures of the king's house; he took all."[7]

---

5. I Kings 11:25
6. II Chron. 13:14.
7. II Chron. 13:9.

If the Synchronized Chronology is correct, Thutmose III would make a campaign into Palestine very early in his reign, and indeed he did.

> The event to which Thutmose harks back again and again and which he evidently regarded as the foundation of all his subsequent successes was his victory at Megiddo, a strongly fortified town overlooking the Plain of Esdralon; this took place in his twenty-third year, the second of his independent reign, and the story is told on some unfortunately fragmentary walls in the very center of the temple of Amon-Re.[8]

Thutmose set out with his huge contingent. After ten days' march they had reached Gaza, which they took, and they continued northward along the coast until a decision had to be made over which route to take to Megiddo. Thutmose had gotten word that the princes of Retenu, led by the king of Kadesh, were assembled at Megiddo to make a stand against him. With characteristic bombast, Thutmose elected to take the most direct and dangerous route to the city, brushing off the warnings of his advisors. His records describe in vivid detail the topography of Megiddo and the surrounding areas.

Preparations for battle are likewise fully recounted and the fight itself was an opportunity for a glorious display of bravery. The enemy was routed and fled headlong for the security of the walled city, Megiddo. The pharaoh's troops could not resist pausing to gather the booty left by the fleeing enemy and thus lost the opportunity for a quick victory. A siege of several months was required to take the city, only to find that the king of Kadesh had escaped.

In all, Thutmose lists 119 cities captured in Palestine, many of them founded only in Hebrew times — an uncomfortable fact ignored by those who follow the Conventional Chronology. First among the cities of Palestine on Thutmose's list is Kadesh. There is no record that Thutmose stormed the city (the details of the later parts of the campaign are missing) but he clearly claimed it. If Kadesh is not Jerusalem, then Jerusalem, being the foremost city in Palestine in the Late Bronze Age, should be recorded separately, near the top of the list; but it is not on the list. And as was mentioned earlier, Jerusalem is referred to as "Kadesh" many times in the Old Testament.

Rehoboam opened the gates to Jerusalem and let the pharaoh in, surrendering sovereignty along with the treasury. Of the great wealth contained within the temple and palace, there can be little doubt. The description of the countless gold, silver and brass vessels equipping the temple staggers the imagination.[9]

---

8. Gardiner, 189.
9. See I Kings 7 and II Chron. 4.

On one large relief panel in the Amon Temple, Thutmose III illustrates a unique collection of spoils taken in Palestine. The collection is of interest not only for consisting almost exclusively of temple items, but also for the incredible numbers involved. For each article there is a quantity listed. If every item were illustrated separately, a wall over a mile long would be required. The panel is divided into 10 horizontal rows with gold items on the upper 5, then silver, bronze, malachite and other materials below. Most of the illustrations are of vessels such as basins and bowls, with some individual items indicated in huge numbers (95 gold basins are indicated by one illustration with the quantity 95 shown below). Candleholders are shown with seven lamps, just as were made for Solomon, and an item named "white bread," made of silver, would be the "shew bread" of the temple.

Except for a few Egyptian-looking items, which may have belonged to Solomon's Egyptian wife, there is a striking absence of idolatry in the collection. Canaanites were as notorious as the Egyptians for the use of phallic elements in their cults; none are shown. And the astonishing level of artistic ability seems to be as much a surprise to Egyptologists as it was to the Egyptians of the day. The artisans were taken captive to Egypt where they made a profound impact on Egyptian arts, language and culture.

> At this time (Thutmosis III, 1503-1449) the Syrians stood at a higher stage of civilization than even the wonderfully gifted race of Egypt. The plunder carried back to Egypt of coats of mail, of gold-plated chariots, of chariots inlaid with silver, witness to an industrial and artistic development that was able to teach Egypt. With all these precious goods went captives, who fell to working in the Nile valley at the crafts to which they were accustomed at home, and as they worked they taught the Egyptians . . . The Syrian craftsmen worked so well in Egypt that their wares changed even the taste of the Egyptians, while the language was semitized, and the method of writing gradually developed into a smooth-flowing and graceful style. Under the great influx of foreign blood even the features of the conquering race were changed into a less bold and more delicate form. Egypt had never known such changes since the beginning of the monarchy."[10]

Thutmose III repeatedly campaigned in Palestine (and beyond) throughout his career. All of Israel fell within his domain as long as he lived, and the momentum of that power carried into the reign of his successor, Amenhotep II, a ruler whose personal strength became the source of legends, but whose political and military life were to meet a different kind of strength.

---

10. R. W. Rogers, *Cuneiform Parallels in the Old Testament*, quoted in V.I 170.

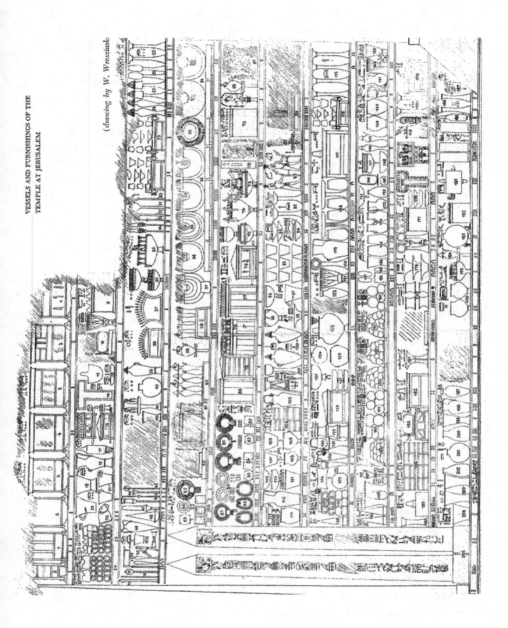

VESSELS AND FURNISHINGS OF THE
TEMPLE AT JERUSALEM

(drawing by W. Wreszinski)

We are informed by the Old Testament chroniclers that the fate of Israel (both halves) is entirely determined by faithfulness to the Lord's commandments. When they are followed, the people are rewarded with peace and prosperity. When the people fail to comply (and clearly the most offensive failure is the worship of other gods), the Lord allows punishment in the form of military defeat and payment of tribute to foreign rulers.

Jeroboam was given the ten northern tribes of Israel as punishment against Rehoboam, the son of Solomon, and although Jeroboam and Rehoboam never battled, the peace lasted only during Rehoboam's life. Meanwhile, Jeroboam had not learned the lesson of Solomon's unfaithfulness that gave him his rulership in the first place. "Yet Jeroboam, the son of Nebat, the servant of Solomon, the Son of David, is risen up and hath rebelled against his Lord. And there are gathered unto him vain men, the children of Belial."[11]

We know that a passage such as this will be followed by a moral lesson. In this case Rehoboam's successor as king of Judah, Abijam, was rewarded for his righteousness with a great victory over Jeroboam, including some territorial gains. And although he only ruled briefly, Judah was on its way back into the Lord's favor, and his son, Asa, carried the spirit forward into one of the more inspiring episodes in the history of Jerusalem.

If the Synchronized Chronology is correct, Asa would have ruled during the reign of the successor of Thutmose III, Amenhotep II, the pharaoh who shot a bow so powerful that the arrow could pierce a "palm's breadth" of bronze. Initially, Amenhotep II was able to maintain Egypt's hold on the Palestinian sources of tribute, but his last campaign there, still fairly early in his reign, was anything but a success.

ASA BATTLES AMENHOTEP II

The last battle of Amenhotep II in Palestine was in a place called Y-R-S-T, and it is significant that he reached it soon after leaving the Egyptian border. He returned to Egypt after a battle in which he managed to take all of the following booty: two horses, one chariot, a coat of mail, two bows, a quiver full of arrows, a corselet, and one more item not readable on the record. The battle was a rout, and for the rest of his reign, he made no further campaigns into Palestine and records no tribute from there.

Keeping in mind the Ethiopian connection of the Amenhotep family mentioned earlier, let us hear what the other party to this battle has to say.

---

11. II Chron. 13:6-7.

And there came out against them Zerah the Ethiopian with an host of a thousand thousand, and three hundred chariots; and came unto Mareshah. Then Asa went out against him, and they set the battle array in the valley of Zephathah at Mareshah. And Asa cried unto the Lord his God, and said Lord, whether with many, or with them that have no power: help us, O Lord our God; for we rest on thee, and in thy name we go against this multitude. O Lord, thou art our God; let not man prevail against thee. So the Lord smote the Ethiopians before Asa, and before Judah; and the Ethiopians fled.[12]

The place of the battle, Mareshah, is called Moresheth-Gath in Micah 1:14. *Moresheth* can be interpreted as "the water of" -reshet. The Egyptians described it as "the arm of water (ford) of arseth."[13] This was no minor victory. Judah had conquered the army of the Pharaoh and threw off the yoke of vassal status for a generation.

Chapter 15 of II Chronicles describes one of the most inspiring episodes in the history of Judah. Following the defeat of Zerah the Ethiopian, the people gathered to make a new covenant and rejoiced together in their oath. But even the most righteous of leaders seems fated to fall from grace, and so it was with Asa. In the 35th year of his reign, he took gold and silver from the temple and palace to send to Ben Hadad, king of Damascus. This was mercenary payment for him to attack Baasha, king of Israel. The ploy worked, but Hanani the seer informed Asa that because he had put his faith in Ben Hadad instead of the Lord, he would have unceasing wars. And so it was.

Actually, the state of affairs in the politics of the Middle East was about to undergo a major transformation. Egypt had never had a serious rival in Palestine. From the time of Saul through Solomon the relationship of mutual respect with Israel made hostilities unthinkable. And no other threat really entered the picture. Then the divided monarchy presented a temptation to the upstart Thutmose III. His records show that he did not stop at Palestine in his campaigns into "Asia." He went far enough north and east to challenge the presence of a new participant on the Middle East scene, the Mitanni.

THE MITANNI, THE KHURRIANS, AND THE RISE OF ASSYRIA

Conventional Chronology sees the Mitanni as the first appearance for an Indo-Aryan people in world history. The names of their gods, in particular, show a link to the names of well-known Persian deities. The only problem is that they show up over a half millennium before the Persians or Hindus, and then they

---

12. II Chron. 14:9-12.
13. Petrie; History of Egypt II,15.

disappear again. The Mitanni were at first adversaries of Egypt, but later entered into close diplomatic ties.

Placed in their correct historical time, the Mitanni can be seen as the forerunners of the Medes. The lake and district of Matienne (Lake Urmia) lie near the heart of the later Medean kingdom. Conventional history has about 700 years separating the Mitanni (14th century BCC) from the Medes (6th Century BC). The Synchronized history requires less than 200, a time during which the Assyrian Empire was to rise to its greatest power, and drive a military wedge between the Mitanni and their western allies.

Yet another new element introduced into the diplomatic mix at about the time of Thutmose III is the so-called Hurrians. They are known mainly by the widespread occurrence of Hurrian (often spelled Khurrian) names. Placed by Conventional Chronology in the 14th century BC, they are ghost-like forerunners of well-known players in the ancient world.

A people that were (by legend) driven from Crete by the Dorians and Ionians appear in history as the Carians, with widespread presence, particularly in the coastal Levant and Asia Minor. Athalia, daughter of Ahab and daughter-in-law of Jehosaphat, had Carians for her royal bodyguard. The "Krete" of David's time, who were also bodyguards, were Carians.[14] In spite of the Greek legends of their Cretan origin, the Carians claimed to be natives of Asia Minor (which was also true of "Khurrians").

We will not be surprised if Assyrian campaigns make "anachronistic" mention of Mitanni long after they were supposed to have disappeared from the world stage. Nor will it surprise us that Carians in Tyre play a similar role to that played by "Khurrians" supposedly hundreds of years earlier in Ugarit!

These two new participants, the Mitanni and the Khurrians, may not be of great interest to the reader interested only in biblical synchronisms, but the scholarly importance of these people is immense. Many of the extensive records preserved in Egypt for the latter part of the 18th Dynasty involve the Mitanni and Hurrians. (One other player, the "Hittites," is a subject that will be treated more or less separately and in much greater detail later).

Israel reacted in a confused manner to the entry of Assyria into regional influence. They did not realize how much difference it would make, being a vassal of Assyria rather than of Egypt. They progressed from internal fighting to alarm over the movement of the Assyrians. Egypt had been content to collect tribute from Palestine and enforce obedience only when resistance was met. "The officers in command had orders to interfere as little as possible in local

---

14. As Velikovsky, for one, explains at some length.

affairs, and to leave the natives unhindered, so long as their quarrels did not threaten the security of the Pharaoh."[15] Assyria changed the whole equation.

In the next chapter we will examine a famous collection of diplomatic correspondence from the Pharaoh Aknaton's royal city, Akhetaton, known today as Tell el-Amarna. The clay tablets found there, written in the Akkadian cuneiform that served as the "diplomatic" language of the day, included many letters from the kings of Jerusalem, Samaria (Sumura, in the letters) and Damascus. In this test of the Synchronized Chronology the Egyptian Pharaoh Amenhotep III and IV would be contemporaries of Ahab in Samaria, Jehosaphat in Jerusalem, and Hazeal in Damascus.

The interactions of these cities is not of great significance in the larger flow of history, but the chance to compare details of the famous Tell el-Amarna tablets to the biblical story is one of the most important synchronisms this work will highlight. The casual reader will find the scrutiny of these events a bit difficult to follow. It may help to examine the way that these letters are treated in standard works on this era. Those already familiar with the tablets know the unique status they enjoy among archaeological finds, not showy like a King Tut's tomb, but truly profound in scholarly concerns.

---

15. Maspero V 16-17.

7. Israel and Damascus at War.
Part 1 of the Tell El-Amarna Letters

If the historian could go back and edit the sources used to assemble the biblical books, a larger variety of material would now be deemed significant and worthy of preservation. Even what we now have is so far superior to the records left by other ancient cultures that it is a little unfair to complain. Still, there are vagaries in the events or their order that have defied generations of scholars. The era that will be explored in this chapter has just such problems. Fortunately, there is an outside source that sheds considerable light on some of them.

The biblical era that corresponds to the Egyptian Tell el-Amarna letters is dominated by one of those personalities that feature so prominently in the moral course of Israel, Elijah. The historical background of his time is overshadowed by the battle for the religious soul of the people. We can concentrate on the sequence of diplomatic interactions in order to simplify this confusing era.

The key diplomatic figures of the biblical sources are: Jehosaphat, King of Judea in Jerusalem; Ahab, King of Israel in Samaria and Jezreel, Ben Hadad, King of Aram (Syria) in Damascus; and Mesha, King of Moab. The events that concern us are the three attacks on Samaria by the king of Syria, a drought that figures in at least one of those attacks and leads to a fight over the important "bread basket" area of Ramoth-Gilead, and raids by the rebel king of Moab.

We will compare the events and personalities presented in Kings and Chronicles with those of the Tell el-Amarna letters. Once again, the Synchronized Chronology is faced with a complex set of data from two eras separated in Conventional Chronology by several hundred years. With the large amount of material from Egypt, the number of variables for comparison is greater than we have examined to this point.

As an overview of the people and places involved, the following table presents the biblical and Egyptian names in their most common forms. There are variations in "spelling" on both sides, especially the Egyptian, which is derived from the Akkadian translations of other languages by using phonetic approximations. In some cases the cuneiforms are meant to be pronounced from an ideographic rather than phonetic translation. With the exception of kings' names (which we are not certain of, even in the biblical record) the identities are more or less obvious. All references to individual letters will be as numbered in Mercer's 1939 edition of the *Tell El-Amarna Tablets*.

BIBLE	TELL EL-AMARNA LETTERS
CITIES	
Jerusalem	Urusalim
Samaria	Sumur
Damascus	Dimasqa
Jezreel (Jezebel)	Gubla
Ramoth-Gilead ("*Aramathea*" In Josephus)	Iarimuta
KINGS	
Jehosaphat	Abdi-Heba (Ebed-Tov)
Ahab	Rib-Addi
Ben Hadad & Hazael	Abdi-Ashirta & Aziru
Mesha	Mes(H)
JEHOSAPHAT'S MILITARY CAPTAINS	
Adnah (Addu Of Dan)	Addudanni
Jehohanan	—
Amasia "Son Of Zichri"	Son Of Zuchru
Eliada	—
Jehozabad	Iahzibada
GOVERNORS	
Amon (Samaria)	Aman-Appa
Namaan (Aram-Amor)	Ianahamu
Adaia (Deputy Of Edom)	Addaia

Of the cities in this table, Jerusalem/Urusalim and Damascus/Dimasqa are unquestioned in their identity. Since the Tell el-Amarna letters are conventionally dated to the 14th century BC, and Jerusalem was supposed to have been re-named only after David's conquest of the city in the 10th century (it was previously known as Salem), it is generally assumed that the scriptures are in error. A 9th-century date for the letters creates no such problem.

A similar difficulty exists with Samaria/Sumur. Sumur is the most frequently-named city in the letters. The biblical city was founded by Ahab's father Omri. The Amarna letters are assumed to refer to a small coastal fortress of that name in the 14th century. Again, a 9th-century date avoids the conflict.

The biblical Ramoth-Gilead presents no real problem in identification with Iarimuta of the letters. It is surprising that no scholar besides Velikovsky has drawn the connection. When we examine the role that this region played during the drought, the similarity between the names becomes more convincing.

It is only with the identification of Jezreel as Gubla that real phonetic difficulties arise. Yet this also has an apparent explanation. The king of Israel, Ahab, had his own palace city, Jezreel, just as his father Omri had with Samaria. Ben Hadad, king of Damascus, repeatedly attacked Samaria. In the letters, the king of Gubla wrote to the pharaoh complaining of attacks by the king of Damascus on Sumur, a city that he, the king of Gubla, claimed was his.

Gubla is assumed by scholars to be Byblos, although in other references in other sources it is known as Gwal. If the original name of Jezreel was Jezebel, named by Ahab for his notorious wife, the phonetic difficulties largely disappear. In II Kings 9:37, suggests that Jezebel's name was blotted out from the land after her death.

The names of the kings present the only real problems, and for the same reason we have encountered in prior eras. Jehosaphat cannot be equated with Abdi-Hiba by any presumed phonetic shifts. On the other hand, since cuneiforms can sometimes have alternate pronunciations (ideographic vs. phonetic), the name was also read as Ebed-tov ("the Good Servant" in Hebrew). It is likely that the name Jehosaphat was created in honor of the king's reputation. It means "Jahwe is the judge," and scripture explains why. "And he set judges in the land throughout all the fenced cities of Judah, city by city. And said to the judges, Take heed what you do for ye judge not for man, but for Jahwe, who is with you in the judgment."[1] For the same reason that Solomon was unlikely to have been known by his contemporaries by the name "Peace," Jehosaphat would probably not show up by that name in his own time.

Ahab does not resemble Rib-Addi in pronunciation, but in meaning they are almost identical. "Ah" signifies brother and "ab" is father. "Rib-Addi" ideographically is "the elder brother (of the sons) of the father."

During the time covered by the Tell el-Amarna letters, the king of Damascus, Abdi-Ashirta, died and was succeeded by a (probably illegitimate) son, Azaru. In the scriptures Hazael is the son of Ben Hadad. Keeping in mind that "l" and "r" are the same letter, the sons' names (*Hazael and Aziru*) are virtually

---

1. II Kings 19:5-6

identical. As for Ben Hadad, we mentioned before that this was a "generic" name for kings of Damascus (meaning "son" of the god Hadad) and would not have been his personal name.

Moab had been a tributary area of Samaria until its ruler, Mesha, rebelled under encouragement by the king of Damascus. We do not need to translate his name because it is virtually identical in scripture and the letters. He left an inscribed tablet (the Mesha Stele) describing his rebellion against Ahab using the same name as occurs in the Amarna tablets. In fact, his name appears so often in complaints against the "amulet-gaz Mes" (people of the rebel Mesh, or Moabites) that he is one of the central players in the letters.

Egypt assigned agents or governors to its tributaries. They were responsible for overseeing the pharaoh's military and economic interests. Vassal kings appealed to these governors for military support when threatened by their adversaries (who often were *also* vassals of Egypt). These appeals seem to have been so often ignored that letters of complaint were sometimes sent directly to the pharaoh asking for help. These also appear to have fallen mostly on deaf ears (especially those to Akhnaton), since Egypt usually kept out of disputes among the vassals. Many letters also seem to have been intercepted by officials and never reach the pharaoh.

The governor of Sumer during the first part of Rib-Addi's (Ahab's) reign was Aman-Appa, who appears to have then returned permanently to Egypt. In II Chronicles 17:7, Amon (an Egyptian name) is referred to as the governor of Samaria: "Amon, the governor of the city." Rib-Addi writes to him in hopes that his sympathies will influence the pharaoh: "Thou knowest my attitude. Whilst thou wast in Sumur that I was thy faithful servant."[2] The three sieges of Sumur by the king of Damascus led to Rib-Addi having the most letters in the whole Tel el-Amarna collection.

The governor (sar) of Aram/Amor (Syria) is mentioned frequently in the letters under the name of *Ianhamu*. His relations with the king of Gubla undergo a change. In the scriptures, the nature of that change is the outcome of a healing of *Namaan* by the prophet Elisha.[3] This is "Namaan, captain (sar) of the host of the king of Syria." The title of "Sar" is the same in the scriptures and the letters.

---

2. letter 73.
3. in II Kings 5

JEHOSAPHAT'S CAPTAINS

Letters to the pharaoh from three of Jehosaphat's five captains are represented in the Amarna collection. II Chronicles 17:14-19 is a brief introduction to these captains:

> And these are the numbers of them according to the house of their fathers: of Judah, the captains of thousands; Adnah the chief, and with him mighty men of valour three hundred thousand. And next to him was Jehohanan the captain, and with him two hundred and fourscore thousand. And next to him was Amasiah the son of Zichri, who willingly offered himself unto the Lord; and with him two hundred thousand mighty men of valour. And of Benjamin; Eliada a mighty man of valour, and with him armed men with bow and shield two hundred thousand. And next to him was Jehozabad, and with him an hundred and fourscore thousand ready prepared for the war. These waited on the king, beside those whom the king put in the fenced cities throughout all Judah.

As with many other positions in society, these titles were hereditary "according to the house of their fathers." One of these captains, Amaziah son of Zichri, is singled out in both the scriptures and letters for his descent from Zichri/Zichru "who willingly offered himself to the Lord." (Actually, Zichri's name does not survive in the letters — only his heritage, "son of Zichru"). Jehozabad of the scriptures is Iahzibada of the letters.

Adna in the scriptures is probably a shortened form of Addu-Dani of the letters. The Assyrian name for the prince of Gaza is Ada-Danu, which Velikovsky explains would be offensive to the biblical scribes since it incorporates the name of an Assyrian divinity "Addu" into the name of one close to the pious Jehosaphat.

Jehosaphat's deputy over Edom would have been Adaia, the father of Maaseiah who was a chief 16 years after Jehosaphat (here again hereditary titles are assumed). In the letters, a deputy with the name Addaia, subordinate to the king of Jerusalem, is mentioned several times.

Just as the scriptures give a severely edited version of this segment of history, so also the el-Amarna tablets present a very lopsided collection of information. One might think that 360+ letters would span a wide spectrum of life, but that is not the case. Almost all of the letters fall into two categories; letters from independent kings who use the term "thy brother" to indicate an equality of stature with the pharaoh, and all the others which are from vassal kings, princes and deputies who refer to the pharaoh as "My lord, my Sun, etc." and include a whole assemblage of subservient gestures. Most of the letters fall into the latter group and are boringly repetitious in the extreme. Strip away the honorifics clustered into the opening address, and little remains other than a profession of faithfulness to the pharaoh and a plea for military help.

Unless a given tablet retains the names of the sender and his city (either or both are sometimes damaged, near the top edge of a tablet, and are unreadable), these must be determined from the content of the letter. This content can go beyond what is actually written into the writing style or even the clay of the tablet itself. A great deal of effort has gone into the sorting of the letters by author, city and time. The locations of many of the cities named in the letters can only be determined by educated guesswork, since the cities are unknown from any other ancient or modern information. Names of people and places often point to a particular language and thus to a probable region of origin.

The assumption of a 14th century BCC date for the letters has prevented the identification of many cities (not to mention governors, captains and deputies) whose names are similar (or identical) to those founded only much later.

The letters also encompass a much larger diplomatic world than the narrow focus of the Books of Kings and Chronicles. The presence of so many letters from areas unknown from scripture should not detract from the fact that the letters from those cities named in the Old Testament reflect conditions, personalities and events exactly as they are presented in the scriptures.

We concluded the historical sequence of the last chapter with Asa on the throne of Judah and Baasha in Israel. Israel was about to sink into one of those violent periods of transition which recur in its history. There were no fewer than four kings in only two years, as Baasha was succeeded by his son Elah, who was then assassinated by Zimri. Zimri lasted only a week before Omri (the popular general of Israel's army) stormed Tirzah and burned the royal palace with Zimri inside. Omri dispatched his only rival, Tibni, and proclaimed himself king.

If Omri were judged only by the number of biblical passages devoted to him (six), he would appear to be rather unimportant. But we know from the Assyrians that he was considered a powerful and important king. They refer to Israel as "Bit Humrai," or House of Omri. Like Solomon, he forged close ties with a Phoenician king of Sidon, Eth-Baal, whose daughter, Jezebel, married Omri's son Ahab.

In about 880 BC, Omri moved the capital of Israel to Samaria, where he built a fortified palace on a hill named for the man from whom Omri purchased the site. The construction of the city was probably completed under Ahab, whose long reign started about 874 BC. This was approximately the same time that Jehosaphat's reign in Judah began in a co-regency with his father Asa.

Hostilities between Israel and Syria erupted as described in I Kings 20:1 — "And Ben Hadad the king of Syria gathered all his host together and there were thirty and two kings with him, and horses, and chariots; then he went up and besieged Samaria and warred against it."

Ahab had nearly decided to capitulate to a demand for tribute from Ben Hadad, when the Syrian indicated that he would take the city even if the price were paid. This stiffened the resistance of Israel. Then the arrival of 232 "young men of the governors of the provinces" made a decisive difference in Israel's favor. Why should 232 "young men" make a difference when 7000 Israelites backed them up? They would have to have been a small contingent of Egyptians (probably archers) at the disposal of the Egyptian governor. We are told, "So these young men (retainers/soldiers) of the governors of the provinces came out of the city, and the army which followed them. And they slew every one his man and the Syrians fled."[4] They seem to have been good shots but, more than that, these detachments of small numbers of Egyptian troops signaled a rare decision by the pharaoh to support one side in a dispute. This, more than the number involved, was the really decisive factor.

The urgency with which these forces are awaited can be seen in the Amarna letters from the king of Sumur. In a missive to a high Egyptian official, Haia, he wrote, "Why hast thou held back and not said to the king (pharaoh) that he should send archers that they may take Sumura?" And he wrote to the governor Aman-appa: "If they perceive that the archers have gone forth, they will leave even their cities."[5]

Ahab's victory over Ben Hadad was to provide peace for only a year, and then another battle was waged, this time at Aphek (a valley site hoped by the Syrians to be of less advantage to the Israelites with their "mountain god"). Again, Ahab defeated the Syrian, who then successfully begs for mercy in exchange for a covenant granting Israel trade concessions within Damascus. Ahab's gullibility in trusting Ben Hadad brought a rebuke from a prophet. " . . . thy life shall go for his (Ben Hadad's) life and thy people for his people."[6]

The peace lasted three years this time and then a dispute broke out over Ramoth-Gilead. The king of Damascus had been taking cities in northern Palestine from Israel. When it came to Ramoth-Gilead, the consequences were too great to tolerate because the region was an important food-producing area. (This is not stated in scripture, but the letters make that clear). Ahab made the

---

4. II Kings 20:19-20.
5. letter 71, letter 73.
6. II Kings 20:42

unprecedented request of Jehosaphat to join together in a campaign to recover Ramoth. Jehosaphat agreed over the warning of the prophet, Micaiah.

The battle apparently did not go well for Israel, as Ahab was wounded and Jehosaphat avoided being slain by the Syrians only by convincing them that he was not Ahab! With the outcome of this battle we enter one of the confusing and contradictory episodes occasionally encountered in the Scriptures.

In I Kings 22:34, when Ahab is injured, he first instructs his driver to take him away "for I am wounded." In the next passage it says that the battle increased all day and the king stayed up in his chariot against the Syrians, and then died.

Added to this contradictory set of passages is a pair of conflicting dates for Ahab's successor(s). His son Ahaziah died from an injury very soon after taking the throne of Israel, and then in II Kings 1:17 it is stated that "Jehoram (another son) reigned in his stead in the second year of Jehoram the son of Jehosaphat king of Judah." (adding to the potential confusion, there are two Jehorams.) This would mean that Ahab died about a year after Jehosaphat, leaving just enough time for Ahaziah's short reign. But then in II Kings 3:1, it is said that, "Now Jehoram the son of Ahab began to reign over Israel in Samaria in the eighteenth year of Jehosaphat, king of Judah." Jehosaphat reigned for 25 years and the difference between these two versions of the date of Ahab's death is about nine years. A few passages later it is stated that Jehoram requested that Jehosaphat ally with him to fight the rebellious Moabites. Still later he fought at Ramoth-Gilead allied with another Jehoram, son of Jehosaphat and was wounded in the battle. The succession of kings of Israel and Judah following Ahab and Jehosaphat has the air of irreconcilable contradictions before which the chroniclers were apparently helpless; they left in all surviving versions.

The sequence, as given, has Ahab succeeded by an Ahaziah and a Jehoram. Similarly, Jehosaphat is followed by a Jehoram and an Ahaziah. Ahab dies in the middle of Jehosaphat's reign in one case and outlives him in the other. For several chapters of II Kings, the chroniclers avoid naming the king of Israel altogether and simply refer to "the king." In all of these same passages the king of Judah is named.

It is not the purpose here to sort out all of the confusion in this series of reigns. The chronological problems have inspired a host of theories. However, there is an outside source that can help us in determining whether Ahab lived those extra nine years. It is stated in II Kings 3:4 that Mesha, king of Moab, rebelled against Israel after the death of Ahab. Not only are we fortunate to have a lengthy inscription from none other that Mesha, the king of Moab, but with the help of the Tell el-Amarna letters we can place the rebellion in the middle of Ahab's reign.

THE MESHA STELE

Considered one of the most important archaeological finds from biblical times, the Mesha Stele (or Moabite Stone) is the earliest inscription in Northern Semitic (of a style very close to Hebrew). A German clergyman found the slab of basalt in the possession of a group of Arabs in Dibon in 1868. He tried to buy it, but then the Arabs who had found it decided the strange writing on it must describe a treasure hidden inside. So they heated and threw water on it, causing it to break into several small pieces — which revealed nothing inside, but did produce more objects for sale! Fortunately, most of the pieces were retrieved, and even more fortunate — a rubbing had already been made, or a cast, and the text was published in 1869, so that it was possible to reconstruct the original (or at least what was found, a chunk about five feet high, which may be just half of the true original). The stone is now in the Louvre Museum.

Moab had been a vassal state of Israel. After the battle of Ramoth-Gilead Mesha rebelled, recovering not only much land north of the Arnon River and east of the Jordan, but sacking Israelite towns also. The inscription begins:

> I am Mesha, son of Chemosh, king of Moab, the Diabonite. My father reigned over Moab for thirty years, and I reigned after my father. . . Omri was king of Israel, and he afflicted Moab for many days, for Chemosh (the deity) was being angry with his land. And his son Ahab succeeded him, and he also said, I will afflict Moab...Omri had taken possession of the land of Mahdabe. And it (Israel) dwelt therein his days and half the days of his son, 40 years; and Chemosh restored it in my day."[7]

If Mesha rebelled after only half of Ahab's reign ("and half the days of his son"), we have a contemporary record which contradicts the opening line of II Kings: "Then Moab rebelled against Israel after the death of Ahab," but which supports II Kings 1:17, which has Ahab living until the second year after Jehosaphat, some nine years later. Apparently Mesha rebelled after Ahab was wounded. Evidence from the Amarna letters show that rumors of Ahab's death were reaching even the pharaoh, causing Ahab to protest that he was still very much alive.

The Amarna letters have the "Rebel Mesh" attacking the cities of the king of Sumur. In one of his last letters to the Pharaoh Akhnaton, the king of Sumur

---

7. CAH III, 372.

describes himself as an old man. Ahab could have been an old man if he outlived Jehosaphat, but his son, in the early part of his reign, could not have been.

The king of "Gubla" (Jezreel) wrote more letters in the Amarna collection (65) than any other writer. In spite of the repetitive theme of his letters, his personality comes through. He is uniformly worried and unhappy.

> Let the king (pharaoh) my lord, know that Gubla is intact, the true handmaid of the king, but that the hostility of the SA.GAZ.MESH-troops (rebel Mesha troops) is very great against me. So let not the king hold back from Sumer that it be not quite annexed to the SA.GAZ.MESH troops. By the deputy of the king, who was in Sumer, Gubla is delivered. Behold, Pahamata the deputy of the king, who is in Sumer, knows the distress which oppresses Gubla. From Iarimuta (Ramoth) we have received provisions.[8]

We can see in the Amarna letters, much more clearly than in II Kings, the hand of the king of Damascus in supporting Mesha. Rib-Addi (Ahab) complains about the king of Damascus, Abdi-Ashirta (Ben Hadad), and his son Aziru (Hazael), in words so similar to those spoken to the prophet Elisha that the idioms are identical: "What is Abdi-Ashirta, the servant, the dog, that he should take the land of the king to himself."[9]

"And Hazael said, And what is thy servant, a dog, that he should do this great thing." (II Kings 8:13, in which Elisha was weeping and prophesizing that Hazael would oppress Israel).

In almost every letter from the king of Gubla, concern for Sumur is mentioned. Sumur is subjected to drought, famine and siege throughout the letters. It is apparent that Rib-Addi is making every effort to keep the city from falling to the king of the Amorites, Abdi-Ashirta (Ben Hadad), and his appeals to Egypt are framed to convince the pharaoh that it is in his best interests to send help. Damascus, of course, is just as much a tributary state to Egypt as Gubla, Sumer or Jerusalem. Rib-Addi tries to convince the pharaoh that Abdi-Ashirta is not faithful and shouldn't be allowed to continue "taking" the cities "belonging" to the pharaoh.

Letters from Abdi-Ashirta complain that others are slandering him and that he is most faithful to the pharaoh. Egypt appears to be unconcerned about those squabbles until claims are made that the "King of Hatti" is starting to encroach on lands attached to the pharaoh.

---

8. letter 68, parentheses added.
9. letter 71.

Sumer is a focus of the conflict between the king of Gubla and the king of Damascus. The second siege is far more serious than the first, because of the famine. The Amarna letters and the scriptures alike paint a vivid picture.

Immediately after Ahab has been introduced as the successor to Omri as king of Israel, we meet an individual whose messages are the real lessons for these times: Elijah. The stories in which he and Elisha play a part fit uncomfortably into the background of historical events, at times seeming completely unrelated to the rest of the chronicles. But there is no question of what is meant by the opening of I Kings 17.

> And Elijah the Tishbite who was of the inhabitants of Gilead, said unto Ahab, 'As the Lord God of Israel liveth before whom I stand, there shall not be dew or rain these years.' . . . And it came to pass after a while, that the brook dried up, because there had been no rain in the land.[10] . . . And it came to pass after many days, that the word of the Lord came to Elijah in the third year, saying, Go shew thyself unto Ahab; and I will send rain upon the earth. And Elijah went to shew himself unto Ahab. And there was a sore famine in Samaria.[11] . . . And Ahab said unto Obediah (the governor of his house), Go into the land, unto all fountains of water, and unto all the brooks; peradventure we may find grass to save the horses and mules alive, that we lose not all the beasts.[12]

Having set the stage, this drought is the backdrop for Elijah's demonstration before the prophets of Baal. Baal (which means "lord") and the female Astarte were the principle deities recognized in Canaan at the time, and the royal family from which Jezebel came were devotees. Not surprisingly, when Ahab married Jezebel, she brought her religion with her. She persecuted the priests of the Hebrew god, thus running headlong into Elijah. He eventually has Israelites gather at Mt. Carmel for a confrontation between him and her 450 prophets of Baal. Two sacrificial bullocks are prepared, one for the prophets, and one for Elijah. The test is to be which God will send down fire to consume the offering.

The prophets of Baal spend all morning praying and pleading for the miracle. Elijah mocks them by declaring that they need to shout louder because their god is away or asleep. So they then cry louder and mutilate themselves in efforts to bring on the miracle. When noon comes and nothing has happened, it is Elijah's turn, all by himself. He lays out 12 stones in a trench and places wood

---

10. I Kings 17:7.
11. I Kings 18:1-2.
12. I Kings 18:5.

and the bullock upon them. He then has four barrels of water poured over all until the trench is filled. Elijah then prays to the God of Abraham, Isaac and Israel, and "the fire of the Lord fell, and consumed the burnt sacrifice, and the wood, and the stones, and the dust, and licked up the water that was in the trench."[13]

Elijah then has the people slay all the prophets of Baal and takes Ahab up to the top of Mt. Carmel to see the rain coming. Elijah runs before Ahab's chariot from Carmel to Jezreel (although the location of Jezreel is not known for certain, the conventional site east of Samaria would make a run from Carmel unlikely. Perhaps it was closer to the coast and to the Canaanite — or Phoenician, to use the Greek term — trading partners he was allied with through Jezebel).

Following Elijah's demonstration, Ben Hadad's first siege of Samaria is described. There is probably no firm chronological connection that can be made here, but the victories over Ben Hadad are then followed by the battle for Ramoth-Gilead (allied with Jehosaphat). The Amarna letters explain why Ramoth is so important during these times as a food source. The drought and famine are centered in Samaria in both the scriptures and the letters; Ramoth was evidently spared.

By the time of Ben Hadad's second siege of Samaria the drought had caused tremendous suffering. "And it came to pass after this, that Ben Hadad king of Syria gathered all his host, and went up and besieged Samaria. And there was a great famine in Samaria."[14] Ahab is absolutely crushed when he hears of a woman crying because another woman would not boil her son to eat after the first woman had kept the deal by boiling her own son the day before. One more time Samaria is spared when the Syrians flee at the sound of approaching chariots, leaving their provisions for the starving Samarians.

In the Amarna letters the king of Gubla (Jezreel) tells the same sad story. His letters begin with the standard honorifics, which include a blessing from the patron deity of his city, "Baal of Gubla."

> Behold, thus have I written to the king, my lord, and he did not listen to my word. Verily, three times, these years, has he opposed me, and two years I measure my grain. There is no grain for our support. What shall I say to my peasants? Their sons, their daughters have come to an end, and the wooden implements of their houses, because they are given to Iarimuta (Ramoth) for the deliverance of our lives.[15]

---

13. I Kings 18:38.
14. II Kings 6:24-25.
15. letter 85.

Here he describes his three battles with the king of Syria, the lack of grain and the selling of household goods to buy grain from Iarimuta. Even the children were sold for food. "Our sons and daughters have come to an end, together with ourselves, because they are given in Iarimuta for the saving of our lives. My field is a wife who is without a husband, deficient in cultivation."[16]

A depressing monotony fills the letters from Rib-Addi to the pharaoh and his advisors. They continue even after the death of Abdi-Ashirta — who is mentioned as sick and likely to die in one letter. The sons of Abdi-Ashirta, especially Aziru (Hazael) continue the attacks that cause Rib-Addi to complain. The son of Abdi-Ashirta, Aziru, is called "the dog," just as his father was. In fact, later on, no other clue as to who is meant is even needed. He is just referred to as "the dog," and everyone knows who is meant!

Before concluding this chapter and moving on to the similar difficulties faced by Jerusalem, a little should be said about this important character in the Amarna letters, Rib-Addi, who, in his biblical alter-ego as Ahab, has been so strongly vilified by history. His name will forever be identified with Jezebel, whose reputation embodies everything evil associated with paganism. Ahab's embrace of the Phoenician deity Baal (reflected in both the scriptures and the letters) was undoubtedly a diplomatic concession of the greatest importance, as was his arranged marriage. Accommodation (and even merging) of deities of allied nations was commonplace in the ancient world. Phoenician temples of this era are indistinguishable from those of the Hebrews; indeed, Solomon's temple was built by Phoenicians. It is likely that the temple services were also similar.

Ahab is presented in the scriptures as a man deeply troubled and willing to humble himself before God. He does not seem to be able to recognize the seriousness of his errors before they occur. But when the ever-present prophets point out his sins, he tears his clothes, puts on sackcloth and fasts in humility. The circumstances of the time in which he ruled offered little but trouble.

The Ahab of the Amarna letters ends his life in exile in Beirut and Sidon, apparently with relatives of his wife Jezebel. This detail in not mentioned in the scriptures but may be responsible for the belief that he was dead. From Beirut, in his last letter to Egypt, he wrote, "When they had said 'Rib-Addi is dead, and we are out of his power,' did I not write to the lands of Egypt."[17]

---

16. letter 74.
17. letter 138.

8. JERUSALEM IN THE TIME OF AKHNATON.
PART 2 OF THE TELL EL AMARNA LETTERS

Jerusalem was not spared the turmoil that marks this particular time, considered by some a "Pax Aegypticus." One cannot help thinking that the Tell el-Amarna letters illustrate a diplomatic policy that prevents a coalition from forming by keeping all the potential members constantly at war with one another. The rivalry seen during much of the divided kingdom is of a kind typical for the letters. Interestingly, the letters show no hostilities between Sumer and Urusalim, a situation reflected also in the scriptures for this singular era.

The tablets from Urusalim describe a state of concern over the advances of a rebel army from the east that is taking the lands (and towns) traditionally belonging to Urusalim. The attackers are called "Habiru,"[1] which in Hebrew means "companions of thieves," "troops of robbers"[2] or "companions of a destroyer."[3]

The term "Habiru" is used interchangeably in the letters with SA-GAZ, which is translated as "cutthroats" and "bandits" in the letters. For some reason the Hebrew word was never connected (except by Velikovsky) to the use in the letters. In fact, when the letters were first translated, the term *Habiru* was considered to be the first literary mention of "Hebrew." In the assumed 14th-century setting, complaints from the king of Jerusalem about Hebrew invaders coming across the Jordan seemed brilliant confirmation of scripture.

---

1. Isaiah 1:23
2. Hosea 6:9.
3. Proverbs 28:24

Unfortunately the time was later seen as just too early for the conquest under Joshua (except to biblical historians who thought the time was just right!) since the Exodus could not have occurred yet. After all, Ramses would not take the throne of Egypt until well into the next dynasty, and there is an inexplicable fixation to identify the Exodus with him. The problem of identifying the "Habiru" gave rise to some interesting speculation concerning the "true" course of Hebrew history.

One theory allows Hebrew tribes who never joined the main body in Egypt to make these preliminary forages into the Promised Land. Never mind that scripture knows nothing of these early tribal movements, Joshua would no doubt have appreciated some allies east of the Jordan. This theory shows the sort of casual contempt for scripture that dominates much of scholarship. Fortunately little attention is paid today to the "Hebrew-Habiru" identity (not nearly as close in the original language as it seems in English). Only a few biblical historians still hold out for an early conquest date "as we shall see there is every probability that these invaders were none other than the Hebrews who had escaped from Egypt some fifty years or more earlier.[4]

The SA-GAZ rebels of Rib-Addi's letters are the Moabites. They were joined by others to go after Jerusalem. The king of Urusalim declares that "there is hostility to me as far as the lands of Seir (Mt. Seir)" (letter 288). "After they have taken Rubuda, they seek now to take Urusalim."[5] Rubuda (also called Rubuta) is Rabbath, in Amman, the modern capital of Jordan.

The impression given in the letters from the king of Urusalim is of a growing alliance among rebellious neighbors east across the Jordan. They are no doubt supported by the king of Aram in Damascus and cause great alarm in their approach to Jerusalem. Letters to the pharaoh complain of his inaction in the face of this dramatic threat to a loyal tributary. "Although a man sees the facts, yet the two eyes of the king, my lord, do not see . . . The Habiru are taking the cities of the king."[6] This is pretty strong language for a subordinate to address to the Pharaoh; the situation must have been getting desperate. (In fact the letters from the king of Jerusalem are unique among those from vassals in refusing to address the pharaoh as Lord.)

The pleas are similar to the letters sent by the king of Sumer. "If there are no archers, then there will also remain to the king no lands and no regents."[7] Suspecting that the pharaoh is not even receiving his pleas, the king of Jerusalem

---

4. Merrill 103.
5. letter 289.
6. letter 288.
7. letter 287

closes his letter with a personal note to the pharaoh's scribe: "To the scribe of the king, my lord, Thus saith Abdi-Hiba, thy servant: Report plain words to the king. I am very humbly thy servant."[8]

In the last chapter the conflicts between Israel and Aram in the times of Ahab and Ben Hadad were compared to events described in the El Amarna letters for the same two regions. The repeated attacks in Samaria occurred in both versions amidst famine and drought. The rebellion of Moab under Mesha was likewise compared. Now we have the opportunity to examine the history of the other capital city of the divided Hebrew Kingdom during the same time frame.

JERUSALEM

The El Amarna letters from Abdi-Hiba, king of Jerusalem, appeal for help against the coalition of rebellious chieftains coming from Moab, Amon and Mt. Seir on their way to the ultimate prize, Jerusalem. If the Synchronized Chronology is correct, Jehosaphat will encounter a similar threat to his city.

The 25-year reign of Jehosaphat yielded only a few events deemed important enough for inclusion in scripture: the makeup of his military command, his alliance with Ahab to retake Rammoth-Gilead, the spread of Yahwist judges throughout Judah, and the miraculous saving of Jerusalem from a terrifying army approaching from the east. The last event serves as the culmination of his devotion and willingness to trust in the Hebrew Lord. Chapter 20 of II Chronicles tells the story:

> It came to pass after this also, that the children of Moab, and the children of Ammon, and with them other beside the Ammonites, came against Jehosaphat to battle. Then there came some that told Jehosaphat, saying, there cometh a great multitude against thee from beyond the sea on this side Syria; and, behold, they be in Hazazontamar, which is Engedi (near the mid-point on the west shore of the Dead Sea). And Jehosaphat feared, and set himself to seek the Lord, and proclaimed a fast throughout all.[9]

Jehosaphat prayed before the assembly in a plea to the Lord to save the faithful people as had been done so many times before:

> If, when evil cometh upon us, as the sword, judgment, or pestilence, or famine, we stand before this house, and in thy presence, (for thy name is in this

---

8. letter 289.
9. Judah 1-4.

house,) and cry unto thee in our affliction, then thou wilt hear and help. And now, behold, the children of Ammon and Moab and mount Seir, whom thou wouldest not let Israel invade, when they came out of the land of Egypt, but they turned from them, and destroyed them not; Behold, I say, how they reward us, to come to cast us out of thy possession, which thou hast given us to inherit."[10]

The El-Amarna tablets preserve only six letters from the king of Jerusalem, all written before the outcome of the city's plight is revealed. II Chronicles supplies the surprise ending. The prophet Jahaziel declares that the Lord will provide salvation, so Jehosaphat tells the faithful to go out to see what will happen. The armies threatening Jerusalem destroyed each other, "For the children of Ammon and Moab stood up against the inhabitants of mount Seir, utterly to slay and destroy them, and when they had made an end of the inhabitants of Seir, every one helped to destroy another."[11]

Jehosaphat was left with nothing to do but go down with his people and gather spoils from the dead, so much that it took three days to collect.

The Tell el-Amarna tablets are a unique survival from so ancient a time. Not only do contemporary witnesses describe events, but those witnesses are the very individuals making the history. Monumental inscriptions from Egypt filter reality through the enormous egos of the reigning pharaohs. Hebrew scriptures reveal only selective details from larger events edited in order to serve a particular spiritual agenda. The *Letters* are an entirely different window on this time.

Because of the wide diplomatic world of the 18th Dynasty pharaohs, the *Letters* do not focus on the events of concern to the Hebrew kingdoms. Granted that 65 of the 350+ letters are from none other than Ahab, they tell us more about his enemies than about him. And the six letters from Jehosaphat are little more than a footnote. But a narrow look at the circumstances surrounding only these relevant cities shows just how closely the histories of the two sources agree. Samaria undergoes the same sequence of sieges during drought and famine from the same attackers, Damascus and Moab. And Jerusalem is threatened by an overwhelming coalition of rebel forces in both sources. Again, the enemies — Ammon, Moab and Mt. Seir — are identical.

In the case of Samaria, the letters help resolve an outcome confused by conflicting scriptural versions. For Jerusalem, the surprise ending to the conflict is missing from the letters, but is supplied by scripture. The only thing we might

---

10. II Chronicles 20: 9-11.
11. II Chronicles 20:23.

wish for from the letters is some link between Samaria and Jerusalem, something to show that some bond connected these two vassal city/kingdoms. That link comes in one of the last letters from Rib-Addi (Ahab).

Ahab is an old man in exile from his palace cities Gubla (Jezreel) and Sumer (Samaria). His letters and messengers get no satisfaction from the pharaoh and he does not wish to stay in exile nor to leave for Egypt, so he asks that he be given another city for his residence. Of all the choices in Palestine he has but one request: "Let him give the city of Buruzalim to me for a residence."[12]

Scholars had no trouble dismissing the typically inconsistent spelling so common in the letters: it was Jerusalem Rib-Addi had asked for. Placed in the 14th century, the request raised no particular interest. How much more significant it is to think that Ahab would entertain the takeover of Jerusalem with the help of Egypt! At this point Ahab was fantasizing about receiving help from a pharaoh who was oblivious to anything but his own religious revolution. But it is fortunate for us that he expressed those thoughts in writing.

In his book *Pharaohs and Kings*, David Rohl proposes a chronology that has been discussed in previous chapters. He links the Exodus to the time of the Hyksos invasion of Egypt for the same reasons as are presented here. But since he keeps the rest of the Dynasties in their same basic order, his remaining chronological reconstruction differs. He places the Tell el-Amarna letters in the time of Saul, a difference of something less than 200 years from that proposed here. In his reconstruction, the "Habiru" are the Hebrew rebels in the time of Saul. (The difference is due to the length of Hyksos rule, which is shorter in Rohl's chronology in order to leave room for all the conventional dynasties.)

Nonetheless, Rohl does give a good example of the problems in Palestinian archaeology that are created by relying on Conventional Chronology. Building techniques specifically mentioned in the Bible for the time of Solomon have been found below strata normally assigned to the Hebrew era. In Megiddo, a city rebuilt by Solomon, the entrance gate walls are constructed with "three rows of hewed stone and a row of cedar beams."[13] The construction technique appears to be intended for earthquake protection (shock absorbing) and is found elsewhere in Assyrian structures. The example from Megiddo (the biblical Armageddon) lies in strata below, and therefore earlier than, a gate normally associated with Solomon. (The first major excavations were by the Oriental Institute of Chicago, 1925-1929 and then by Yigael Yadin from 1960-1970. After finding triple gates at both Hazor and Megiddo, Yadin predicted he would find one also at Gezer —

---

12. letter 137.
13. I Kings 6:36.

and he did. That one was later found at Ashdod is seldom allowed to spoil the theory.)

One of the "benchmark" archaeological features in Palestine is a unique triple-chambered gateway, examples of which have been found in three cities mentioned as having been built by Solomon. At Megiddo, it is above (and therefore later than) the gateway built according to I Kings 6:36. Rohl points out that a triple gate is nowhere in scripture identified with Solomon. Other archaeologists have also questioned the dating of the triple gates.

The biggest problem with this part of Rohl's theory is that it is pegged on the identification of *Labaja* of the El-Amarna letters with Saul. Regardless of any similarity between a battle involving Saul and the Labaja of the tablets, the letters state explicitly that Labaja served in his position of authority at the will of the pharaoh and that his father and grandfather had held the same kingship. This situation cannot possibly be made to agree with scripture, and Rohl will get little support for this identification from biblical scholars.

But Rohl has questioned the assumptions of Egyptian chronology and rightly points out the lack of written evidence for dating sites in Palestine. Disagreements have been so common that they are more the rule than the exception. David Rohl has proposed the idea of a Late Bronze Age date for Solomon, and there will be sympathy for this idea because the Solomon of scripture does not fit the meager Iron Age sites found in Palestine.

IVORY

The time of the el-Amarna letters can be linked with the era of Jehosaphat and Ahab by another mode of comparison entirely. A single line in the concluding verses of Ahab's story reads, "Now the rest of the acts of Ahab, and all that he did, and the ivory house which he made, and all the cities that he built, are they not written in the book of the chronicles of the kings of Israel.[14]

Excavations in Samaria turned up large quantities of ivory. Letters inscribed on some of them were identical in form to those on the Mesha stele, thus dating them to the time of Ahab.

Ivories found in the tomb of the Pharaoh Tutankhamon (who ruled just a few years after Akhnaton) were found to be surprisingly similar to those of Samaria. Motifs such as winged sphinxes (cherubim, to the Israelites) were executed in such a similar manner that objects inadvertently cross-mixed probably could not be assigned to either collection on stylistic grounds alone.

---

14. I Kings 22:39.

Samaria is not the only place that such ivories have been found in Palestine. A large hoard was also found in Megiddo, in strata assigned to the 18th dynasty era. Again the objects are executed in a style identical to those found in Samaria 500 years later on the conventional time scale. Scholars actually suggest that Israelites of the 9th century BC copied Egyptian art forms from 500 years in their past — presumably some deep-seated longing for the experience of bondage in Egypt is played out in the revival of the art forms of that era.

Ivories identical to those of Samaria have also been found in Assyria, at least some of which had been looted from cities in Palestine. Interestingly, the powerful force of Assyrian art, which so influenced its other neighbors, does not show up in the ivory; only 500-year-old Egyptian designs are copied.

AKHNATON

The Tell el-Amarna letters document the closing chapters of the great 18th Dynasty of Egypt. The decline began when Akhnaton broke with the Theban priesthood that had groomed him and his predecessors for the throne. Many theories have been put forward to explain the reasons for the schism. Most see Akhnaton as a visionary mystic driven to cleanse Egypt of its degenerate polytheism. Many scholars have seen him as the inspiration for the monotheism of Moses. The full irony of that conception can only be appreciated in light of the Synchronized Chronology, which places Akhnaton in a time when monotheism was breaking down in Israel! A closer examination of this "heretic" pharaoh's life presents a rather different impression to that imagined by his fans.

Elements of the Mittani culture had already made an impact on the Egyptian royal family in the time of Akhnaton's father, Amenhotep III (they both took Mittani brides). That culture is seen as a "Hurrian/Indo-Aryan" mixture. We have already identified these "14th century" Mittani as the predecessors of the Medes. Some innovative "mating" practices for the Egyptian royal family probably came from these Mittani. It is known (if seldom mentioned) that Amenhotep III mated with his own daughter.

For some reason, Amenhotep III never shows his son on any of his royal inscriptions. It is totally out of character for a pharaoh to "hide" his offspring. Perhaps he was raised with distant relatives of his mother, Queen Tiy, who is suspected of being related to the Mittani. Akhnaton's physical characteristics are so unusual that he may have been considered an embarrassing freak. His face is long and thin, his chest emaciated, and his hips and thighs grotesquely enlarged. With no other prince to replace the deceased Amenhotep III, Tiy may have exercised her authority in forcing the recognition of her son. El-Amarna letters to and from her show that she was indeed the power in Egypt upon her husband's death.

It is not difficult to guess that the Theban priesthood of Amon was uncomfortable with the idea of Akhnaton representing god on earth. The fact that Akhnaton made a complete break with the priesthood early in his reign points to some hard feelings. He stripped them of not only the priority of their deity in the public observations, he also stripped their budget.

When he moved the capital of Egypt to a brand new city, he changed his name from Amenhotep IV to Akhnaton. He also named the city Akhetaton for his deity Aton, the disk of the sun. He didn't stop at rejecting his father's name; he had the name chiseled out of his father's inscriptions on buildings. This act of vengeance was taken seriously in Egypt because there was a "life" in the inscribed name that could be "killed" by erasing it.

Things appear to have gone along pretty well for a while in the new city. Buildings, palaces, temples and tombs were constructed. The pharaoh's unusual physique was not only openly depicted, it became an artistic fashion that turned Egyptian art on its head. His features were even exaggerated to the point that depictions of the entire royal family assumed his profile and slouching posture. It actually had a liberating effect on Egyptian art as a whole, such that the period has its own name, the El-Amarna period (named for Tell el-Amarna, the mound of archaeological remains of the city and the famous collection of diplomatic letters).

The bust of Akhnaton's wife, Queen Nefertiti, is one of the great archaeological treasures of all time, but her life seems to have had an unusual turn of events. At some point during the middle of Akhnaton's 17-year reign, Queen Nefertiti just seems to have vanished from the scene. She stops appearing on murals and is replaced by another woman who is referred to as the "Great King's Wife and Queen." We know this other woman, because she appeared in the same role during the reign of Amenhotep III, Akhnaton's father. It is none other than Tiy, Akhnaton's mother (whose brother Ay was the highest official in Egypt). This does not appear to be a symbolic depiction to fill in after the death of Nefertiti (there is no indication that she had died). Tiy is actually shown with young daughters. They cannot be children of Amenhotep III, because he has been dead too long. No, Akhnaton depicts them as if they are her children!

Now Egypt has long been known to have accepted and even expected brother/sister incest in the royal family to preserve the purity of the bloodline. But the mating of father with daughter, as Amenhotep III had done, makes us uncomfortable. How then are we to deal with mother/son incest?

In addition to daughters, Akhnaton had at least two sons, Smenkhare and Tutankhamon. The former served briefly as co-regent with his father before his

own reign of (probably) only one year. Certain depictions of the father and son showed such intimacy that more than a few scholarly eyebrows were raised. Tutankhamon's following reign was not much longer, and he clearly held the throne under the dominance of old Uncle Ay, who managed to make the transition from Tell el-Amarna back to Thebes and remain the High Priest and the power behind the throne.

Virtually nothing is known of Tutankhamon's reign other than his famous burial. He is depicted in battle scenes on his tomb walls and may have even died in battle. Since he was very young, probably still in his teens, he had no business being in combat unless his great uncle saw this as a way of getting him out of the way. No sooner had Ay conducted burial ceremonies for the boy king than he married one of the lad's sisters in order to gain the right to the throne for himself!

Tutankhamon's tomb was sumptuous and seemingly out of proportion to his importance. Perhaps Ay was making up for a twinge of guilt. On the other hand, Smenkhara was found in an unlooted tomb assembled from a bizarre collection of funerary articles borrowed from other family members. The tomb was vandalized soon after the burial, and then resealed. One can see in these two burials retribution against the Atenist Smenkhare, who stayed faithful to Akhnaton, and a reward to Tutankhamon who served the Theban god Amon (he even changed his name from Tutankhaton to Tutankhamon).

Ay was able to control Egypt only briefly before the whole 18th Dynasty collapsed in disorder.

This detour from our story into the inner details of Akhnaton's family has been made for a purpose. At the beginning of this chapter Jehosaphat of Jerusalem was writing to Akhnaton to plead for help against marauding rebels. The pharaoh displayed astonishing indifference to the collapse of the empire he had inherited. He was so obsessed in his religion of sun worship that he failed to see the impending doom at home also. His legacy is the brief flowering of a narcissistic art form and his famous "Ode to the Sun," which is so similar to the 104th Psalm that the psalm has been suspected of borrowing from the ode. Could it not be the other way around?

At this point in Conventional Chronology we would have reached the time usually assigned to Moses (c. 1350 BCC). There is a sizable body of scholarship devoted to the notion that Moses received his inspiration for monotheism from Akhnaton (there is even one silly Hollywood movie that depicts Atenists much like pious early Christians). One does not have to be a specialist to recognize that the family relations of this would-be hero were unusual, if not unique, and likely to be accompanied by some conflict and misgivings. And in that a larger significance could be recognized.

Before he took up history, Velikovsky was a psychologist. In Freud's last book, *Moses and Monotheism* (which was unabashed idol worship on the part of Freud), Velikovsky observed a perverse rejection of his own Jewish roots on the part of Freud. So engaged was he in this religious self-immolation that the very man who had "discovered" the Oedipus Complex failed to recognize *the historical person whose life was the basis for the Greek drama.* Akhnaton, his parents, uncle, sons and daughter played the exact rolls portrayed in the Theban Trilogy (Oedipus Rex, Antigone and Oedipus at Colonus).

The word "Oedipus" in Greek means "swollen legs," and one look at Akhnaton provides a humorous confirmation of the appropriateness of the nickname. Of course, Thebes in Greece is merely a transplanted setting for the true events of Thebes in Egypt. A detailed look at the intricate similarities between the family of Akhnaton and the story of Oedipus is the subject of Velikovsky's wonderful book *Oedipus and Akhnaton.* If he were remembered for nothing else, a book of this quality is a fine legacy.

We will not here delve any deeper into the life of Akhnaton. But there is a point to be made concerning the history of religion that was hinted at earlier. Moses was a product of the Middle Bronze Age. Several hundred years of Hebrew life in Palestine passed before Akhnaton's influence was a factor, and then it was to prove a disappointment to everyone. Perhaps if he had become a high priest, he might have exercised some discipline and elevated the spiritual life of Egypt constructively. Instead he immersed himself in his self-glorifying religion while the country fell apart.

As an example of a scholar blinded to the moral contradictions in this pharaoh's life, it would be hard to exceed the following eulogy:

> There died with him such a spirit as the world had never seen before, a brave soul, undauntedly facing the momentum of immemorial tradition, and thereby stepping out from the long line of conventional and colorless Pharaohs, that he might disseminate ideas far beyond and above the capacity of his age to understand. Among the Hebrews, seven or eight hundred years later, we look for such men; but the modern world has yet to adequately value or even acquaint itself with this man, who in an age so remote and under conditions so adverse, became the world's first idealist and the world's first individual.[15]

---

15. Breasted 392

9. THE END OF THE BRONZE AGE

The end of the Theban Dynasty is approximately the mid-point of the revisions required by the Synchronized Chronology. The Bronze Age is also nearing its end. Conventional Chronology has the 18th Dynasty followed immediately by the 19th, 20th and 21st. This is based on the assumption that the dynastic lists given by Manetho (the priest who under Ptolomy I and Ptolomy II wrote up the history of Egypt, in around 300 BC) and bequeathed to us through the vicissitudes of passing centuries, different cultures, and second- and third-hand transcriptions and translations, are to be understood as a linear succession. Abundant archaeological material exists for pharaohs of all these dynasties, making the surmise seem safe. But the 18th Dynasty cannot be brought down to end in the 9th century BC without something being wrong with that assumption.

If the 19th Dynasty indeed follows the 18th, some shift in emphasis in the arts and writings can be expected. However, major changes in the manner of language and artistic expression took place in the transition between these two dynasties, suggesting that a substantial interval had passed.

> After recovery from the religious revolution Egypt was a changed world. It is not easy to define the exact nature of the changes, since there are many exceptions; yet it is impossible not to notice the marked deterioration of the art, the literature, and indeed the general culture of the people. The language which they wrote approximates more closely to the vernacular and incorporates many foreign words; the copies of ancient texts are incredibly careless, as if the scribes utterly failed to understand their meaning.[1]

There is powerful evidence here that something is wrong. The scribal tradition in Egypt appears to have suffered a break that cannot have occurred over a single generation. The assumption that the 19th Dynasty immediately followed the 18th is grounded solely on the assumption that we can take Manetho's lists at face value. Can we be sure that that is valid? In fact, the native sources used by Manetho in creating his lists were undoubtedly similar to those used by modern scholars in their studies, and the king lists found at Karnak and Abydos, as well as the Turin Papyrus and Palermo Stone, reveal that the Egyptians were all too willing to omit names or even whole embarrassing dynasties from their history.

The hiatus in styles between the 18th and 19th Dynasties is similar to that which separates the 12th and 18th Dynasties. We know that the entire Hyksos era separates the 12th and 18th Dynasties and the differences in art and language are understandable. But the native Egyptian king lists at Abydos and Karnak omit the Hyksos Dynasties entirely. How would the hiatus in artistic traditions be reconciled if we did not know that a lengthy interval had elapsed?

MANETHO

The Synchronized Chronology understands Manetho's 18th-21st dynasties to be a list of the *native* pharaohs from the end of the Hyksos rule to the time of Alexander. It is the sort of list that the Egyptians themselves would have made, deleting non-native dynasties and monarchs whose legacies were less than glorious. Appended onto the end of this list are the non-native dynasties and the garbled lists that emerged from Alexandria.

Manetho was almost certainly the important Egyptian priest that he purports to be. He was approximately contemporary with Berosus, "who was priest of Marduk at Babylon, lived under and wrote for Antiochus I . . . The works of Manetho and Berosus may be interpreted as an expression of the rivalry of the two kings, Ptolomy and Antiochus, each seeking to proclaim the antiquity of his land."[2]

While Manetho appears to have successfully brought the Egyptian Serapis Cult to Alexandria, Egypt never accepted the city. Alexandria became an intellectual center in Hellenic times, but it did so without the participation of greater Egypt. The writings of Manetho survive only by reference in other authors: Josephus, Eusebius and a few other fragments. The Egyptian names were so severely distorted in these translations that some are completely

---

1. Gardiner 247
2. Weddell-Manetho X

unrecognizable. It is unfortunate that we do not have an original of Manetho's writings; it is easy to blame him for the poor quality of what passes for his work. "Manetho introduced into an already garbled series of dynastic lists a number of popular traditions written in the characteristic Egyptian style. No genuine historical sense had been developed among the Egyptians."[3]

The mistake that has been made in past treatments of Manetho's lists is in not recognizing the end of the native list, to which were appended non-native kings (Dynasties 22-25) and the Alexandrian collection (Dynasties 26-31). The 22nd through 25th belong between the 18th and 19th (the 19th is the same as the 26th). And the 27th through 29th belong between the 19th and 20th (the 20th is the same as the 30th). *See the Dynastic list on page 18*.

All attempts at squeezing the 19th, 20th and 21st Dynasties in between the 18th and 22nd are doomed to distort history. This is true of *Centuries of Darkness* by Peter James. As mentioned earlier, he attempts to shorten the interval between the 18th and 22nd Dynasties by 200 to 300 years without removing any dynasties. In doing so he shows how the histories of surrounding countries, whose events are dated by Egyptian Chronology, can be relieved of their uncomfortable "Dark Ages."

The flaw in James' solution is that the lengths of the dark ages have already been "fudged" at both ends. For example, the end of Mycenaean Greece has to be dated about 150 years later than concrete evidence would suggest is appropriate. And Geometric (Archaic) Greece is similarly pushed back in time by about 150 years to make the 550-600 years in between seem like only 300. There is no reason for making these chronological accommodations other than to artificially shorten the span.

In the Conventional Chronology, the 18th Dynasty ends in turmoil. A military commander from Lower Egypt, Haremhab, is promoted to pharaoh, commencing a new dynasty or at least providing a bridge to the 19th Dynasty (since no blood links have been found). He was probably the most important official in Egypt outside of the priesthood and his power in the military certainly insured strength behind the throne. If he were chosen to be pharaoh by the priesthood that had groomed pharaohs throughout history, it seems strange that he would be allowed to move the capital of Egypt from Thebes to Memphis. Thebes was the most powerful city in the world at that time and its priesthood had successfully forced the heretic Akhnaton from the throne, *and had caused the abandonment and destruction of his capitol city.*

---

3. Weddell-Manetho XXVI.

The Synchronized Chronology identifies the 19th (Tanitic) Dynasty with the 26th "Saitic" Dynasty and places it following the Ethiopian 25th. Those Ethiopian kings were unable to resist a takeover by Assyria, and the constant rebellion against that rule led to the eventual crushing reprisals by Assurbanipal, including the looting of Thebes. (Assurbanipal must have felt secure after ensconcing Necho on the Egyptian throne, but Necho's son broke free soon after.)

The native rulers of Egypt who served, originally at least, as vassals of Assyria, came from the ranks of the military in lower Egypt. The Dynasty known as the 26th was friendly to Assyria. What started out as a subservient relationship evolved into the status of equal allies as both countries, Egypt and Assyria, faced the growing power of Chaldea.

In identifying the 19th Dynasty with the 26th, the true order of history can be restored. The turmoil of the 18th dynasty resulted in the takeover of Egypt by Libyans. Bringing the end of the 18th Dynasty from the end of the 14th century to the middle of the 9th also frees the Libyan Dynasty of filling an extra 100 years beyond the 120 given by Manetho. Instead of ruling from 945 to 730 BC, the 22nd Dynasty (concurrent with the 23rd) began about 845. By the same token, the archaeological remains of early Libyan pharaohs have consistently shown up in foreign contexts about 100 years later than the Conventional Chronology places their reigns. Under the Synchronized Chronology, the necessity of assuming several additional Osorkons and Shoshenks to fill that 100 years is eliminated. The evidence and international relationships for the Libyan Dynasty will be presented in Chapter 13, *The Third Intermediate Period in Egypt.*

At the risk of confusing the non-specialist reader, an explanation of the concept of duplication of dynasties is indispensable to the reconstructed chronology. The focus of the entire problem of ancient chronology is the end of the 18th Dynasty. Libraries full of books have been written about the course of history following the Theban Pharaohs. There are so many links with other cultures throughout the ancient world that pass through a transition at this same time that it is critical to pin down the absolute date that it occurs.

In the Synchronized Chronology, generation after generation of 18th Dynasty rulers have been compared with their contemporaries in Judah and Israel. Since the archaeology of Palestine is hopelessly interwoven with dates derived from Cyprus and the Aegean, it will be necessary to examine the impact of Egyptian dating on these and other countries. The degree to which circular arguments are used to reinforce Conventional Chronology cannot be overemphasized, so it will be interesting to see how the same type of dating problem reappears in a variety of areas.

ITALY

Italy can serve as an ideal test case for the transition following the 18th Egyptian Dynasty. The Bronze Age in Italy is known as the Apennine Culture. Imports from Mycenaean Greece fix the date of this culture and its bronze industry, which extends northerly into Europe and provides a further widening of the cross dating. The Late Apennine is firmly dated by Conventional Chronology to about 1300 BCC. Some will place it as late as 1200 BCC, but that is simply an attempt to shorten the gap between the Apennine and the culture which succeeds it, the Villanovan (i.e. "fudging").

The Villanovan Culture is identified with the arrival of the Etruscans, who are almost universally acknowledged to have migrated from Anatolia, bringing a tradition of cremation burial with them. Although some experts insist that the Villanovans are native to Italy, most will see a large measure of truth in the story told by Herodotus of their ancestors' decision to leave Asia Minor during a famine. The beginning of the Villanovan Era is archaeologically indicated and by tradition accepted as approximately contemporary with the founding of Rome (c. 750 BC).

Although there are sites in Italy where a transition from Apennine to Villanovan Cultures can be subdivided into Sub-Apennine and Proto-Villanovan, there is no break in occupation across the transition and there are sites where late Mycenaean pottery is found intermixed with these transitional strata. Any efforts to see a "Dark Age" in between the Apennine and Villanovan cultures (in order to absorb the time differential) are faced with the challenge of explaining why the archaeological remains across the transition do not appear to allow for much (if any) time to have elapsed. What is going on here?

Efforts to bridge the hiatus between 1300 BCC and 750 BC have resulted in endless confrontations between archaeologists refusing to accept that the Apennine lasted so late or that the Villanovan started so early. An uncomfortable number of centuries are occupied by Sub-Apennine and Proto-Villanovan ghosts, each scholar drawing a dividing line somewhere in the span and daring anyone to cross it.

ROME

The Etruscans established Tarquinia at approximately the same time as the founding of Rome. In fact legend places the origin of both Rome and Tarquenia in Asia Minor in the early eighth century BC. Rome is closely associated with the Trojan War, in tradition. Aeneas fled from Troy when that city was defeated by the Greeks. He stopped for an extended stay in Carthage, where he eventually spurned the affections of its queen "Dido," and chose to flee. After leaving Carthage he went to Rome. As the ancestor of the Roman kings, he carried the seeds of future conflicts between the two cities.

Clearly, the conventional date for the Trojan War (c. 1200 BC) cannot be reconciled with a visit to the North African city that was founded about 300 years later. Timaeus gives a date of 813 BC for the establishment of Carthage. If the Trojan War took place two or three generations later (in the early mid-eighth century), Aeneas could have visited an already existing Carthage on the way to founding Rome in 750 BC. At one stroke, ancient legend is made compatible with a compelling synchronism.

SICILY

Sicily is plagued by the same type of hypothetical hiatus in occupation as that seen in Italy. The Thapsos Culture that had grown through Middle Bronze times into Late Bronze ended at a time corresponding to Mycenaean IIIB. The culture that succeeded the Thapsos is known as the Pantalica Culture and is made up of Greek and Phoenician colonists. This new culture is assumed to date from 1250 to 650 BCC, but the earliest Greek and Phoenician archaeological remains date to the late 8th century BC.

As a rational for the hiatus, it is theorized that the Thapsos Culture abandoned the coastal areas and clustered into urban areas of the interior, but there is no real evidence that the interior sites date later than those on the coast, which are overlain directly with Greek occupation. Thucydides tells us that the Greeks expelled the natives from Syracuse in 733 BC, a date that would be consistent with the archaeological finds — if it was indeed the earlier Thapsos Culture that was expelled! Then the Pantalic Culture needn't have lasted more than 730-650 BC, a duration that is more in line with the remains; and the dark age of Sicily disappears.

SPAIN

Further to the west, the Phoenician settlements at the entrance to the Mediterranean are assumed to have been established in the 12th century BC by classical sources that reference it to the Trojan War. Solomon's Phoenician merchants are also believed to have been trading with Tarshish in the 10th century BC, and Tarshish has been equated with Tartessos in Spain. However, this assumption is questioned by many ("Tarshish" is actually a term for a type of trading ship, not a city[4]). No evidence of Phoenician presence in Spain prior to the 8th century BC has actually been discovered. Ivories found at Carmona are so similar to those from Megiddo in Palestine that one scholar, Albright, attempted to back-date the site to the 12th century on the basis of the style of ivory alone. No one else has been willing to date those ivories earlier than the 8th century (the Megiddo Ivories are dated too early, due to Egyptian chronology).

The Bronze Age of Spain, with no direct links to datable Mycenaean items, does not have the kind of clear hiatus in occupation found further to the east. But this is only because no Mycenaean remains have been discovered. Sooner or later one will show up and it will either throw the chronology into the chaos of the eastern Mediterranean or it will be dismissed as an "heirloom."

TROY

The nearer one gets to the Aegean, the more closely the archaeological picture mirrors the Dark Age found in Greece. With the Mycenaean Age closely identified with the Trojan War, there should be evidence at Troy that could shed light on the hiatus. The discovery of Troy by Heinrich Schliemann was a watershed in Western understanding of history. Until that time, Homer was considered the author of pure mythology, and few historians believed that the Trojan War had actually occurred, or even that Troy had ever existed. Nonetheless, setting out in 1879 with the *Iliad* as his guide, Schliemann uncovered stunning treasures under the mound. (Many of these treasures made their way to museums in Berlin, and at the end of World War II found their way into Russia, ending up in the Pushkin Fine Arts Museum.) The site, now known as Hissarlik, left no doubt about the existence of Troy. The subsequent discovery of Agamemnon's city of Mycenaea forced a further reevaluation of Homer.

Troy was situated on a strategic site just outside the Straits of Bosporus, the narrow passage linking the Mediterranean and Black Seas. A protected beach below the city was the last safe harbor before entering the currents of the Straits. The mound was built up of occupational strata over thousands of years. Of the successive strata, those numbered VI and VIIa vie for identification with destruction during the Trojan War. Although some still consider the war a myth, the city was destroyed twice during the broad interval during which the War could have taken place.

City VI had magnificent walls more like those described by Homer, but shows signs of earthquake damage and (archaeologically) pre-dates the time conventionally assigned to the War (c. 1200 BCC). City VII was destroyed by fire but does not match the grandeur of the Homeric description.

---

4. Hyde 41.

Mycenaean pottery helps to establish the relative dating of these strata with VIIB being linked with the last Mycenaean remains, LH IIIC. The next occupation level, VIII, is contemporary with Archaic Greece of about 700 BC. The attentive reader will be able to predict the sort of comment that experts are forced to make:

> There is nothing at Troy to fill this huge lacuna. For 2000 years men had left traces of their living there; some chapters were brief and obscure, but there was never yet a chapter left wholly blank. Now at last there is silence, profound and prolonged for 400 years; we are asked, surely not in vain, to believe that Troy lay 'virtually unoccupied' for this long period of time.[5]

It could be assumed that there was actually a Dark Age at Troy and that, however unlikely, the site was simply unoccupied. But the situation is complicated by the fact that shards of Geometric pottery (of the 8th century BC) were found in level VIIb and at least one house remained occupied from VIIB into VIII. Scholars have considered down-dating VIIb to the 9th century, but the LH IIIC links make that impossible.

It is almost painful to observe the gymnastics forced on scholars as they try to reconcile such conflicting data. But do they ever question the chronological framework that creates these absurdities?

Several Greek scholars of the 19th and early 20th century were unwilling to place a gap between Mycenaean and Archaic Greece. Similarities in many aspects of the cultures imply that the end of the Mycenaean Age should be brought down to the 9th or even 7th century BC. But the Greek scholars were overwhelmed with evidence for the link between Mycenaean Greece and the 18th Dynasty of Egypt. Greek archaeology stands against Egypt as a very junior partner. Nothing from Greece can compare with the written evidence from Egypt. The current popularity of books challenging the accuracy of Egyptian dating is a refreshing contrast to the debate over the "Long, Middle or Short Chronologies" which argue over 10- to 30- year variations in a timescale warped by over 500 years.

Several ancient authors arrived at dates for the Trojan War, some by generational counts, others by unknown means. The dates range from c. 1100 BC to over 1300 BC. Those who have examined the foundations of those dates realize the hazard of using them for serious purposes. "Sober historic judgment must discard the ancient chronological schemes in toto. . . . Not until the fifth century

---

5. Denys, quoted in James 61.

BC did the historic Greek world come to date even contemporary events on a coherent scheme."[6]

So where does this leave the date of the Trojan War? It occurred toward the end of the Mycenaean Age, which all non-Egyptian evidence places in the eighth century BC, immediately before the Archaic Age in Greece.

THE END OF THE BRONZE AGE

This chapter has been looking at areas dated by links to the 18th Egyptian Dynasty and the problems created by the Conventional Chronology. Connections through Greece are often the strongest ties in the cross dating. But Greek dating will be treated separately; it is too vast and important to be dealt with in this overview chapter. Instead, one aspect of this "mid-point" in the Synchronized Chronology should properly be examined here because it is a factor in all of the cultures examined so far: the End of the Bronze Age.

This particular subject has been covered in depth by Robert Drews in a work entitled, *The End of the Bronze Age: Changes in Warfare and the Catastrophe c. 1200 BC.* This well-written work tackles the problem of the collapse of the Bronze Age civilization and the resulting "Dark Age" that descends on the northern and eastern Mediterranean. Although the fall of Mycenaean Greece is of particular interest, all of the Aegean, Anatolia and the Levant are affected. Since the Synchronized Chronology eliminates the fictitious Dark Age that this collapse of civilization is supposed to have caused, the collapse itself should also be regarded as spurious. Nonetheless, the subject is a popular one and needs to be put into synchronized context.

Drews surveys the variety of theories that have been put forward over the years to explain the cause of the event. Since many of these theories are still current, and show up in almost every discussion of the era, a review is in order.

Earthquakes

A team of French archaeologists led by Claude Schaeffer excavated the remains of Ugarit (north of Beirut, now in Syria) after a member of the local Alaouite tribe stumbled upon a tomb site in 1928. They found evidence that the site had suffered destruction by earthquake and a resulting catastrophic fire. Because so many other cities had suffered a similar fate at about the same time, Schaeffer believed that an "act of God" ended the Bronze Age. All of the northeastern and eastern Mediterranean can be considered an active seismic

---

6. Starr 61.

zone and almost every area is subject to earthquake damage every few generations.

When put to the test, however, several problems arise in the argument that earthquakes could have caused the end of civilization over such a wide area. Examined more closely, the destructions prove to have been spread out over at least several decades. Cases of violent destruction were, if not common, at least regular enough to be somewhat routine. Most often the destruction layer was simply leveled out and the city would be rebuilt. The argument for a natural disaster causing the end of the Bronze Age also fails to explain why widespread depopulation should occur when most cities were not destroyed by earthquakes.

Migration

Almost all current theories on the end of the Bronze Age involve the migration of people from the north invading and destroying on their way south. The origin of the theory can be traced to inscriptions in Egypt describing warriors with names reminiscent of European/Mediterranean peoples, "Northerners coming from all lands," who helped the king of Libya attack Merneptah. The Shardana, Shekelesh, Denyen and Tursha suggest Sardinians, Sicilians, Danaans and Etruscans.

These references are specific to the 19th and 20th Dynasties, which have nothing at all to do with the time following the 18th Dynasty and will be covered later in Chapters 14-18. Nonetheless, Drews point out, quite rightly, that in a Bronze Age context the islands of Sicily and Sardinia were at best a collection of independent cities and could hardly have achieved a collective identity.

The real standouts among the migrating people theory are the Peresett (or Pelesett), who were stopped by Ramses III from a full-scale invasion. It was pointed out earlier that the Peresett have been misidentified as the Philistines who led a failed invasion attempt on Egypt and then settled in Palestine. They were, in fact, the Persians (P-r-s-tt on the Canopus Decree), who employed Aegean mercenaries in their attempt to re-take Egypt in the time of Nectanebo (Ramses III in 375 BC). There are problems to the invasion theory that Drews doesn't cover because he accepts a 12th-century time frame for the events.

Drought

The drought hypothesis for the end of the Bronze Age was renewed in 1965 by Rhys Carpenter in *Discontinuity in Greek Civilization*. The theory proposes that a severe drought in the Aegean region and Anatolia led to desperate attacks by the city populations on the governing palaces. Egypt plays a part in the theory also since the wealth of Nile grain became an enticing target for the hungry northerners.

At certain Mycenaean palaces (such as Pylos), tablets written in Greek Linear B reveal the social and economic situation immediately prior to the destruction of the city. No evidence of drought has been found. There may have been limited areas subjected to local droughts that forced migration similar to that described in Herodotus for the Etruscans, but Homer knew of no drought, and climactic studies are equivocal at best for drought at the end of the Bronze Age (even if it *did* occur 1200 BC).

Political Collapse

One can always count on the Marxists to find a political angle to any major social change, and archaeology has not been spared its Marxists. They see the end of the Bronze Age as a culmination of social forces brought about by the collapse of a top-heavy palace-based bureaucracy. The elites of the royalty, priesthood and military were replaced by the "Democracies" of the Iron Age.

This theory has two problems that only a revision in chronology can fix. First, the democracies didn't show up until at least 500 years after the end of the (Conventional Chronology) Bronze Age. And second, this only happened in Greece, whereas the Dark Age collapse covered a much wider area. Furthermore, the pottery evidence (which is the only evidence) for Greece that bridges the gap between the Mycenaean and Geometric (archaic) stages is comprised of an exceedingly small number of specimens. And since the time span supposedly involved is so large (500+ years), even the few items are subdivided by style, however subtle. Those pottery types are referred to as Sub-Mycenaean, and they are followed by Early, Middle and Late Proto-Geometric. Each of these is given 100 years or so and, behold, the 500-year dark age is filled. A cynic might propose a similar system of jargon to designate the political stages in between Palace (Mycenaean), and Democratic (Geometric/Archaic). These phases would be the Sub-Palatial, followed by Early, Middle and Late Proto-Democratic. This will allow the circular logic of chronological cross-dating to be buttressed by yet another reinforcement.

In all seriousness, one can see in Greece a truly profound political change, but it did not take 500-600 years to occur. Also, what was happening in Greece did not occur elsewhere, least of all Anatolia (except the west), the Levant, Egypt or Assyria.

Warfare

Drews dismisses one by one the arguments outlined here for the end of the Bronze Age and focuses instead on the changes in warfare that altered the power structure of the ancient world. He shows that actual written descriptions of battle from the Late Bronze Age are dominated by chariot warfare. In particular, he demonstrates that the old concept of the chariot as a vehicle used to transport fighters to the battlefield is not supported by the facts. Rather, the chariot is universally portrayed as a mobile archery platform. Battles were dominated by this type of encounter, with infantry playing little part.

Drews pictures the chariot warfare of the Bronze Age giving way to foot soldiers in the Iron Age as larger and larger armies are used in battle. His logic is no doubt biased by the type of sample used in creating his picture of Bronze Age warfare. The writings are largely penned from the point of view of a king or pharaoh participating in the battle, with bow in hand, riding a chariot. The lowly foot soldiers get short shrift in the press coverage. Of course, in the Synchronized Chronology the battle descriptions of Ramses II and III and Hattusilis, referred to by Drews, date from c. 600 and 400 BC and have nothing to do with the Bronze Age.

Iron

Of all the arguments for the cause of the end of the Bronze Age, the one that begs the issue most is the argument that iron weapons changed the balance of power and led to the collapse of the old Bronze Age centers (whatever they were). The fact is that there is no evidence for the use of iron weapons prior to the time of Sargon II at the end of the 8th century BC. If any kingdom had the power and resources to exploit iron for use in warfare, it was the Assyrians. Sargon's predecessors placed great emphasis on controlling metal resources, yet mastery of the new metal did not occur until his time. Needless to say, a technological innovation that occurred c. 700 BC could not have caused the collapse of the Bronze Age c. 1200 BC.

This chapter focused on links to the 18th Dynasty with cultures that show a dating problem before and after a distinct transitional point. Typically, a culture that ends c. 1200 BC when cross dated to Mycenaean evidence is succeeded by a culture dating to the 8th century BC, according to similar cross dating. The transition may show no break in occupation, but intervening stages are either meager or missing altogether.

At the root of this phenomenon is a tacit acceptance of Manetho's dynastic list showing the 18th Dynasty separated from the 22nd by the 19th, 20th and 21st. The Synchronized Chronology sees this sequence as a relic of a typical Egyptian list that recognizes only native pharaohs, skipping over the foreigners. Appended onto the Egyptian list is a compilation that emerged from Alexandria, including Libyans, Ethiopians and Persians.

Egyptian archaeologists so dominated late 19th century scholarship that they effectively bullied Greek and Palestinian scholars into submission. Initial resistance to the contradictions imposed on Greek history gave way to resignation and acceptance. The status quo is so ingrained now that to question it invites the resistance of entrenched theories.

Before rejoining biblical history, one more chapter on the Greek Dark Ages will be presented. Greece has a literary tradition that buttresses the Synchronized Chronology in a particularly vivid manner. Historians have been forced to warp the flow of Greek history so profoundly that it is awkward to follow. Only specialists grapple with this confused assemblage, robbing an interesting time of its real history.

10. New Light on the Greek Dark Ages

Early Greek writers may have differed on many details of their history, but they generally agreed on the broad outline. When their ancestry is pushed back as far as it can go before entering the realm of Gods, the relative time frame is, at most, a few generations before the Trojan War. Presumably this is someplace towards the end of the "Mycenaean Age," also known as Late Helladic.

Of course the Greeks did not know this era as Mycenaean, even if its famous King Agamemnon played a leading role in legend. Hesiod, a contemporary of Homer, ranked Greek history mostly by metal ages: Gold, Silver, Bronze, "Heroic," and Iron. Mycenaeans would be of the Bronze and Heroic Ages. It should be pointed out that Hesiod, who considered his own age as Iron, did not include a "Dark Age." None of the Greek historians regarded several centuries of reversion to primitive life to be a part of their history.

The Trojan War stood as a benchmark for the Greeks in charting ancestry. The names identified with Oedipus and his contemporaries occur about two generations before the War. This is not far from the time of Jason and the Argonauts, and lineages quickly retrograde into Olympian figures.

The famous "Catalogues" of Homer broaden the social and geographical landscape of Greece tremendously, providing the backdrop for later generations' pride of ancestry. The Greeks may have won the Great War, but they returned home to a changing world. They tell us that the "return of the Heraclids" occurred two generations after the war. These were the Dorians who moved south into the Peloponese, driving out the Achaeans and destroying their "Mycenaean" palaces.

Immigrants driven out of the Peloponese by the Dorians placed great pressure on Attica and Boetia. Greek climate and soil will not support dense populations, so the only place to go was offshore. The Aeolians were the first to leave, founding colonies along the northern coast of Turkey and into the Propontis. The region became known as Aeolia, and its cities carried a common identity throughout their history.

Ionian colonization (largely from Attica) followed quickly in settling the rich sites along the central Aegean Islands and coast of what is now Turkey, founding cities whose fame would nearly overshadow those of mainland Greece. Even the Dorians continued their push southward into Crete, the southerly Aegean Islands, and southern Turkey.

This age of colonization fills later Greek history with celebrated names. The colonies were established in such rapid succession that their foundation dates are closely interrelated. Many of these sites have been excavated and provide confirmation of the legends. They began in the 8th century BC and continued through the 7th and 6th. Colonies in the West, in Italy and Sicily, began as early as those in Asia Minor and also have well-documented histories.

By the late 6th century BC, Greek history is interwoven with that of Egypt, Persia and the Near East in an ever-widening complex of increasingly reliable dates. It would not be long before the likes of Herodotus established "History" as the kind of discipline we think of today. But what happens when modern Greek historians are confronted by an understanding of historical chronology based on received ideas about Egypt?

By the end of the 19th century, most Greek scholars were resigned to Egyptian dating by virtue of Mycenaean links to the 18th Dynasty. As was mentioned in the previous chapter, those historians acknowledged this situation with extreme reluctance. Enough was known about the Greek pottery sequence to know that the flow of Greek history was being forced to include a "Dark Age" of several hundred years' duration.

Even the normally dependable study of pottery became a frustrating subject because it refused to shed any light on these Dark Ages:

> ... extensive synchronizations between the physical evidence of the Aegean and the orient exist only in eras when large-scale commerce throve — i.e., only at the height of the Mycenaean age and again from 700 BC onward. For the long stretches of time which intervened, our bases for absolute dates are inferences from archaeological stratification, which is not easily come by in the poverty of Aegean sites. . .
>
> Archaeologists have not thus far succeeded in discovering a site at which men left a continuous stratified deposit all the way from the height of the Mycenaean Age on down into the Dark Ages.[1]

---

1. Starr 1991, 79.

This is not the sort of Dark Age that we think of in European history where noteworthy achievements in the arts and literature were scarce. At least in those days, people went on with their lives and left behind the debris of occupation to prove it. No, the Greek Dark Age was of an altogether different sort. We are expected to believe that the people either disappeared completely or adopted a lifestyle that left nothing behind.

There is an almost token gesture made to the Greek version of history in acknowledging that the legendary "Return of the Heraclids" and subsequent migrations were a reality of the 13th and following centuries.

> The oral traditions of the Greeks preserved a story of a series of movements into Greece at very much this time (two generations after the Trojan War, which should probably be assigned to the middle of the thirteenth century), originating in the northwest districts which lay outside the Mycenaean world, properly speaking. The chief of these movements was that of the Dorians, led by kings of Mycenaean descent, and the main target was the Peloponese, where the invaders warred against local Mycenaean rulers and emerged victorious. So far the tradition is acceptable, but it goes on to tell us that the invading groups immediately settled in many areas of the mainland; and for this, as we have seen, there is no archaeological evidence at all. [2]

The Mycenaean cities were attacked and destroyed. They had attempted to stem the invasion near Corinth. Desbrough says, "As one leaves the Peloponese, at the isthmus, there are stretches of a wall with projecting towers at intervals, unconnected with any settlement, built in the thirteenth century, its precise purpose unknown, but evidently defensive in character."[3] This author says the purpose of the wall is unknown because the "invaders" left no remains, at least for several centuries.

Thus the invasion of the Peloponese in the 13th century BCC is supported by archaeological evidence, suggesting that tradition is correct concerning the Dorians. But then we are told that there is no occupation of the Peloponese until several hundred years later, as if the invaders conquered the land and then disappeared. And a Dark Age descended over all of Greece.

HOMER

It is impossible to consider the Mycenaean Age without Homer. Time and again minor details of life described in the Iliad and Odyssey are confirmed by

---

2. Desborough 23.
3. Desborough 19.

archaeology. Yet Homer lived and wrote in the late 8th or early 7th century and his subjects date supposedly to the 13th century BCC. "Nowhere dare we rely upon the Iliad and Odyssey as independent evidence for conditions in the second millennium. Between the thirteenth century and the eighth century, in which the epics assumed their present shape, lay virtually aeons of unrest and even chaos; and, as I shall try to show later, the basic spirit of the Homeric poems accords chiefly with the closing stages of the Dark Ages."[4] This author sees the *society* described by Homer in the generations just preceding the poet's time.

Homer was recreating a heroic age in contrast to his own. The Mycenaean Age was over and a new one had replaced it. The pottery of this new age is known to us as "Geometric," a style as unique and accomplished as anything from the Mycenaean. Starr sees the meter and rhythm of Homeric poetry in the geometric patterns of the pottery. "The most conclusive grounds, however, are the close relations in style and outlook between Ripe Geometric pottery and the Iliad."[5]

Between Mycenaean times and Geometric, in terms of pottery, there is a transitional stage known as "Protogeometric." This is sub-divided into early, middle and late. Formerly, there were even theories of a transitional phase between Mycenaean and Proto-geometric, which was dubbed the Sub-Mycenaean.

> Within the past decade, however, Desborough has argued that sub-Mycenaean pottery was not common to the whole of Greece but was rather a local style confined to Western Attica and particularly the cist-tomb cemeteries of Salamis and the Keramicos. Elsewhere, he believed, Mycenaean pottery evolved directly into the protogeometric style. [6]

With a Sub-Mycenaean era removed from the long time span dividing Mycenaean and Geometric, Protogeometric is forced to stretch over a longer interval, 1200-750/800 BCE. This is a genuine problem because of the very small amount of material representing all of the Protogeometric stage. Some scholars are willing to grant only 100 years (or less) for the whole span of Protogeometric. If the material were judged without the preconception of a required 300-400 year evolution, it could fit about the way we would expect into somewhat less than a century.

It should also be pointed out that even the Geometric has been pushed further back than many scholars are happy with, only because Protogeometric

---

4. Starr, 1991, 46.
5. Starr, 1991, 161.
6. Kelly, 21.

cannot be asked to last even longer. In my view, Geometric should really begin about 700 BCS. And to top off the confusion, the evidence from Troy shows *Geometric* mixed with *Mycenaean IIIC*, suggesting that the Geometric at least overlapped the final stage of Mycenaean, leaving no vacant span for Protogeo-metric. (Protogeometric is actually closest to Middle Helladic in appearance.)

It is the premise of this work that the Trojan War took place around the beginning of the 8th century BC at the earliest and that, stripped of an artificially stretched history, a more reasonable course of events can be observed.

The colonization inspired by the disturbance brought both cremation and the new geometric inspiration from Asia Minor. Starr says, "The virtually new custom of cremation penetrated from Asia Minor into Greece of Attica and secondarily Boeotia, regions closely connected with the Greek expansion eastward across the Aegean in the eleventh and following centuries."[7]

The 11th-century BCC Greek expansion that Starr notes here is a "fudged date," a ghost-like preview of the true event that occurred in the 8th and 7th centuries. In a work devoted to the Ionian colonization, Roebuck writes:

> In this complex historians have chosen to stress one or other of the two strands and have presented us with two contrasting pictures of early Ionia; either a migration in the late eleventh century, which brought a selection of Mycenaean refugees to Ionia with the memories of their past still strong or a struggling migration across the Aegean from various parts of Greece in the ninth century; out of these disparate elements the new Ionia had to be formed. [8]

Roebuck is acknowledging the conflicting dates for the migration versus the settlements, much like the Dorian invasion of the Peloponese. And it forces him to use creative language to integrate archaeology with Greek tradition. Yet both the 11th-century Mycenaean date and the 9th-century Ionian migrations noted here are already pulled together in time (without justification) to minimize the discrepancy. Two generations after the Trojan War by Conven-tional Chronology would be 13th century and an "Ionian migration" would be 8th or 7th.

The association of cremation with Geometric pottery is an important point. The evolution of Geometric pottery culminates,in existing artifacts, in the magnificent "Diplyon" cremation vases from Athens. By placing the origins of the Geometric style into the time frame of Aeolian and Ionian migrations and coloni-zations, the phenomenon of cremation (previously alien to Greece) is also brought into agreement with the larger sweep of events. There were actually

---

7. Starr 1991, 86.
8. Roebuck 26.

cremation burials found associated with Mycenaean remains at Tell Atchana, where Asia Minor meets Syria on the Orontes River. It would not be unexpected to find more evidence of cremation at sites in Ionia and Aeolia associated with the first Greek presence at those colonies. The traces of Mycenaean pottery that are found at almost all Greek colony sites are not evidence that Mycenaeans were there hundreds of years earlier and then left. No, the colonies were founded by Greeks in the transition from Mycenaean to the new Geometric style. They were one and the same people.

OTHER PEOPLES OF ASIA MINOR

There are other aspects to early Greek history that reflect on the Dark Age problem. Ancient Greeks understood history in a manner incompatible with the Conventional Chronology. For example, Mycenaean Greeks are often linked to peoples or events whose true historic time falls several hundred years after the Conventional date for the end of Mycenaea. Among the allies of Priam in the defense of Troy were the Phrygians, a people whose homeland was distant from Troy. Their famous King Midas is a well-known legendary character. The Phrygians (a people closely related to Greeks) moved into central Asia Minor in the ninth century BC.

Locating Phrygians in Asia Minor in Mycenaean times creates a difficulty that leads to the use of some creative terminology. Without any hint of tongue in cheek, one author writes of Proto-Phrygian, Proto-Lydian and Proto-Carian. These rightfully belong in the same category as the term Proto-Democratic facetiously suggested in the last chapter.

In a reference to the "Amazons" (who were probably the Hittites, who are depicted on reliefs in western Asia Minor that show them garbed in kilt-like skirts), Strabo writes, " . . . now the Amazons would not fight on Priam's side because of the fact that he had fought against them as an ally of the Phrygians."[9] This presents a very interesting footnote to history. Here we have the possibility that the Hittites (actually the Chaldeans or Calybes) fought against the Phrygians, who had drawn in the Trojans as allies. The Phrygians and Trojans probably have ancestral links that would make such an alliance possible. However, Phrygians in a 13th-century setting is clearly impossible. In Chapters 14-16, the true time frame of the Hittites/Chaldeans will be examined in greater detail.

Greek colonization of Asia Minor did not go unchallenged. The Cimmerian invasion of Asia Minor about 700 BC put an end to the Phrygian kingdom. Until

---

9. Strabo 12.3.24.

that point, Lydia had probably been a part of that kingdom, providing a conduit across western Asia Minor for goods traded with Assyria and Urartu. As Roebuck describes it, "Ionian colonial expansion overseas began early in the seventh century. At that time the Ionians were attempting to break into the river valleys which led to Lydia and the interior. Land in Asia Minor, however, was hard won, and any possibility of expansion inland was soon blocked by Gyges' consolidation of Lydia."[10]

> The invention of coinage has been convincingly ascribed to the generation after Gyges and to the Lydian-Ionian area, if not to Lydia itself. In a study of the coins from the Basis of the Ephesian Artemision and from the related deposits, Robinson traces the development step by step from dumps (pellets) of electrum (and some silver), through unpunched dumps, through punched and striated dumps, dumps with a type to coins proper. The whole series is convincingly attributed to a rapid development which starts in the third quarter of the seventh century and reaches its climax c. 600, when the Basis deposit was made. [11]

The sequence of coin development noted above must have happened very quickly, and resulted in an item that was so revolutionary that it is still in use today. And precisely because coinage was such a deliberate and rapid invention, a number of chronological anachronisms can be traced to the Lydians and their contacts with other peoples. When one of the phases of that sequence showed up in a Mycenaean context, Roebuck was quick to back away from the clear inference: "Dumps of metal without punches or striations were found at Enkomi in Cyprus in Mycenaean contexts; apparently the practice could develop in various places at various times, and there need be no connection between them."

The art on that early coinage displays a seeming anachronism just as curious as the existence of Mycenaean coins, that is, Hittite art. The famous Lion Gate at 13th century BCC Mycenaea has been compared to similar 8th century BC gates in Phrygia. Phrygians were contemporary with (and their archaeo-logical remains thoroughly intermixed with) the Hittites/Chaldeans. There should be no surprise, then, that "The lion head on the Lydian coins is the Assyri-anized Hittite type which appears in Greek Art c. 650."[12]

However trade to Assyria was accomplished, either overland through Lydia or more directly from Al Mina (see Tel Atchana above), Greek items found their way to the Assyria of c. 700 BC. "We cannot determine how Greek fibula

---

10. Roebuck 105
11. Roebuck 55
12. Roebuck 55.

(basically big safety pins) made their way to the palace of Sargon (G. Loud, The Palace of Sargon II, [Chicago, 1938], pl 59) or Greek vases (one sub Mycenaean, one Protogeometric, one Rhodian) to Ninevah (R.W. Hutchinson, J.H.S. LII [1932], 130)."[13] Here we have Greek items conventionally dated to c. 1100 BCC showing up in Assyria 400 years later. Taken alone, they could be explained as a fondness for antiquities on the part of Assyrian kings. But the Synchronized Chronology makes no such demands on credibility. 700 BC is just about right. The Sub-Mycenaean and Proto-Geometric pottery phases were contemporary during early Greek colonization.

LITERACY

If any one aspect of the Greek Dark Ages secretly bothers scholars more than any other, it is surely the apparent loss of literacy for so many generations during the presumed "Dark Ages." Mycenaean Greeks employed a script (known as Linear B) that appears to be totally unrelated to the Phoenician alphabet used in archaic and later times. How could such an intellectually forceful people give up writing? Some scholars have refused to believe it and have proposed that perishable materials were substituted for the clay of Mycenaean times. Presumably this was to go along with the perishable building materials they used for their homes, which also disappeared without a trace.

All Linear B tablets thus far discovered on the mainland have been found in a Late Helladic IIIB context, with the possible exception of Pylos, where destruction took place perhaps at the very beginning of the Late Helladic IIIC period. Clay tablets can be preserved only under certain conditions, it is true, but it is worth noting that none of the inscribed pots and potsherds that have come to light can be dated later than Late Helladic IIIB.[14]

The Synchronized Chronology places the LH IIIB in the early 8th Century BC, freeing Greece from that most egregious *faux paux*, lapsing into illiteracy. By this time, Cadmus the Phoenician had probably already adapted the Hebrew/ Phoenician alphabet to the Greek language. (In Chapter 11, evidence for identifying Cadmus with the time of Shalmanesser III will be presented.) Its superiority over the old Linear B that had been in use for Palace inventories made a changeover inevitable.

---

13. Starr, 1991, 201 footnote.
14. Kelly 13.

Attempting to place the earliest Greek alphabetic writings into the proper point of borrowing from the Phoenician script has not led to unanimous agreement.

> Efforts to fix the date of the Greek alphabet by comparing Greek and Semitic letter forms must face the lack of established canons either in Phoenicia or in early Greek scripts; such attempts have resulted in very divergent dates; B.L. Ullmann, 'How old is the Greek Alphabet,' AJA XXXVIII (1934), 359-81, eleventh or twelfth century (as Wilanowitz and others) . . . mid-ninth century . . . late ninth to mid eighth century . . . and elsewhere, about 700.[15]

John Forsdyke is of the opinion that the evolution of the Greek alphabet can be both chronologically and sociologically fixed:

> The alphabetic script doubtless had its origin in the commercial relations of Ionian and Phoenician traders . . . A hundred years do not seem to be too many for the consecutive processes of professional formation and use, general diffusion in Ionia and overseas, and popular application as it appears on the common pottery of European Greece at the end of the eighth century. [16]

The script at the end of the eighth century BC was not just the application of a known alphabet to a new language. Forsdyke goes on to say, "the Greek system . . . was not . . . a mere adoption of Phoenician letters. The vowels were differentiated, and signs for some consonantal sounds, which the Semitic languages did not possess, were added at the end of the alphabet."[17]

In a later chapter, the full extent of confusion over the evolution of the Semitic alphabet will be highlighted with reference to the famous Tomb of Ahiram, a Phoenician royal burial containing a sarcophagus inscribed with dedications and warning curses. The tomb contained both 7th-century Cypriot pottery and a 13th-century Egyptian vase with the cartouche of Ramses II. It is no wonder that opinions are so divided over the date of that Phoenician script. It should come as no surprise to the reader that the script on the sarcophagus is usually dated to the 10th century, splitting the difference!

It bears mentioning repeatedly that the chronology for Greece following its Dark Ages has been pushed back in time to minimize the enormous discrepancy between conventional date for the end of the Dark Ages, 900 BCC, and the cultural and literary milieu of Archaic Greece (c. 750 BC). The Greeks themselves used vastly inflated estimates for the ages of their ancestors, and

---

15. Starr, 1991, 170 footnote.
16. *Greece Before Homer*, p. 20.
17. *Greece Before Homer*, p. 19, 20.

modern scholars struggle with the necessity of choosing between irreconcilable options.

Archaeological finds have placed the colonization of Asia Minor no earlier than the 8th century, but Greek historians themselves would place that colonization hundreds of years earlier, tempting modern scholars to accept the early dates. Unfortunately, many of the Greek sources that supply chronological clues are very late, such as Pausanias in the 2nd century AD. Even Herodotus, in the 5th century BCC, places the Trojan War 800 years before his own date. He was most likely basing that on genealogies that are no more reliable than the date itself. As was pointed out earlier, the Greeks did not date even contemporary events correctly until the 5th century. Very far before that the Greeks supplied confused and contradictory data.

ARGOS

Argos provides a good example of the problems that arise when trying to reconcile the three cornerstones of Greek chronology legend, native history, and archaeology. Legend tells us that Argos was within that portion of the Peloponese that was the "Lot of Temenos." Temenos was one of the three sons of Aristomachus (and descended from Heracles) who led the Dorians in the conquest of the Peloponese. Argos was the seat of power over the other cities of the Argive plain.

The oldest written inscription from ancient Greece (excluding Linear B) is the "Parian Marble," which gives chronological information going back hundreds of years before its 5th century date. The first (surviving) entry on the Parian Marble is a reference to Pheidon, the most celebrated king of Argos. He is noted as having established weights and measures and minting the first coins. The date given is 895 BC.

In his "Chronica," Eusebius dates the establishment of weights by Pheidon to 798 BC. He is also noted as being seventh in descent from Temenos, a generational point that would be approximately contemporary with Lycourgous of Sparta. He is also noted for having briefly usurped control of the Olympic Games (in the 8th Olympiad) and regaining the Lot of Temenos by military might.

The problem of dating Pheidon is one of the great enigmas not only of Argive history but of all Greek history. It is not exclusively a modern problem. Ancient writers were equally uncertain about when he lived and ruled Argos. By the fourth century BC, no fewer than three dates spanning a 300-year period were already current.[18]

Mycenaean

Protogeometric pottery is assumed to follow Mycenaean but stylistically it is closest to Middle Heladic

Protogeometric

The burial mound at Marathon (490 BC) is filled almost exclusively with Black Figure Ware, offering the earliest reliable ceramic date for Greece

Geometric

Black Figure

Greek Pottery from Mycenaean times to the Battle of Marathon

There is good reason for believing that Pheidon was actually associated with weights and measures and also for the introduction of coinage to Greece. There were even measures named after him. Since the Basis deposit of the Artemesion in Ephasus gives a concise record of the development of coinage starting about 625 BC and culminating about 600 BC, the most likely date for Pheidon is the early 6th century BC, a far cry from the 895 BC date supplied by the Parian Marble.

The Greeks should not be singled out for their chronological exaggeration; it was common in the ancient world. Even Egypt and Babylonia, possessing legitimate rights to great antiquity, nonetheless claimed tens of thousands of years.

The archaeological remains of Argive, like other cities in Greece, suffer a hiatus following the Mycenaean Age. Scholars are troubled by the discrepancy between archaeological "reality" and tradition that makes Argos a powerful and important city following the Dorian invasion. It must be that the Dark Ages struck Argos as well. It is not until the 8th century that (archaeologically datable) activity picks up again and surprisingly, Argos emerges as a political power in the area, constructing the famous Heraeum cult center about five miles from Argos in the geographical center of the Argive Plain. This was a time of religious revival for Greece and Argos was making a statement of confidence by building such a large undefended project so far from the city.

The temple was built on irregular ground, which required the construction of a retaining wall (still standing) known as the Old Temple Terrace Wall. One may be excused for thinking that the distinctive building style could be considered, when attempting to date the remains. "The size of some of the stones used in its construction cannot pass unnoticed; some were as large as five meters in length and two meters high. The wall is strongly reminiscent of the Cyclopean architecture style used during the Mycenaean period, which deceived the excavators of the site into believing that the wall was contemporaneous with the walls at Tiryns."[19]

Kelly had spent his previous chapter showing that the traditions of Argos being an important city soon after the Trojan War was flatly contradicted by archaeological evidence. Argos was actually so unimportant that it left almost no occupational evidence during the Dark Ages. He was impressed, but he does not even question the likelihood that Greeks could have abandoned the art of

---

18. Kelly 94.
19. Kelly 54.

building with stones that weigh as much as a freight car for 500 years and then pick it up again, out of the blue:

> For its day, the construction of this complex was a gigantic undertaking; not since the great days of Mycenaea nearly 500 years earlier had construction on such an impressive scale been attempted. . . . before the latter half of the eighth century had passed, it seems clear that Argos was, at least in a limited sense, master of the Argive plain.[20]

Kelly has outlined a scenario where the legend of Argos becoming the ruler of a region encompassing the cities of the Argive plain after the Trojan War was contradicted by the hard reality of archaeological evidence. With a 13th century Trojan War, Argos must be seen as sinking into the Dark Ages for centuries, only to finally emerge again in the 8th. This scenario also has Argos constructing the famous Heraeum Temple complex using prodigious building practices abandoned 500 years earlier.

By contrast, a Trojan War date early in the 8th century BC allows Greek legend and archaeology to make a comfortable fit. The Heraeum was probably built toward the end of the 8th or early 7th century. No pottery earlier that Late Geometric has been found associated with this building phase. The early and middle Geometric styles are absent and it appears that Argos was not a major trading factor with the Asia Minor colonies that inspired the geometric movement.

Argos was Dorian. The exiled Mycenaean kings who led the Dorian invasion went on to build in the familiar Mycenaean style. But the Argive potters appreciated the fast pottery wheel introduce along with the geometric style, and eventually adopted the new decorative techniques as well.

Greek history offers one of the most compelling arguments for the Synchronized Chronology. Modern scholars have recognized the exaggerated dating that Greeks gave their early history. The dates were mainly derived by counting generations, using as many as 40 years per generation. Those techniques sometimes support the Conventional Chronology, for example the Trojan War. Other times they are demonstrably far off the mark, such as the Parian Marble date for Pheidon. There are also many examples of generational counts from different sources contradicting and otherwise failing to mutually support each other. At times names appear within a genealogy that have obviously been inserted for political reasons, making links with other powerful families.

---

20. Kelly 60.

It will be found that a more reasonable generational count using 20- to 25-year generations (and the elimination of spurious entries) makes Greek tradition closely agree with the Synchronized Chronology.

Argos is just one example that could be multiplied all over Greece, the Aegean Islands and Asia Minor. The Dark Ages are a fiction created by a misreading of the chronological records of Egypt. It is time to restore Greek history to its correct order.

11. THE RISE OF ASSYRIA. PART 3 OF THE TELL EL AMARNA LETTERS

The last two chapters have been an additional buttress to the new chronology between Egypt and Israel and will not be the last detour in this study. Since it is impossible or, at least not very useful, to isolate the history of any one country or region of the ancient world, we will go on to examine the effects of the chronology on the other neighbors.

The Mycenaean links to the 18th Dynasty were one natural area of study. In the chapter on Israel and Damascus at war, Samaria suffered a combination of a severe and prolonged drought coupled with a siege at the hands of the Syrians. In the midst of the ensuing famine, when pitiful substitutes for food items were selling for a fortune, the prophet Elisha made a prediction that on the following day the cost of food would drop. This was to be evidence of an act of God, who would intervene to break the siege.

> For the Lord had made the host of the Syrians to hear a noise of chariots, and a noise of horses, even the noise of a great host: and they said one to another, Lo, the king of Israel hath hired against us the kings of the Hittites, and the kings of the Egyptians, to come upon us. [1]

The Syrians had fled in such a fearful hurry that they abandoned all their provisions in camp. The besieged Samaritans were able to salvage so much food that they could sell "Two measures of barley for a shekel and a measure of fine flour for a shekel."[2]

---

1. II Kings 7:6.

		Chronology to Chapters 11-13		
DATE	EGYPT	PALESTINE		ASSYRIA
	THEBAN DYNASTY	JUDAH	ISRAEL	
				SHALMANESER III
840	(AKHENATEN)	JEHORAM	JEHORAM (?)	
	LIBYAN DYNASTY	AHAZIAH/ ATHALIA	JEHU	
820	SHOSHENK I	JOASH		
			JEHOAHAZ	ADADNIRARI
800	OSORKON I	AMAZIAH	JEHOASH	
780			JEROBOAM	SHALMANESER IV
		UZZIAH		
760				
	OSORKON II		ZECHARIAH/ SHALLUM	TIGLATH-PILESER III
740			MENAHEM	
	SHOSHENK II	AHAZ	PEKAHIAH	
720		HEZEKIAH	HOSHEA	SARGON II
	NUBIAN DYNASTY			
700	TIRHAKA	MANASSEH		SENNANCHERIB
	(SETI I)			
680				ESARHADDON
	(NECHO I)			ASSURBANIPAL
660				

This little incident is a hint that there are new entities for the Israelites to deal with. No longer will it be just Egyptians and neighboring city-states. The international situation was changing and would never be the same again.

---

2. II Kings 7:18.

Even if the feared Hittite mercenaries were only imagined, the possibility of this event must have been real. Now, the Hittites had disappeared as a *united* force about 300 years earlier, according to Conventional Chronology. In the Synchronized Chronology, the Hittites of this era were the city-states north of Syria who occupied a large area known as "Hatti." They were not united as a kingdom and were comprised of an assortment of ethnic and linguistic types. Were it not for the rising power of the Assyrians, the groups making up what we call the "Hittites" might have remained small and independent. Instead, in the face of the new reality, they were pressured into forging new alliances just as were the Syrian and Palestinian states.

A more likely course of Hittite history will be the subject of later chapters. But for now the consequences of Assyrian expansion on the Israelites will be examined. It is unfortunate that the biblical records edited out so much from this important time so that we must rely solely on outside sources for information. If it were not for the annals of Shalmaneser, we would not know that Ahab contributed the largest contingent to a regional defense of northern Syria in Shalmaneser's early campaigns.

This chapter will examine several important events from the records of the Assyrian king Shalmaneser (859-824 BC). They will be compared with biblical history and, once again, the Tell el-Amarna letters (1375-1345 BCC). Specifically:

- Shalmaneser appears in the El Amarna letter from the King of Tyre as "Shalmaiati" who forced the abandonment of the city.
- Shalmaneser's pressure on Ugarit led to the expulsion of its king and his Aegean contingent.
- The expelled king of Ugarit ("Nikdime" in Shalmaneser's records and "Nikmed" in the El Amarna letters) left for Greece with his college of linguists and became known as the "Cadmus" who applied Phoenician letters to Greek.
- Leaders of the coalition against Shalmaneser's first attempt to conquer Syria are also named in the El Amarna letters.
- Damascus had originally sided with the Assyrians against the allies of Egypt but, evidently, could not tolerate the tribute and other demands of Shalmaneser and became a leader of the opposition.
- The "Suppiluliuma" of the El Amarna letters is the "Sapalulme of Hattina" mentioned in Shalmaneser's annals.
- The Mitanni of the El Amarna period were Carians with Aryan overlords who migrated to the Lake Matiene area and became known as "Medes."

THE INTERNATIONAL SCENE

The El Amarna letters give us interesting and puzzling information about the state of international relationships at the time. The informed reader will recognize some problems in the Assyrian and Babylonian areas. The Synchronized Chronology identifies the Assur-uballit of the El Amarna letters as preceding Shalmaneser III of the 9th century; Conventional Chronology places Assurnasirpal on the throne. The only way such a state of affairs could be explained is by the existence of collateral rulership in Assyria, a situation for which Peter James provides evidence. Babylonian king lists have a different but related problem, and both can be traced to the forced extrapolation of a distorted Egyptian chronology onto their history.

The middle of the 9th century BC is a time of rich documentation from Assyria, beginning with Shalmaneser III. His chronicles will be closely compared with the political environment in northern Syria described in the El Amarna letters. It will also be necessary to examine the interrelationship of Assyria and Babylon in terms of relative and absolute chronology. Both are mentioned in the El Amarna letters and they share a long and richly documented history as neighbors in the Tigris and Euphrates Valley.

The El Amarna tablets include letters from Suppiluliuma of Hatti and Assur-uballit of Assyria, as well as references to a Shalmaiati in a letter from Abimilki, the king of Tyre. From Babylon (Karduniash in the tablets) several letters are represented. In the Synchronized History, the letters as a whole would span the last ten years of the reign of Assur-uballit and the first twenty years of Shalmaneser III. We know that Shalmaneser had military contact with a "Sapalulme" of Hattina (referring to his city, Alisar). He also conquered Babylon.

Placing the El Amarna letters in the time of Shalmaneser (859-824 BC) allows the comparison of events from both Assyrian and Egyptian records, separated by over 500 years in Conventional Chronology. Each gives a one-sided version that, when combined, sheds light on some profoundly significant historical moments.

BABYLONIA

Before we go on, let's look at the Babylonian problem. The references to Babylonia (Karduniash) in the El Amarna letters are a difficult area for the Synchronized Chronology, one that will be discussed but not resolved here. Kings of Babylon are listed in the native sources by dynasty. These are not dynasties by family as we usually think of them, but rather by the city or region of origin. Within the meager records that constitute the Post-Kassite era (between 1158 and 722 BCC), the mid 9th century falls in the "uncertain dynasties" span (called by archaeologist the "various dynasties"). Many problems surround this whole Post-Kassite era, not the least of which is the absence of stratified archaeological remains.

While the El Amarna tablets mention four kings of Karduniash (Kariandash, Kurigalzu, Kadashman-Enlil and Burnaburiash), only Burnaburiash is the sender or recipient of extant letters. The Babylonian kings listed for the time before and during the reign of Shalmaneser III are Nabu-suma-ukin I, Nabupallidin and Marduck-zakir-sumi I. Notably missing from the list is Shalmaneser himself, who conquered Babylon and performed the religious rites reserved for the installation of a king. His name should appear on the list. In other cases of an Assyrian holding the throne of Babylon, the Babylonian records confirm it. This inconsistency raises a question over that portion of the Babylonian king list assumed to correspond to this period.

> "This Post-Kassite era of Babylonian history is another "Dark Age." There are virtually no archaeological remains that distinguish this era, which begins with the end of the Late Bronze Age Kassite kings (conventionally 12th century BCC) and lasts until the Chaldeans of the Neo-Babylonian (7th century BC). As scholars have noted: "We are frequently handicapped by the lack of distinctive archaeological remains of the Post Kassite period, i.e. remains that can readily be distinguished from those of the preceding Kassite or the following Neo Babylonian periods."[3]

The time span here is over 400 years, and Brinkman elaborates regarding the Babylonian king lists, noting that:

> The 400 years are not apparent from King List A alone, but must be calculated from the synchronisms with Assyrian history, which has a more chronological framework.[4]

In other words, the Babylonian evidence is being forced to conform to the Assyrian "framework." And unspoken in this comment is the underlying fact that the Assyrian history is forced to conform to the accepted Egyptian timeline. As for the Babylonian kings of the El Amarna letters,

---

3. Brinkman 22.
4. Ibid 38 fn.

As these five Kassite rulers are dated to the 14th and 13th centuries BC, the synchronisms would seem to provide an impressive array of evidence supporting the conventional Egyptian dates. Closer analysis reveals, however, that the placement of Kassite kings of these names in the accepted Babylonian chronology actually depends principally on the Egyptian and Hittite evidence rather than on native documentation. *None of these '14th to 13th century' Kassite rulers is given in any Babylonian king list or chronicle*, with the exception of a problematic reference to a Burnaburiash.[5]

The impression that I get from my own (admittedly limited) study of Babylonian king lists is that the regional dynasties may be just that, concurrent (at least some times) ruling dynasties from regions of greater Babylonia. We try to see modern historical discipline in the lists, and in doing so, overlook the real problems. I predict that the whole "Kassite" era (1595-1157 BCC), stripped of spurious Egyptian synchronisms, will be allowed to move downward in time to merge with the Neo-Babylonian or "Chaldean" dynasty and eliminating the "Dark Age" of Post-Kassite Babylon. As mentioned before, a resolution of Babylonian chronology will not be attempted here.

ASSYRIA

Reason to question Assyrian chronology has already been given, for instance with Peter James who exposes the circular reasoning for the seeming agreement between Assyrian and Egyptian time scales. Since this chapter is examining the international scene at the close of the 18th dynasty of Egypt (conventionally, the first half of the 14th century BCC, but 870-820 BCS here) the same latitude for dealing with lists of names will be required as with the names of Hebrew and Egyptian monarchs in previous chapters. For example, the name Assur-uballit appears on two of the El Amarna letters. An Assyrian king of that name occurs in the 14th century BCC (Assyrian king names are frequently re-used by later kings — a habit not unknown in modern times; there were five Shalmanesers!). But the Assur-uballit who wrote to the pharaoh gives his father's name as "Assur-nadin-ahe." Descendants of this presumed 14th century Assur-uballit give a genealogy going back several generations without ever naming an Assur-nadin-ahe. Granted, "The word 'father' may here have the meaning 'ancestor,' as it often does in the Assyrian texts, but even so our difficulties are not all cleared up. In the texts given below, Assur-uballit does not

---

5. James 307, italics added

include Assur-nadin-ahe among his ancestors although he carries his line back six generations."[6]

It should be mentioned that in royal correspondence with the king of Egypt, the El Amarna Assur-uballit mentions *only* his father and "may be a king descended from a collateral royal line."[7]

Another interesting anomaly concerning the El Amarna Assur-uballit is his use of the title "King of Assyria." *Assyrian* inscriptions of the Assur-uballit assumed to be the same person *never* use the title "King." Only in his grandson's reign is the title king found on writing from Assyria.

> In one respect, indeed, Arik-den-ili had been forestalled by his grandfather Ashur-uballit, who did call himself "king of Assyria, great king" in correspondence with the king of Egypt, and identified himself as "king of Assyria" on his seal; this, however, was not quite the same as using the same terminology in official inscriptions formally intended for the eyes of the gods.[8]

Without stating it explicitly, the same source is trying to reconcile the use of the term "king" by Assur-ubalit in the El Amarna letters. The Assyrian kings had not yet adopted that term, as far as we can tell from any of their known remains.

The extant Assyrian lists can only support the accepted reconstruction by resorting to numerous "corrections." Enormous lengths of time must be filled in order to make the lists fit the preconceived spans. Any inconsistencies in the genealogies offer a chance to insert "missing links" such as repeating sequences of names (grandfather-father-son) to fill spans created by (what may be) faulty assumptions or scribal errors. Keep in mind that a very heavy reliance on Egyptian chronology is forcing Assyrian scholars to accommodate lengthy spans for which no archaeological remains exist. One would think that the enormous hiatus in the archaeological data would present a caution to those who might try to force the king list to fill a presumed time span.

ANOTHER DARK AGE

The chapters on the dark ages in Greece and its neighbors have provided some evidence of the scope and nature of the chronological problem created by Egyptian dating. The clarity and simplicity of the Greek dark age hiatus should serve as a warning of just how obvious the dating problem can be and yet still

---

6. ARAB I 21.
7. James 393.
8. Saggs 44.

remain unrecognized (or suppressed). To think that *several hundred years* of occupational strata could be missing from entire areas that *had* to be occupied ought to be unthinkable.

The lack of Post-Kassite remains in Babylon is a similar problem and has more than just local implications. All of southern Mesopotamia is affected, even to the Arabian Gulf and Bahrain. And it does not end there. Elam has the same gap of several hundred years in occupational remains. Well, it could be assumed that some widespread drought depopulated this vast area; and such a theory has been examined.

But there should be no serious consideration given to theories of depopulation. We have abundant Assyrian textual records going back to at least the reign of Shalmaneser III. The fortunes of Assyria varied from one king to the next. Unchanging through it all was a relentless pressure from neighbors and a rivalry with Babylon. It was no different in the times before, during and after Shalmaneser. The people were clearly there.

SHALMANESER

Shalmaneser was the dominant personality in the mid-9th century BC. We may find the names of people to the north and east of Assyria to be strange and unfamiliar. Many campaigns against these people are recorded in Shalmaneser's records. But he placed a high priority on access to the Mediterranean and that gives us more familiar names to identify: Tyre, Sidon, Israel and Damascus.

These areas had long enjoyed the mild Egyptian dominance that tolerated inter-city rivalries as long as trade and tribute did not suffer. But the weakness of Egypt under Akhnaton invited a challenge to this complacency. The great Phoenician trading cities of Tyre and Sidon were subjected to such terror from Shalmaneser that major portions of their populations elected simply to leave, forming new colonies in Carthage and elsewhere.

SHALMANESER ATTACKS PHOENICIA

Shalmaneser relates the following military campaign: "Year four. To the cities of Nikdime and Nikdira I drew near. They became frightened at my mighty weapons and my grim warfare, [and] cast themselves upon the sea in wicker (?) boats —. I followed after them in boats of — — fought a great battle on the sea, defeated them, and with their blood, I dyed the sea like wool."[9] The reference to dying wool seems to be an allusion to one of the chief Phoenician industries, the

---

9. ARAB sec 609.

wool dyes made from the extract of Murex shells. But what cities could these be? The city of Nikdime refers to a personal name, not the name of a city. Placed in their correct time of the 9th century, the El Amarna letters might shed some light.

A letter from Abimilki, king of Tyre says, "And fire has consumed Ugarit, the city of the king; half of it is consumed, and its other half is not; and the people of the army of Hatti are not there [any more]."[10] Tablets found in Ugarit of the same type and age as the El Amarna tablets describe the events just prior to the destruction. The king (Nikmed, in the Letters) and several foreign population groups were expelled, among them Cypriots, Hurrians (Carians) and Jm'an. This last group could only be Ionians, since the term familiar from Assyrian writings for them was used. The attentive reader might wonder how Ionians could have been in 14th century Ugarit; scholars wondered, too.

Ugarit was an international city with extensive archives of writing in several languages, including alphabetic Hebrew/Phoenician cuneiform (more about that later). There were lexicons in bilingual and even trilingual versions. King Nikmed was apparently a scholar of writing and languages. With his expulsion and the destruction of Ugarit in the middle of the 9th century instead of the 14th, the possibility exists that his destination was of some importance. His name was written in various ways: Nikmed, Nikmes and Nikmedes — so similar to the Greek name Nikomedes that it gave scholars another thing to fret about. And by the inversion of consonants (as so frequently occurred in translations), the name could also be given as Nikodemas.

So we have Shalmaneser conquering the city of Nikdime, almost certainly a northern Phoenician city. A letter from the king of Tyre describes the destruction of Ugarit (Ras Shamra) and at about the same time a king Nikmed of Ugarit is expelled along with foreigners, including Ionians. The letter says that he was expelled, not killed. Where did he go?

At some time prior to the eighth century BC, a Phoenician linguist by the name of Cadmus arrived in Boetian Greece and adapted alphabetic Phoenician to the writing of Greek, an event that was surely one of the watershed moments in Western civilization. This is not the sort of feat to be attempted by the average scribe. If this was not our Nikmed, Nikdem, Nikodemas (Ni-Cadmus), then it must have been his namesake!

SHALMANESER'S SYRIAN WAR

---

10. Letter 151.

After a few more years spent consolidating his territories east and north of Assyria, Shalmaneser was confronted, in his sixth year of reign (854 BC), by a coalition of armies in northern Syria. In his annals, Shalmaneser names the kings and/or cities in the coalition: Adad idri of Aram, Ihruleni of Hamath, Ahab the Israelite, the Gueans, the Musreans, the Irkandeans, Matinu-Ba'il the Arvadite, the Usanateans, Adunu-bail the Shianean, Gindilbu the Arabian and Ba'sa son of Ruhube, the Ammonite. The battle is described as a great victory for the Assyrians, but historians know better. The annals are written in a special code where pretend victories or outright defeats are barely discernible from true conquests. Subsequent events are not consistent with victory.

Shalmaneser apparently collected no tribute as a result of this confrontation and returned again in his tenth year to face the same coalition. This is one of the periods for which Assyrian records must be compared with the El Amarna letters. Assyria was trying to control a region that Egypt had depended on since very ancient times. Without appreciable timber in Egypt, the cedars of Lebanon were a staple for Egyptian construction of everything from boats door frames to furniture. The relationship between Egypt and the Phoenician cities appears to have always been friendly, based on mutually beneficial trade. But Assyria needed access to the Mediterranean and was unconcerned with diplomatic subtleties. The Phoenician cities knew that they would not be able to maintain their traditional lifestyle under Assyria.

If the El Amarna letters date from the 9th century, some of the same rulers we know from Shalmaneser should be represented on the tablets. The following table compares the 9th century records of Shalmaneser with the presumably 14th-century Amarna tablets.

SHALMANESER (ARAB Sec 609)	EL AMARNA LETTERS
Matinu-Ba'il the Arvadite	Mut-Bahlu ([a])
Metten-Ball, a grandson of Ithobal and nephew of Jezebel (Josephus, Against Apion, 123-125)	Ruler of a (Phoenician port?) city where caravans depart to Hanigalbat and Babylonia (Letter 255)
Usanateans	Usa A city that Tyre depended on for water, wood and burial grounds (Letter 149)

Adunu-Bail the Shianean ([b])	Aduna — of Irquata [([c]) killed by mercenaries] (Letter 75)
Biridri (Adad-Idri)(Bir-Adad) Leader of the forces of 12 kings ([d])	Biridia Commander of Megiddo

(a) *The city is not named.*
(b) *Perhaps the kingdom of Sihon.*
(c) *There is a lacuna after Aduna.*
(d) *Luckinbill gives as Hadad-ezer. Pritchard shows both Bir-Adad and Adad-Idri. Velikovsky notes the name as Biridri without explanation. Most of his sources are German.*

It is commonly assumed that Adad-Idri was Ben Hadad of Damascus. In fact, in several later campaigns into this region, Shalmaneser names Hazael, son of Ben Hadad, and names his city as Damascus. It was argued that Ahab would never have allied with Ben Hadad and that Ben Hadad may have fought with Ahab to force him into the coalition, but Damascus was not named in the year six and year ten campaigns, it was *Aram*. During these campaigns the leader of the Aramaic coalition against Shalmaneser is Biridri, based in Megiddo.

Aram was a regional term for the area from northern Palestine to the Euphrates north of Hamath and west to the coast. The leader of the armies of the twelve kings allied against Shalmaneser was supported by a relatively small (1000 troops) Egyptian contingent, just the sort of token force described as being so effective in the El Amarna letters.

Megiddo was the military fortress of northern Palestine that served the northerly extents of the pharaoh's armies. The El Amarna letters give us insight into the political scene at this time where Damascus is flirting with the new power in the area while Israel and Phoenicia rely on Egypt. Later on, Damascus realized the heavy burden the Assyrians imposed in tribute and joined the Aramean coalition.

Biridri, commander of Megiddo, could lead the Aramean armies only with support from Egypt. Under Akhnaton, that support dwindled to the extent that the people of Megiddo were actually under attack and could not leave the city gates. Taanach was already taken.

Shalmaneser's conflicts with Aram continued for years, leaving this record:

> In my eighteenth year of reign I crossed the Euphrates for the sixteenth time. Hazael of Aram trusted in the masses of his troops. He mustered his troops in great numbers. Mount Saniru, a mountain peak which is in front of Mount Lebanon, he made his stronghold. I fought with him. I defeated him.[11]

Hazael was trying to halt Shalmaneser's march down the valley leading into Damascus from the north. Tunip guarded the approach to Baalbeck at the foot of Mt. Lebanon and the Amarna letters tell the same story: "The king of Hatti is staying in Nuhasse, and I am afraid of him. Heaven forbid that he come into Amurru. If he attacks Tunip, then it is only two day-marches to where he is staying."[12]

THE KING OF HATTI

Fear of the "King of Hatti" is a common theme in the El Amarna letters from northerly Palestine and Aram (Syria) and the threat progressed during the interval covered by the letters. Hatti, or "the Hatti Lands," was a geographical term covering the area north of Aram, south of the Black Sea, the east half of Asia Minor, west of the Euphrates and portions east. When Shalmaneser boasted of conquering "the Hatti lands to their farthest extent," this was a matter of great pride. The "mother lode" of metals in the Middle East (excepting Cyprus) was in Pontic Cappadoccia, south of the Black Sea, the legendary home of metalsmithing. Shalmaneser, like all Assyrian kings (and no doubt anyone else who thought it might be within range), coveted this land most of all.

The king of Hatti who is mentioned in so many letters is assumed to be Suppiluliumas, who calls himself "King of Hatti" in the one letter of his that has come to hand. That innocuous letter whines about how few gifts he receives from the king of Egypt compared to what his father received. Could this be the feared King of Hatti? In his first year campaign into Asia Minor, Shalmaneser (on his monolithic inscription) names Sapalulme the Hattinite among those he conquered.[13] In the next section he describes how Sapalulme summoned allies from as far away as Carchemish to defend his stronghold at Alisar. At this point, Shalmaneser is deep into Asia Minor, almost to Boghazkoy (Hattusilis), which may be the city that he says the Hattinans called Petru (Pteria?).

Shalmaneser had a reputation for ruthlessness, piling up pyramids of severed heads in front of besieged cities, imposing crushing tribute on those that surrendered, and burning cities that he conquered. The king of Hatti of the El Amarna letters conducted his wars in the same way. We read, "Why is nothing given to me from the Palace . . . the Hittite troops and they have set fire to the country."[14] Cities like Ugarit were burned.

---

11. ARAB Sec 663.
12. Letter 166.
13. ARAB Sec. 599.
14. Letter 126.

Sapalulme was one of the kings of the Hatti lands. There were others also, but he may have been the dreaded king of Hatti of the El Amarna letters. Perhaps, but more likely it is the powerful king who called himself "King of Hatti": Shalmaneser.

None of the letters is signed by Shalmaneser. On the other hand, the King of Tyre, Abimilki, writes a letter to the pharaoh in which he suggests that his new master is someone named *Shalmaiati*. Abimilki wrote typical letters to the pharaoh pledging his loyalty and determination to guard the king's (pharaoh's) city. But in his last letter he conceded that he had failed, and was abandoning the city:

> Let the king set his face toward his servant and Tyre *the city of Shalmaiati* . . . Behold the man of Beruta has gone in a ship, and the man of Zidon goes away in two ships and I go away with all thy ships and my whole city.[15]

The significance of this letter should not be lost. Here are Phoenician kings leaving cities under siege to found new colonies, such as Carthage, and not in the 14th century BCC, but in the 9th.

In a previous chapter the time of the Phoenician colonization was considered from an archaeological point of view. The legendary association of that colonization and the time of the Trojan War has not been supported in the field. This should have been a clue that perhaps the underlying chronological assumptions were faulty. The founding of Rome is dated to the early 8th century BC with a strong legendary association with both Carthage and Troy. Carthage was founded in 813 BC, according to Timaeus, a date that is reasonably close to Shalmaneser's reign of terror on the Phoenician coastal cities and in respectable agreement with archaeological data.

Setting the El Amarna letters in their conventional place in the 14th century BCC would mean that the Phoenician cities of Ugarit, Tyre, Sidon and Beirut were all attacked to the point of abandonment. Yet there is no *14th century* archaeological evidence to indicate that this led to colonization.

THE AGE OF THE AMARNA SCRIPT

The El Amarna Tablets have formed such a large element in this chrono-logical study because of their unique status among historical records. They betray many points in common with 9th century Assyrian and biblical texts. If the tablets actually date from the 9th century rather than the 14th, then the script itself should present anomalous dating.

---

15. Letter 155, italics added.

In the introduction to an early compilation of Assyrian and Babylonian literature, the opinion of two early scholars is given. Budge and Bezold describe it as follows: "The writing on the Tel-el-Amarna tablets resembles, to a certain extent, the Neo-Babylonian — i.e., the simplification of the writing of the first Babylonian Empire, used commonly in Babylonia and Assyria for about seven centuries B.C."[16]

The gap in time between the conventional date of the Amarna tablets and the Neo-Babylonian empire is over 700 years (1360-620 BC). In the Synchronized Chronology, it is only 200, a believable span for the minor changes in writing over the interval.

MITANNI

One party to the El Amarna letters, the Mitanni, was at the end of what was most likely a fleeting role on the stage of history. The uncomfortable juxtaposition of backgrounds implicit in the language, names and religion of the Mitanni imply the imposition of a ruling class by an invading culture on another people, in this case Aryan on Hurrian (Carian).

> "The first and very important stronghold of Hurrian civilization is known as the Kingdom of Mitanni (the Huri-Mittani). The Mitanni were an Aryan aristocracy ruling over the Hurrian settlements, and the names of Mitannian gods, such as Mitra, Varuna and Indra of the Hindu Rigveda, indicate their Oriental origin."[17]

The land occupied by the Mitanni was called Hanigalbat in the Amarna letters. It was a geographical region lying east of Carchemish and west of the Tigris. Theories have been concocted to cover the ensuing blank spot:

> "The ancient Mitanni to the east of Carchemish, which was so active in the times of the later Amenothes, had now ceased to exist, and there was but a vague remembrance of its former prowess . . . Its chief tribes had probably migrated towards the regions which were afterwards described by the Greek geographers as the home of the Matiene on the Halys and in the neighborhood of Lake Urmiah.[18] (Lake Urmia is also known as Lake Matiene.)

---

16. Harper XII.
17. Chahin 13
18. Maspero VI 130.

The author here assumes that the Mitanni disappeared in the 13th century but retained their identity until they reappeared in the 8th (as the Medes), with the same cultural dichotomy that characterized the Mitanni of the 14th century BC still present after the supposed hiatus.

> Curiously enough, with the Median tribal union proper, only one out of six tribes was called "the tribe of the Arya" ("Arizanti" in Herodotus, or in Iranian, "Aryi-Zanti").[19]
>
> Even in the Assyrian inscriptions of the 9th and 8th centuries B.C. relating to the campaigns in the western part of the historical regions of Media, the number of non-Iranian place names exceeds the Iranian, and the number of non-Iranian personal names of rulers falls short of the Iranian by only a few of the Iranian.[20]

The Mitanni did not disappear from history for 400 to 500 years only to reemerge with the same internal struggle for cultural dominance unresolved. No, the Assyrians became strong enough to challenge their immediate neighbors to the northwest. Those who would not submit to Assyrian rule migrated to the northeast (and northwest) to the area near Lake Urmiah (also known as Lake Matiene), where the next generation of Assyrians found them.

The son of Shalmaneser (Shamshi-Adad V 823-810 bc) wrote, "Against the land of the Matai (Medes) I marched. Before the terrible weapons of Assur and my mighty battle onslaught, which none can stop, they became frightened, they forsook their cities, they went up into the white mountain."[21]

This chapter began with the end of the siege of Samaria when the camp of the attacking army of Damascus thought it heard an approaching army of Egyptians or Hittites. For the people of the Kingdoms of Israel and Judah, a watershed moment in history had arrived. There had never been a superpower neighbor to deal with other than Egypt. For the next 300 years, Assyria was going to make life miserable for the Hebrews and their neighbors.

That same Assyrian pressure caused the people of Hatti to move their "capital" further to the north and west into Asia Minor. The so-called Hittite Empire was not a 13th-century expression that was later reflected in the north Syrian Neo-Hittite kingdoms. Rather, it was the other way around. The "empire" grew from the regional city-states into the Neo-Babylonia Empire under Nabopolassar and Nebuchadnezzar, Chaldeans who were the People of Kaldu from Asia Minor.

---

19. Cambridge History of Iran, 57.
20. Ibid. 56.
21. ARAB Sec 720.

12. SAMARIA AS A BENCHMARK FOR ARCHEOLOGY

If ever there was a source of motivation for archaeological inspiration, surely the Bible ranks at the top. No sooner had the theory of evolution stirred the controversy over the reliability of the Bible than the opportunity to support the ancient document with the new scientific evidence appeared. Early cities in Mesopotamia mentioned in the Bible proved that the sources were far older than ever suspected.

The glory days of 19th-century archaeology amounted to little more than treasure hunting. At least a pretext of recordation was managed, but scant attention was paid to detailed stratification. Modern excavations of sites previously dug in the 19th or early 20th century often expose gross errors on the part of the early reports. Mistaking an Early Iron Age palace as a "Macabbean Fort" may seem laughably sloppy today, but debris of this sort litters the archives of some of the ancient world's most important sites.

Many Egyptian cities were stripped of all materials from critical eras, leaving nothing for modern techniques to salvage. Of course, looters would have stripped many of those sites anyway, if some effort were not made to survey them. Gezer was an important biblical city that suffered this fate. Fortunately, much of the work in Palestine has been conducted with a greater emphasis on scientific archaeology and less on treasure hunting.

One might expect that Palestine would be an archaeologist's dream, with dozens of cities with recorded histories covering hundreds of years. Many of them were even mentioned in newly-deciphered Assyrian and Egyptian records. Jerusalem and Jericho were natural targets for verifying the Bible, and each, in its own way, served to fuel the unending controversy that is biblical archaeology. Jericho, as mentioned earlier, frustrated the early hopes that were raised by

Samaria as a Benchmark

ARCHAEOLOGICAL LEVELS

ABSOLUTE DATES	SAMARIA	LACHISH	MEGIDDO	RELATIVE AGES
1000 BC			VIII	LB I
900 BC			VII	
			VI	LB II
	I	VI		
800 BC			Vb	
	II	V		
	III		Va	I 1a
		IV		
700 BC	IV		IV	I 1b
	V	III		I 2a
	VI		III	
600 BC				I 2b
	VII	II		
500 BC				
			II	I 2c
		440 NEHEMIA		
	VIII			
400 BC				
		I		
300 BC	IX			

claims that the famous collapsed walls had been found. Jerusalem defied its excavators in a multitude of ways.

Hopes of recovering remains of Solomon's Temple or Palace were quickly dashed as it became obvious that the confines of the Temple Platform left nothing even of Herod's Temple, much less any earlier construction. The topography of Jerusalem, which necessitated terraced construction, provided archaeologists with a scrambled jigsaw puzzle of layering. Terraces frequently collapsed, from a variety of causes, leaving otherwise datable remains almost hopelessly mixed. Although excavations have continued to the present, Jerusalem has failed to live up to early expectations.

ARCHAEOLOGY IN "CANAAN"

Even by the early 20th century, Egyptian chronology was making life miserable for archaeologists in Palestine. One site after another revealed an astonishingly sophisticated "Canaanite" culture in the Late Bronze Age, replaced by a much lower level of material culture for the following Iron Ages, which were presumed to be the Hebrews. Could the Bible be so wrong about the nature of Canaanite vs. Hebrew culture?

The contrast between Iron Age and Bronze Age cultural levels was overshadowed by controversies regarding the chronology of presumed Hebrew-era strata. One can read archaeological works on areas of the old and new world and see respectful acknowledgments of previous digs; but Palestinian archaeology is characterized by a degree of acrimony unlike anything displayed elsewhere. The reason is not too hard to understand. Those who took the scriptures seriously, as a legitimate historical document, were attacked by the mainstream of scientific archaeologists who could see that hard data from excavations was incompatible with the "historical" record of the Bible.

A school of archaeology evolved around a principle figure in Palestinian archaeology, William F. Albright. Whenever data from a site was subject to interpretation one way or another, the Albright school leaned in favor of the biblical cause. He was such a powerful and authoritative figure that a deferential attitude accompanied any scholarly reference to his opinions. That tone was to last only during his lifetime and didn't necessarily extend to his contemporaries. Some of the difficulties with Palestinian archaeology have been emphasized in previous chapters. As the time frame passed into the province of Assyrian records, one can expect that really serious disagreements would arise. Indeed the evidence has been the subject of some of the most impolite discourse imaginable.

LOOKING FOR A BENCHMARK

Although it is nowhere stated explicitly, the hope was held out that a site would emerge as a prototype for vindication of biblical history. Jericho was already spoiled, and Jerusalem was far too complex, so all eyes turned to Samaria as the ideal benchmark site. This is where King Omri purchased a hill owned by Shemer and built his capital city. If ever there was an ideal city on which to base biblical chronology, Samaria was it. Construction periods could be compared with their corresponding pottery assemblages and reference points established for important moments of biblical history.

Samaria was a focus of attention when Harvard University conducted excavations in Palestine in the early 1930s. Lessons had been learned from earlier campaigns into similar sites, and the hope remained that this site would reward expectations.

The archaeologist most often identified with the Harvard excavations is Kathleen Kenyon, a renowned archaeologist and a gifted writer.

The approach to the fieldwork at Samaria was specifically aimed at avoiding the problems associated with the Gezer excavation by Macalister. Not only was that site fully excavated over most of the occupational periods, but details of stratigraphy and find spots were not recorded. As Kenyon puts it:

> The answer to this is observed stratigraphy, the visual evidence (recorded in drawn sections) that a surface ran to a wall, sealing the foundation trench cut when its foundations were laid; that a rubbish pit was cut into this surface at a later date; that a wall of a room was completely removed when its successor was built; and, most important of all, the digging methods must provide the evidence to enable one to say which objects come from the foundation trench, from the pit, from the robber trench of the wall...This excursus has been necessary to show why the results of the excavations a Gezer are almost worthless today.[1]

The final published report of Kenyon's (and Crowfoot's) work at Samaria brought early praise for "thorough publication of the pottery and other small objects" so important to scholarly research, and "all future students of Israelite pottery chronology must start with [Kathleen Kenyon's] results."[2]

This may appear to be acknowledgment of a job well done — which it is, but it is also the calm before the storm that broke as the implications of her results ran into the hard realities of Conventional Chronology. A comprehensive

---

1. Kenyon 1986, 2.
2. Albright 1958, 21.

critical review of Kenyon's work published in 1992 is the latest and most complete attack yet. First the author pays Kenyon a compliment on the quality of her work:

> Though our aim in this study consists in examining Kenyon's conclusions with a critical eye, we wish to state at the outset that the comprehensive notes she recorded daily over the duration of the project attest to her perceptiveness and thoroughness as a field archaeologist.[3]

The controversy surrounding Kenyon's work at Samaria concerns the identity she asserted between building periods and their associated pottery. As will be shown later in this chapter, Palestinian pottery sequences are strictly relative, lacking written links to established absolute dates, and therefore are subject to scholarly interpretation. It should come as no surprise to the reader that the experts found Kenyon's pottery dates to be in error. Nobody challenges her assertion that the first construction was started by Omri (c. 879 BC), but the ceramics she related to that phase were consistently identified with similar objects at other sites dated earlier.

Without going into too much detail, there are several cities such as Megiddo, Gezer, Hazor and Lachish that were found to have distinctive gateways built at around the same time. Experts believed that these were Solomon's, since accepted chronology placed them at about that time and scripture specifies that he rebuilt Megiddo, Gezer and Hazor. The fact that an identical gateway was found at Philistine Ashdod complicated but did not overturn the theory.

Even though she recognized and acknowledged the similarity of her Period I pottery to that found elsewhere in 10th- and 11th-century contexts, Kenyon refused to alter her opinions. This invited the kind of blunt criticism so common in Palestinian archaeology.

> The recent work of G. J. Wrightman, for example, has brought into graphic relief the dangers inherent in an uncritical acceptance of Kenyon's chronological framework. His proposals also demonstrate the negative implications which a mishandling of the evidence holds for properly understanding the historical archaeology of other significant Iron I-II sites.[4]

A "mishandling of the evidence"? So much for Kenyon's "perceptiveness and thoroughness as a field archaeologist."

---

3. Tappy, 7.
4. Tappy, 6.

Tappy proposed that pottery periods and building periods for Samaria be treated separately. Kenyon identified the first two pottery phases with Omri and Ahab:

> Since Omri's rule in Samaria was so short, it is very reasonable to expect that Ahab's buildings were a direct continuation of those of his father's. There was certainly a very direct continuation for on the limited grounds of archaeo-logical dating by pottery, Period I and II at Samaria cannot be distinguished. Stratigraphically they can be very clearly distinguished, and functionally the distinction is very important on sociological grounds. Stratigraphically, the distinction between Period I and II is absolute.[5]

Tappy insists that Pottery Periods I & II predate Omri. By examining the evidence with the help of Kenyon's unpublished excavation notebooks, Tappy claims to expose her faulty judgment. Although there is no evidence of previous building activity at Samaria (except for a few EB artifacts), Tappy still believes that there must have been some sort of private estate on the site before Omri. By comparing the Samarian pottery with that from other sites he is simply compelled by the dating.

Tappy is not alone in his criticism of Kenyon; in fact, other experts are apparently unanimous in contradicting her. How could such a reputable archae-ologist, determined to make her excavation a model of careful attention to detail, be so wrong in her conclusions? As mentioned before, the virtual absence of written evidence from anywhere in Palestine forces scholars to determine the ages by judgment alone. Destruction layers and changes in material culture are the guideposts used to make a chronological fix.

Since the Conventional Chronology places the entire history of the pre-exile Hebrews in the Iron Age, it is no wonder that controversy reigns and that so little confidence in the Bible as a historical document survives. In order to make a more reasonable assembly of the sequence of archaeological remains for Palestine, we will work backwards from a fixed point toward the end of the reconstruction.

THE LACHISH OSTRACA

Ostraca is a generic term for writing on broken pieces of pottery, a readily available surface in a land where papyrus and parchment were scarce. A collection of ostraca, written in ink, were found during a British archaelogical dig in the gatehouse of Lachish in the 1930s and have become famous. These

---

5. Kenyon 1971, 81.

"Lachish Letters" were believed by their excavator, J. L. Starkey,[6] to date to the level terminated in destruction by Nebuchadnezzar in 587 BC. The letters were turned over to a scholar who identified some of the names found with those in the book of Jeremiah relating to a situation of danger to Lachish and neighboring Azeqah — seemingly, a pat case.

As other scholars examined the letters, some of the initial identifications were found to be in error. Years of dissection in journal articles eroded the original assumptions so completely that they became just another interesting dead end. But what was lost in all the debate was the faulty dating assumed for the original find. To this day, the Lachish Ostraca are cited as the earliest *collection* of Hebrew writing ever found.

Peter James presents the case for identifying the Letters with the time of Nehemiah. There is a much larger percentage of name matches, and the troubling attacks by Nehemiah's enemies fit the tone of the letters quite well. That would put the time at 440 BC, rather than 587 BC. James summarizes the case:

> An incursion from nearby Philistia seems the most likely explanation for the destruction of Lachish II, as the material culture of the succeeding settlement (Lachish I) includes new pottery forms, altars and figurines known principally from coastal sites. Lowering the date for the end of Lachish II would also eliminate the long gap interposed by the conventional chronology before the beginning of Lachish I in the mid-5th century BC.[7]

Placing the destruction of Lachish II 150 years later means that Lachish III was also destroyed later than normally figured, and not by the Assyrians but by Nebuchadnezzar. This destruction was massive, leaving a three-foot layer of ashes burying the city. This destruction is normally ascribed to Sennancherib in 701 BC. But even though that Assyrian king depicts the attack of Lachish on his reliefs, he does not claim to have burned the city, something that was virtually always noted, if it was true. Rather, the city attacked by Sennancherib would be Level IV.

The Level IV & V cities at Lachish follow a gap after the massive destruction of Level VI, the last Bronze Age city. In the Synchronized Chronology, the end of a Bronze Age Lachish would be placed at the end of the 9th or early 8th century BC. King Amaziah died there, having fled the conspirators in Jerusalem. Perhaps the city was razed as an act of retaliation.

---

6. Starkey was killed by Arabs mistaking him for a Jew, leaving the excavation incomplete. Olga Tufnel, a member of Starkey's staff, spent twenty years publishing the results.

7. James 175.

Level VI Lachish would then be contemporary with Period I at Samaria (Lachish is numbered from the top down, Samaria from the bottom up). Critics of Kenyon's dating of Samaria I and II noted that some pottery was similar to Late Bronze Age types found elsewhere. Since there is enough regional variation in forms to make exact parallels rare, the consensus was that they dated perhaps to the 12th century, still far too early for Omri's time.

Kathleen Kenyon refused to budge from her position linking the pottery and building periods at Samaria. She even presented an outline of chronology for other cities having pottery sequences similar to Samaria.[8] Her meticulous attention to detail so greatly impressed her fellow archaeologists that her techniques and strategies were adopted for training new generations of excavators. It must have been difficult, at least at first, to question her opinions.

MEGIDDO

In the last chapter the case was presented for Biridri, as commander of Megiddo, leading the coalition of Aramean states against Shalmaneser at the battle of Karkar. Interestingly, Ahab's army was the largest contingent of forces among the allies, but Samaria would be an unlikely base for the troops. It was a Royal Palace city. On the other hand, Megiddo was a military fortress of great renown. Using both her archaeological insight and historical acumen, Kenyon arrived at the same conclusion:

> From this historical evidence, there seem clear grounds for ascribing the Stratum IV lay-out of Megiddo to the time of Ahab. On the basis of the Samaria pottery evidence, a date in the 850s B.C. would be perfectly suitable. A base such as the Royal City of Megiddo of Stratum IV would be very suitable for the launching in 853 B.C. of the great expedition of "2000 chariots and 10,000 soldiers" for the battle of Karkar.[9]

Her opinion is based on first-hand archaeological experience, and it shows in her confidence. But once again the assumptions based on Egyptian chronology have forced scholars to deny otherwise convincing evidence (Kenyon's) when even a remote Egyptian connection exists. Excavations at Ta'anach, a city near Megiddo and closely connected by history, have been recently and expertly studied.

In light of the depositional history at the site of Ta'anach, the correlation which Rast has clearly demonstrated between the pottery of Period IIB at

---

8. *Megiddo, Hazor, Samaria and Chronology;* Bulletin of the Institute of Archaeology, 143-56.
9. Kenyon 1971,105.

Megiddo has had a devastating affect on Kenyon's proposed date of 850 BCE for the Megiddo assemblage. We cannot date the Ta'anach material that late inasmuch as a century-long occupational gap would then be ensconced squarely in the 10th century BCE, at exactly the time during which the records of Pharaoh Shishak inform us of his successful attack upon both Ta'anach and Megiddo.[10]

It is unnecessary to understand the technical basis for this quotation. Underlying Tappy's criticism of Kenyon is not only a tacit acceptance of Egyptian chronology, but unblinkingly gives credit to "Shishak's" inscription record, many parts of which are *known* to be fabrications, ahead of a reputable archaeologist's analysis based on the Bible.

In a previous chapter, the "Shishak" who attacked Megiddo and Ta'anach was identified with Tutmosis III, the resentful junior companion of his half-sister, Queen Hatshepsut, who had seen the riches of Solomon. He returned, as Pharaoh, to conquer the country that had helped free Egypt from the Hyksos.

The pharaoh that archaeologists assume to be the biblical "Shishak" is the Libyan pharaoh Shoshenq, whose dynasty is extended 100 years farther back in time than evidence would support in order to overlap with the time of Rehoboam. In the Bible, he is the Pharaoh "So." Hoshea, King of Israel, "Had sent messengers to *So*, King of Egypt, and brought no present to the king of Assyria, as he had done year by year: therefore the king of Assyria shut him up and bound him in prison" (II Kings 17:4). Shalmaneser V then besieged Samaria for three years, culminating in the carrying off of the people and ending the Kingdom of Israel forever.

The Egyptian pharaoh "Shoshenq" (So) lists Megiddo and Ta'anach on his reliefs at Karnak. They are among the cities he "conquered." Ironically, the list is blatantly copied in the style of those of Thutmose III. Apparently most of the cities are fairly insignificant sites in the north; only a few are identifiable. Jerusalem does not appear on the surviving lists and surely it would have been noted at or near the top, if he were indeed the "Shishak" who sacked the Temple of Solomon.

Scholars have had a problem in reconciling the fact that the Jeroboam had evidently been sheltered from Solomon by the very pharaoh who then attacked only Israel, not naming a single Judean city. So firmly entrenched is the identification of Shoshenq with Shishak that it is virtually the only accepted correspondence between Egyptian and Hebrew histories for hundreds of years,

---

10. (Tappy, 12)

and it has been so hallowed that the chronology of the Libyan Dynasty is warped and forced to fit! And also so hallowed that some of the finest work by one of the greatest archaeologists (Kenyon) can be treated with disdain.

The episode of Hoshea sending messengers to the pharaoh was another of the dreadful experiences the Hebrews had with the Assyrians. The Hebrew prophets warned constantly against trusting in Egypt. But the Hebrew Kings were repeatedly tempted to regain a "Pax Aegyptica."

After conquering all of the northern kingdom, the king of Assyria turned his attention to Judah and sent messengers to Hezekiah, King of Jerusalem, taunting him about reliance on Egypt. ". . . Thou trusteth upon the staff of this bruised reed, even upon Egypt, on which if a man lean, it will go into his hand, and pierce it: so is Pharaoh king of Egypt unto all that trust on him."[11]

So do modern archaeologists trust in the chronology of Egypt. Lean on that reed, and it will also pierce the hand.

---

11. II Kings 18:21

13. THE THIRD INTERMEDIATE PERIOD IN EGYPT

The year was 1973, and an important book for Egyptology was published. The long-overlooked era that Kenneth A. Kitchen had dubbed "The Third Intermediate Period (1100-650 BC)" was launched into the forefront of awareness by sheer force of scholarship. This was not a book destined to become fashionable among the otherwise "well-read;" rather, it presented a density of information on minute genealogical links from minor figures of Egyptian nobility, providing a trove of detail on which further research could be based. Endless lists of unpronounceable names may make for difficult reading, but for specialists this work was a landmark event.

The title of the work is an analogy to the gaps between the Old and Middle Kingdoms and between the Middle and New Kingdoms, now known as the "First" and "Second" Intermediate Periods. These were interruptions in the united kingship by native pharaohs. The Third Intermediate Period covers the 21st through 25th Dynasties, conventionally placed alongside the era of the Hebrew monarchies.

One would expect that the rich history of Hebrew interaction with Egypt as told in the scriptures would be paralleled by the Egyptian sources; but, in these pages, the reader has been led through an alternate version of the course of Egyptian history that brings us now to the mid-point of the time covered by Kitchen's work. Either the reconstruction has been wrong to this point, or evidence will be found to bring further support.

It must be emphasized that the "Third Intermediate Period" breaks no new ground in the overall picture of Egyptian history. Actually, Kitchen's intent is to contrast the period with its earlier namesakes whose histories are truly shrouded in mystery. He does this by lifting some of the obscurity of the 3rd period. But nowhere is there any question that the time span involved is firmly fixed at both ends and the dynasties must fill that span!

According to Kitchen (and convention), the 21st through 25th Dynasties were, with certain exceptions, sequential. One dynasty begins where the last ended. They are as follows:

21st Dynasty	"Priest Kings"	1069-945 BC
22nd Dynasty	Libyan	945-715 BC
23rd Dynasty	Libyan	818-715 BC
24th Dynasty	Libyan (2 kings)	727-715 BC
25th Dynasty	Nubian	715-664 BC

Following the Nubian Dynasty is "the resumption of more precise history with the Saite kings from 664 B.C."[1] The irony in this last statement will be left for a later chapter. For now, the moment of transition from the 25th to 26th Dynasties is not an issue and Conventional and Synchronized Chronologies are in full agreement.

Until Peter James' *Centuries of Darkness*, criticisms of Kitchen's work had been argued entirely within the "fixed" endpoints of Conventional Chronology. The beginning point varies over about a 20-year span between the "Long" and "Short" chronologies with the end fixed at 664 BC. Even the most severe critics, who found the evidence for a given Libyan pharaoh too weak to warrant including in the list, found it necessary to add years to the reigns of other pharaohs to fill the voids created. Never is there a questioning of the assumed span involved, that is — until Peter James.

James proposes that the 20th Dynasty ended about 820 BC, to be followed by the 22nd and concurrent 21st. By deleting Libyan pharaohs for which there is little or no evidence, he shortens the length of the 22nd and 23rd by 100 years, bringing it into line with the figures given by Manetho. He provides compelling evidence for dating the earliest Libyan pharaohs to the early 8th century rather than the 10th and early 9th. This means that Shoshenq I, founder of the 22nd Dynasty, *cannot* be the biblical "Shishak" who captured Jerusalem and took the treasures of Solomon's temple in the early years of the Divided Kingdom.

In an earlier chapter Shishak was identified with Thutmose III of the 18th Dynasty. The treasures taken from the temple were depicted on the reliefs of Thutmose III. The dynasty itself ended about 825 BC. James identifies Shishak

---

1. Kitchen 1973, xi.

with Ramses III of the 20th Dynasty; David Rohl identifies him with Ramses II of the 19th. Both claim that "Sisi" was short for Ram*ses*, becoming the "Shishak" of the scriptures. Since neither James nor Rohl recognizes the duplication of the 19th and 20th Dynasties with the 26th and 30th (or, rather, their ghost-like foreshadowing), their view differs from the Synchronized Chronology by over 200 years.

The Synchronized Chronology places the 21st Dynasty not in the 11th and 10th centuries BCC but rather parallel with the time of the Persians (525-330 BCS). Just as the Hebrews were allowed to restore and maintain a *theocratic* rulership under the Persians, so also were the Egyptians allowed their "Priest Kings." Evidence for this placement will be presented in Chapter 17. The present chapter will examine the span of the Libyan and Nubian Dynasties and their historic context. The difference with the Conventional Chronology is only about 100 years for the start of the Libyan kingship, but it is critical for the elimination of a historical distortion and restoring the true course of history.

The collapse of the Egyptian Empire at the end of the Theban Dynasty coincided with the ascendancy of Assyria. No longer were the Hebrews' problems limited to foreign powers of comparable size to Israel and Judah or Damascus. Assyria became the international superpower that Egypt once had been. But, unlike Egypt, Assyria's heavy-handed treatment motivated resistance. Even with the demonstrated reality of brutal retaliation, resentment against Assyria led to almost unceasing rebellion. There was always the hope that Egypt would come to the rescue. Under the Libyan pharaohs, Egypt did its best to maintain its international position and the all-important Levantine trade, but it was no match for Assyria.

THE CASE FOR SHOSHENQ AS SHISHAK

So firmly accepted is the identification of Shoshenq I, the founder of the 22nd Dynasty, with Shishak of the time of Rehoboam that evidence for an alternate dating is bound to be controversial. Only two objects clearly identifiable with Shoshenq I have been found in Palestine and both were found "out of context," meaning that the dating cannot be determined by normal stratigraphic position.

A stele of Shoshenq I was found at Megiddo and is noted in virtually all references to "Shoshenq as Shishak." And while it will be pointed out that the find was "out of context," it proves that Shoshenq I was there at Megiddo, just as his reliefs claim. What is played down is the lack of agreement between Shoshenq's campaign lists and the biblical version of history.

During the reign of Solomon, Jeroboam had lived in exile in Egypt as the guest of (presumably) "Shishak." He returned to take the throne of Israel. Rehoboam had fortified Judean cities against the anticipated campaign but was forced to surrender Jerusalem, the richest prize in all of Palestine. Why then does the "Shoshenq as Shishak" of Conventional Chronology list only cities (actually mostly obscure villages) in Israel and the Negev, curiously omitting Judah and especially Jerusalem? The fact that Shoshenq attacked only his ally and not the enemy of his ally (as we are about to discuss) has not prevented the identification of "Shoshenq as Shishak."

SHOSHENQ IN THE SYNCHRONIZED CHRONOLOGY

In the Synchronized Chronology Shoshenq I would have been welcomed to Megiddo since the Egyptian contingent that aided in the battle against Shalmaneser III at Karkar was typical of the alliance that prevented Assyria from extending its domain further south at that time. As shown in the last chapter, the alliance for the battle of Karkar was based in Megiddo. The pathetic lists of cities on Shoshenq's reliefs at Karnak are the only occurrences for most of the names. They provided a showy display for the Egyptian audience, rather than a legitimate empire.

Besides the Megiddo Stele, the only other object found in Palestine with Shoshenq's name is a statue fragment found at Byblos, again "out of context." But around the cartouches of Shoshenq's name on the statue, the local king of Byblos, Abibaal son of Yehimilk, added his own inscription in Phoenician. Another statue, this time of Shoshenq's son Osorkon I, was also found with a Phoenician inscription by another son of Yehimilk, Elibaal. The two Phoenician texts were identical in form, as would be expected if they were nearly contemporary. The evidence suggests that the two kings of Byblos ruled sequentially and that their Egyptian contemporaries were likewise successive pharaohs.

The problem here for Conventional Chronology is the dating and identity of the kings of Byblos who would have to reign in the late 10th and early 9th centuries BC. Elibaal, whose inscription coincides with Osorkon I, was followed on the throne by his son Shipitbaal. Tiglath Pilesar III, king of Assyria from 745-727 BC, received tribute from Shipitbaal of Byblos in 740 BC. This places Shipitbaal about 100 years too late to be a son of a contemporary of Osorkon I, so scholars have argued that there must have been two kings of Byblos by that name. But removing 100 years from the Libyan Dynasties eliminates many problems, and is just what is called for by the Synchronized Chronology.

THE PHOENICIAN SCRIPT

Even more important for the history of Palestine is the dating of the Phoenician inscriptions themselves. Their form was similar to that on the Mesha Stele (Moab, 840 BC). But the presumptions of Conventional Chronology prevailed and Albright placed them in the 10th century BC. Confusion could only follow. The group of inscriptions known as "Proto-Canaanite" were slightly earlier stylistically than the Abibaal and Elibaal inscriptions mentioned above, forcing them to be pushed back to an 11th century time frame. On the other hand, their forms are so similar to the earliest Greek letters that another dilemma was created. Did Greece receive the Phoenician alphabet in the 11th or 8th century BC?

One other Phoenician inscription, on the tomb of Ahriman, has been similarly controversial and has led to more confusion about the evolution of Hebrew/Phoenician script. The date of this Ahiram cannot be determined historically, so the remains found in his tomb are used to fix the era by cross reference. An alabaster vase with the cartouche of Ramses II was found along with 7th century Cypriot pottery. Almost six centuries separate the dates. Confusion won.

It should not surprise the reader that after decades of controversy, the consensus has been to split the difference on the Ahiram script, and so it is most often placed in the 10th century BC in modern references. Of course, there were no 10th century artifacts found in the tomb. A recent study of the artistic features of the sarcophagus finds similarities to Assyrian motifs of the early 9th century and later.[2] In Chapter 16, evidence for showing agreement between Ramses II and the 7th century Cypriot pottery will be presented. For now, the important points concern the true evolution of Hebrew/Phoenician writing and the assignment of Shoshenq and Osorkon to the late 9th and early 8th centuries BC.

SAMARIA AS THE BENCHMARK

In the last chapter the critics of Kathleen Kenyon's dating of Samaria were shown to have questioned her judgment because the pottery in the earliest levels had to predate Omri. Kenyon herself used the most conservative dates possible, but refused to separate the building and pottery phases. While she dated the first two building levels to Omri and Ahab, the Synchronized Chronology would place only the first period in that time, since Omri only ruled there six years and

---

2. Dornemann, in Douglas 1981.

there would be little time for stylistic changes. Kenyon might just agree with this but she recognized the problem of similar pottery found elsewhere that other experts had dated earlier, and so refused to raise the earliest date.

The famous Samaria Ivories have long been held out as an indication of the time of Ahab. An alabaster vase found with the ivories bearing the name of Osorkon II reinforced the dating with an Egyptian link in full agreement with Ahab's reign. The mention of Ahab's "House of Ivory" has fixed the linking of the ivories to his time. They were mostly found in a Period III context, lending support for the argument that Pottery Periods I and II predated Ahab and Omri. On the other hand, experts in ivory styles find a strong similarity between the Samarian items and 8th century ivories found in Phoenicia, Syria and Assyria. Indeed, the collection of ivories found in Khorsabad (Sargon II 722-704 BC) includes many pieces undoubtedly from Israel, and they are very similar to those from Samaria. James suggests that the ivory style should fix the date of the ivories and the alabaster vase that was found with them, rather than the vase dating the ivories.

So far, the evidence for items relating to three of the early Libyan pharaohs has been found in non-Egyptian contexts of the 8th rather than 9th century. James assembles a longer list of 22nd and 23rd Dynasty pottery and scarabs found outside Egypt with their independently dated contexts. *In no case* is the Conventional Chronology supported! Naturally, the argument could be made that any one of the items might have been an heirloom. The odds against this go up exponentially when many different pieces in different locations are involved.

It is a testament to the importance of the "Shoshenq as Shishak" identifi-cation that the weight of all the evidence has failed to break the link. Indeed, there is such an unquestioning acceptance of the identity that a hint of doubt is never expressed. Even in a work as meticulous as Kitchen's, the first entry on a list of "ultimately interlocking data" for the 22nd and 23rd Dynasties is "(i) Ascension of Shoshenq I in 945 B.C. *on Near-Eastern evidence*."[3] This can be none other than the "Shoshenq as Shishak" assumption, since the only other evidence, the statue inscribed by Abibaal of Byblos, points to the early 8th century! A hint of the uncertainty surrounding some of the dubious Libyan pharaohs (whose reigns are necessary to make up the elongated dynastic length) can be gained by Kitchen's opening of the chapter enumerating the Libyan kings. "Over the years, there has been much confusion as to the identity and number of *real kings* at this period."[4]

---

3. Kitchen 1986, 179, italics added.
4. Kitchen 1973, 85, italics added.

ISRAEL

The Libyan pharaohs, in their correct time frame, ruled from the time of the revolt of Jehu to the end of Israel as a kingdom. This was also from Shalmaneser III to Sargon II of Assyria. The Hebrews began this era with one of the bloodiest episodes of their long, checkered history.

The prophet Elisha initiated a purge of Baalism from Israel by selecting a new king to replace the "House of Omri" (as the Assyrians called it). He chose one of the "children of the prophets" to take a box of oil to Ramoth-Gilead and anoint Jehu, one of Ahab's captains, as the new king. He gave him the command to smite the house of Ahab. Jehu's zeal in carrying out his task was so extreme that biblical commentators are left to speculate on God's use of such a man in accomplishing his will.

Joram had returned to Jezreel to recover from wounds suffered at Ramoth-Gilead in battle with Hazael of Syria. (Some scholars consider Ahab's wounds at Ramoth-Gilead to be an erroneous and confused borrowing of this episode.) By coincidence Ahazia, king of Judah was also there. Jehu shot and killed Joram and had Ahazia chased and killed when he tried to flee. Jehu then assembled the 70 sons of Ahab and the friends and partisans of Ahab's house. Naturally, he had them all killed. Such slaughter is reminiscent of some of the excesses of Patriarchal days.

To complete his purge, Jehu pretended to be a servant of Baal and called for a ceremony to be attended by all the priests and followers of Baal. When they were all assembled, he had them killed as well, and destroyed the temple and pillar of Baal.

There is at least a little bit of irony in the fact that Jehu was actually depicted on the "Black Obelisk" of Shalmaneser III in the act of kneeling and bowing before the Assyrian king as he delivered tribute. This occurred very early in his reign, 841 BC, according to Assyrian chronology. Jehu would probably have accepted that indignity more readily than the fact that he is listed there as being the king of "Bit-Humri," which translates as "House of Omri." The subtleties of local politics were probably of little interest to Assyrian monarchs. What is significant is the importance implied in using the name of Omri to represent Israel, a king whose representation in the Bible is surprisingly brief.

The mother of Ahazia, the executed king of Judah, was Athalia — daughter of Ahab and Jezebel — and she took this opportunity to claim the throne of Jerusalem for herself. In the spirit of the times, she had all other family heirs to the throne killed in order to protect her claim, except for one. A young son of Ahazia (Joash) was hidden away until he was seven years old and could take the throne, with the help of the faithful priesthood. The first act, of course, was to kill Athalia. The young Joash began his reign with a hope of renewal for Judah, but fell short as a ruler and even surrendered the temple treasury to pay off Hazael, king of Syria.

Hazael was also making inroads into Israel, taking all the lands east of the Jordan from Jehu. It would be during Jehu's reign that the Libyan dynasty came to power. This is the true time of Shoshenq I and his "campaign" through Palestine. Hazael was at the peak of his power, remaining in control of an Aramean "empire" that had withstood Shalmaneser III in 851 BC and was a problem for the Assyrian king for many years. Jehu may indeed have welcomed Shoshenq I, for the first time since Amenhotep III there was a pharaoh virile enough to attempt foreign exploits.

Before he came to the throne, Shoshenq I was "great chief of the Meshwesh," a Libyan people already living in the Delta. It took a ruler of substance to bring a new dynasty to power. The grandiose fanfare with which he touted his accomplishments cannot negate the fact that he did sponsor substantial construction projects and left a stele in Megiddo to prove he had been there.

Artifacts of both Shoshenq I and his son Osorkon I were found at Byblos with inscriptions added by the local kings in a manner indicating anything but fearful submission. Egyptians had always depended on cedar timber from the mountains of Lebanon for shipbuilding and other lumber needs. The bond between Egypt and Phoenicia was already thousands of years old at the time of Shoshenq.

Of course, the links inland from Phoenicia to Israel were already hundreds of years old, too, and the dangerous international scene would have brought Israel closer to Egypt. Shoshenq's Palestinian campaigns have remained problematic to historians as long as they have been assumed to be the same as those ascribed to the biblical Shishak of 100+ years earlier. Shoshenq never took on a formidable enemy such as Assyria or even Damascus. When he created the reliefs to memorialize his reign, he used the panels of Thutmose III as a model. They were not 500 years old at that time, as Conventional Chronology would make them, but only 100. Shoshenq was no Shishak!

LIBYA WITH A DISTRACTED ASSYRIA

The vigor of Assyria went through one of its down cycles following Assurnasirpal II and Shalmaneser III. A fight over the succession was only one aspect of this decline. The constant attacks and raids into Armenia had managed to unite the tribes there into an empire that we know as Urartu (the Mt. Ararat of the Bible should probably be Mt. Urartu). The kings of Assyria that followed

Shalmaneser were far too pre-occupied fighting with Urartu and Babylon to bother with Palestine. Until Tiglath Pilesar, in 745 BC, Israel and Judah had a reprieve from Assyria. So did Egypt.

After an opening flourish, the Libyan Dynasty did little more than retain power, and even that was divided. If James is right (and the chronology suggests he is), the overlap between the 22nd and 23rd Dynasties was almost complete. Two delta cities, Bubastis and Leontopolis, coexisted with rival pharaohs of the 22nd and 23rd Dynasties respectively. The drop in cultural level from the 18th Dynasty was profound.

Libyan kings continued to rule in the eastern delta region even during the 25th or Nubian Dynasty (the 24th Dynasty was a single Libyan, Bochoris, ruling from another Delta city, Sais). Their hold over upper, or southern, Egypt was maintained by the appointment of a high priest of Amon (patron deity of Thebes), who was also military commander. Whatever feelings the traditional priesthood may have had for this arrangement will never be known. The Libyan pharaohs spent little time in Thebes. They performed the necessary rites there and returned to the Delta. They made no effort to be buried in the Valley of the Kings.

With the ascension of Tiglath Pilesar III to the throne of Assyria, a new ascendancy for that empire was to begin. In spite of the warnings of the prophets, Hoshea made one last overture to Egypt in rebellion against Assyria (it was to a pharaoh called "So," who could only be the Libyan Shoshenq II). Tiglath Pilesar II (Pul, in the Bible) laid siege to Samaria. This siege lasted three years and was concluded under his son Sargon II. The tribes of Israel were crushed, deported, and lost forever, "punished by God" for prolonged unfaithfulness.

The weakness of the Libyan pharaohs betrayed the trust of the Israelites abroad, but it also invited a challenge from within. The Nubian cousins of the 18th Dynasty royal family saw the opportunity to reclaim Egypt from the foreign usurpers (the Libyans). At the close of the 8th century BC, Egypt was once again ruled from Thebes. The Nubian kings had as strong an allegiance to the god Amon as their 18th Dynasty forbears. The later Nubian kings of Cush maintained that faithfulness. What they were unable to do is gain the complete support of the Delta, indeed an assortment of local dynasties remained there, each holding power as a pretend pharaoh. It was Assyria who finally determined their fate.

This chapter has been meant to place the so-called third intermediate period of Egypt into the true historic context of the Synchronized Chronology. The period seems a lot less obscure when made to cover only the 200 years of the Libyan and Nubian Dynasties instead of 450 per the Conventional Chronology. The breakdown following the 18th Dynasty in 825 BCS allowed a particularly strong prince of one of the Libyan tribes that had infiltrated the Delta to take control of all Egypt. The names of the Libyans who ruled for the next 120 years — the Shoshenqs, Osorkons and Takelots — have an alien sound to them. Rounding out the Third Intermediate Period were the Nubian pharaohs, whose rule was seldom uncontested by Assyria. Assyria finally prevailed, but only to establish native vassals who eventually asserted their independence as the 26th Dynasty. The Saite pharaohs of the 26th Dynasty may not have been any more "native" than the Libyan, but they have gone down in the history books as such.

14. Who Were the Hittites?

Throughout Western history, the major players on the stage of the ancient world have been familiar: Egyptians, Babylonians, Assyrians, Chaldeans, Persians, Hellens and Romans. Modern scholarship has pushed back the Babylonians toward the earlier Sumerian and Akkadian roots. Rather than really surprising us, the discoveries there largely vindicated biblical representations of Patriarchal times.

Yet, one area forced scholars to add a previously unsuspected name to the list of major powers of the ancient world: the Hittites, in Asia Minor. Greek, biblical and other early historical sources knew nothing of a Hittite empire. The relations between the 18th and 19th Egyptian dynasties with a world class power in central Anatolia could not have been ignored — how could their name have been forgotten from history? Sure, Hittites were mentioned in the scriptures as a minor people of the ancient world, but nothing would indicate that they were ever anything more than that. Could it be that the same chrono-logical alchemy that forced a dark age into Greek history is at work also in Turkey?

Not that the Hittites are unreal. We just know them by another name: the Chaldeans. The ancient historical sources had much to say about these people, who conquered Babylon and ruled most of the known world from there. The opinions of Strabo, Homer and Herodotus will help guide this search.

The Archive

The cornerstone of Hittite scholarship is the collection of clay tablets found in the ruins of an ancient city in what is now central Turkey. Near the

		Chronology to Chapters 14-16		
DATE	EGYPT SAITIC DYNASTY	CHALDEAN-HITTITE	ASSYRIA	EVENTS
660	SETI-PSAMMETICH	SAPALULME-	ASSURBANIPAL	663 THEBES FALLS TO ASSURBANIPAL
640		NABOPOLASSAR-MURSILIS		
620				
	RAMSES II-NECHO		ASSURUBALLIT	612 FALL OF NINEVEH
600		NEBUCHADNEZZAR-HATTUSILIS		605 BATTLE OF CARCHEMISH
				CA 588 EGYPTIAN-KHETA TREATY
580	MERNEPTAH-HOPHRA			587 FALL OF JERUSALEM
560		NERGILISSAR		560 CROESUS KING OF LYDIA
		NABONIDUS		CYRUS KING OF PERSIA
540				546 CROESUS SACKS BOGHAZKOI
		BELSHAZZAR		546 CYRUS CONQUERS LYDIA
520				525 CAMBYSES CONQUERS EGYPT

modern town of Boghazkoy (100 miles east of Ankara, in the bend of the Halys River) is the site of a large fortified city and palace. Spilling down a slope from a collapsing archive room, thousands of cuneiform tablets and fragments lay ready for the picking. They were indeed picked up and collected with such reckless abandon that little stratification data was preserved. However, one find eclipsed all others and made headlines.

The official discoverer of the archives, Hugo Winckler, was reading the cuneiform texts as fast as they could be brought to him — by the wheelbarrow load! Among the other finds was a Hittite version of a text found in Egypt. It was the treaty between Ramses II, pharaoh of Egypt, and Hattusilis, king of Hatti. As archaeological finds go, this ranks close behind the Rosetta Stone. Now, there was no longer any question about the age of the archives and the rulers named in them. The similarity of some of the local artwork to late Assyrian forms was swept aside in the "landslide" of chronological evidence.

Ramses II and Hattusilis had fought an important battle around a city referred to as "Kadesh," by a river "R-N-T." Kadesh is a generic term for "holy city" and could be applied to numerous sites. Which one was meant, this time? We know this was not Kadesh Naphtali or Kadesh Barnea, because Kadesh-Naphtali is too far west of the Jordan River and Kadesh-Barnea is an oasis in the wilderness of Zin. It cannot be the Jerusalem Kadesh of Thutmose III, because of the river. The true time and place of the "Battle of Kadesh" will be the subject of Chapter 16, concentrating on Ramses II. For now, the important factor is the linguistic nature of the tablets themselves and what they tell us about the Hittites.

A MIXED PEOPLE

No fewer than eight languages are represented in the texts, first among them Babylonian, the diplomatic language of the time. The second most frequently found language was assumed to be "Hittite." Only later was it found to be called "Neshili." The Indo-European roots of this language served to popularize the idea of Hittite as an ancestor to later European languages. When one of the other languages was discovered to be called "Khatili" (the language of Hatti), it was too late to undo the confusion. This new language appears to have been used mainly for religious purposes and within the palace. It is unrelated to any other known language.

Phrygian, Etruscan, Medean and Lydian can be expected to figure among the remaining languages (Lydian "seems to be Hittite," notes McQueen[1]). Placed in correct time, the cosmopolitan capital of the "Hatti Lands" would have diverse diplomatic correspondence. These ties will later be compared to those of Nebuchadnezzar, the powerful Chaldean king of the "Neo-Babylonian" empire who called himself the "King of all the Hatti lands."

The language issue has presented a mixed set of data. On the one hand, the two principal languages used locally indicate a possible elite class employing

---

1. P. 59.

"Khatili" in the palace and for ceremonial purposes, ruling over the native speakers of "Neshite" (now known as "Hittite"). Another possibility is that Neshili is the language of the people from Kanesh (Kanesh=Kultepe, southeast of Boghazkoy), who play a large role in Hittite legends. Khatili might then be a vestigial language like Sumerian in later Babylon (or like Latin in later Europe, for that matter).

Most likely, the Hittites were the ancestors of the people there today:

> The typical Armenian of today is, on the physical side, what his ancestors were in the age of the Vannic Kingdom. Broad-skulled, with black hair and eyes, large and protrusive nose and somewhat retreating chin, he represents the "Armenoid" type which extends throughout Asia Minor, embraces a section of the Jews, and is characteristic of the Hittite monuments . . . Languages change readily; racial types are extraordinarily permanent.[2]

Within the regions covered by the Armenian type, Strabo described a bewildering density of cultures. The mountainous country surrounding the Black Sea on the south and east provided isolated valleys that defied millennia of passing conquerors.

The Vannic kingdom referred to above was the 8th century kingdom of Urartu, whose art has such a similarity to that of the Hittites. As mentioned earlier, Urartu is a more correct pronunciation of the word from which Mt. Ararat gets its name. And Mt. Ararat lies near the center of this region of incredible cultural diversity, as if the font of humanity were the very landed family of Noah.

HITTITE ORIGINS

Attempts to trace the origin of the Hittites by their art has been complicated by the fact that it seems to begin and end with the same style, with 500+ years in between. This problem in Hittite art will be dealt with in detail in Chapter 15. For now, the matter of origins is the issue and scholars are really no closer to an answer today than when the Boghazkoy archives were found:

> Generally speaking, the Hurrian hypothesis viewed in connection with the problems of the origins of Hittite art is a solution born of despair, amounting as it does to an explanation of the obscure by the yet more obscure.[3]

---

2. CAH III 173
3. Vieyra 14

The Hurrians had in common with the Hittites a cosmopolitan city with diverse lexicons. At Ugarit we recognize the Hurrians (Khurri) as the alter egos of the Carians of classical times. Likewise, the Hittites are the alter egos of a people known in classical times. In their religion, which comfortably encompassed the deities of all subject peoples is the clue to their identity:

> Hittite religion was very hospitable, so long as the foreign deities who were admitted into it acknowledged the supremacy and fatherhood of Khaldis.[4]

Khaldis was the Supreme Being for all the Armenian people who were "Children of Kaldu." And therein lies the secret to the identity of the Hittites. They are "children of Khaldu" or Khaldeans. The word "Chaldean", used for the Neo-Babylonian kings, is a modern artifact of spelling intended to present a difference where there is none in the originals! The concept of Chaldeans as a separate people from the Khaldeans is fundamental to modern scholarship, yet there has also been an occasional voice suggesting some remote relationship between the two.

THE KHIRBET KERAK PEOPLE

A type of pottery found first at Khirbet Kerak in Galilee has an interesting story to tell of the history of the Hittites. From the Old Testament we learn that Hittites were present in Palestine already in Patriarchal times and were still among the peoples of the hill country from the times of Joshua until David. The early history of the Hittites is presented in broad outline in Sir Leonard Wooley's trail of Khirbet Kerak pottery.

> . . . a single example of characteristic Khirbet Kerak pottery was found in each of the Hittite Royal Tombs at Alajahuyuk in Cappadocia. Those tombs date from about 2000 BC and at the time the Khirbet Kerak ware was no longer in current use amongst the Hittites, so that the examples of it found in the royal tombs must be a survival perhaps due to ritual notions . . . The Khirbet Kerak people originally lived in the south Caucasus area where, starting from the Neolithic stage, they had built up a chalcolithic culture of their own of which the pottery is the outstanding feature.[5]

---

4. CAH III 183.
5. Wooley 32

Wooley traced their migration from their original center north of Mt. Ararat to the Amuq Valley (Antioch) on the boundary between Turkey and Syria. From there they moved north and west, into the Hatti lands:

> For in the Khirbet Kerak people we must recognize the ancestors of the Hittites.[6]
> Moreover, the scanty historical records that survive to us are sufficient to show that the Hittites made their way up into central Anatolia from the south, establishing a new capital with each stage of their advance . . .[7]

These "Hittites" who moved into central Anatolia were adding another layer to the ancient mix of cultures. Few places on earth show as long a sequence of habitation as this region (including neolithic villages as old as Jericho). It is no wonder that so many languages were represented in the Boghazkoy archives.

THE HATTI LANDS

It is important to remember that "Hatti" is more of a geographical than an ethnic or linguistic term. Whether or not the present work successfully proves that Hattusilis is the same person we know as Nebuchadnezzar, both claimed to be king of all the "Hattilands." And whichever age the claim is assumed to represent, 13th century by Conventional Chronology or 7th Century by the Synchronized Chronology, a vast area is encompassed, from central Anatolia to east of the Euphrates and south to some part of Syria.

An analogy could be made between Hatti and Babylonia. The name Babylonia implies a region of the ancient world that evolved around the city of Babylon. Dynasties from a variety of cities alternated on the throne, each honoring the tradition of Babylonian centrality. The Hatti lands encompassed a much larger area than Babylonia and often splintered into territorial rivalries. Babylonia and Hatti would have abutted and overlapped at times.

In whatever age the Hatti Lands are examined, metallurgy ranks high in importance. The cuneiform records found at the Assyrian trading colony Kultepe in the 20th-18th centuries BC are just the earliest to reflect the principal commodity of the region. By the time the Greeks get around to cataloguing the natural history of the area, the term Chaldea was identified with ironwork, and more anciently, silver.

---

6. Wooley 33
7. Wooley 34

Kinnier Wilson equates the *selap(p)aju*, a group of foreign metalsmiths working in Assyria, with the Chalybes, a people living in the Pontic region whom later Greek tradition associated with early mastery of iron, and views them as highly specialized traveling craftsmen.[8]

Strabo, whose own homeland was just to the west along the Black Sea Coast from the Calybes, tells us more about them.

The Chaldaei of today were in ancient times called Chalybes . . . their territory on the land, has the mines, only iron mines at the present time, though in earlier times it also had silver mines.[9]

In book 12 of Strabo's geography, the Greek author launched into a description of tribal people called Chaldaei or Chalybes, also known to Aeschylus and Xenophon. These coastal people lived in much the same way as the modern descendent tribal Laz of Black Sea Turkey. Having come from this region of Anatolia, Strabo knew them well, as well as the narrow and mountainous seaboard of mines and forests from which they gained their livelihood. These were the same Halizoni who in Homer's catalogue of ships were identified with the birthplace of silver.[10]

At this point the term Chaldean has described both the people whose principal deity is Khaldis, including not only the "Hittites" but also the "Urartu" of the kingdom of Van. On the other hand, Strabo names the Chaldaei as one of several peoples inhabiting the Pontic region of northeasterly Asia Minor, although they are singled out for special attention. Assyrians fought against the "Kaldu" to the west of Assyria and some tribes of the Chaldeans settled south of Babylon in the area known as the "Sea Lands."

Scholars have been somewhat mixed in their treatment of the origins of the Chaldeans who formed the Neo-Babylonian Dynasty. Were they the same as the Kaldians of Asia Minor? (Remember, the differing spelling is merely an artifact for purposes of distinction.) Maspero, one of the great early authorities, could not say for sure:

The tribes from which, soon after, the Kaldi nation was formed, were marauding round Eridu, Uru, and Larsa, and may have already begun to lay the foundations of their supremacy over Babylon: it is indeed, an open question whether those princes of the Countries of the Sea who succeeded the Pashe dynasty did not come from the Stock of the Kaldi Aramaeans.[11]

---

8. Wertime and Muhly 90.
9. Strabo 12.3.18
10. Wertime and Muhly 18.

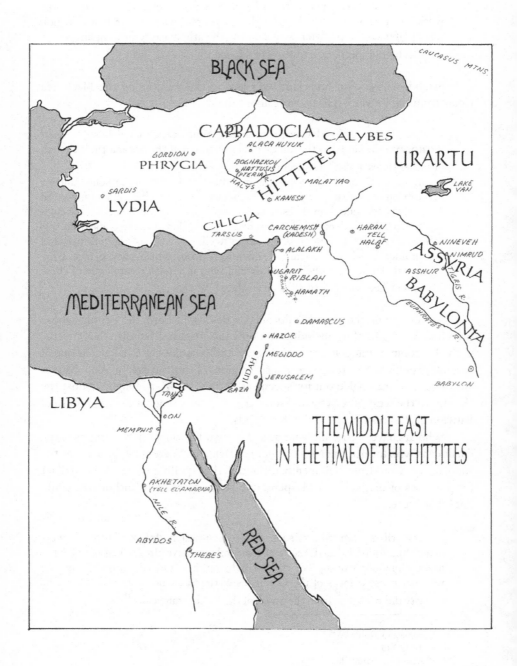

THE MIDDLE EAST
IN THE TIME OF THE HITTITES

Maspero did not use the current spelling. A modern scholar notes an important Chaldean tribal name as a link between the southern and northern branches:

> The name Adinu, attested both for a ninth-century individual and for a clan Bit-Adini in southern Babylonia in the time of Shalmaneser V invites comparison with the well-known Aramean tribe of Bit-Adini in upper Mesopotamia in the ninth century. But whether or whence the Chaldeans are likely to have come from the West Semitic area cannot as yet be established.[12]

In later classical times the word *Chaldean* was virtually synonymous with *Astrologer*. The priesthood of Babylon was famous for their knowledge of astronomy and occult sciences. Add to this their fame as metallurgists. No doubt their secretiveness in the occult is mirrored in those "highly specialized traveling craftsmen."[13] After the fall of the Neo-Babylonian empire to the Medes and Persians, the only region in which Chaldeans are clearly attested is Eastern Asia Minor, as "neighbors of the Armenians," as noted by Cyrus. 100 years later Xenophon wrote of Chaldeans living between Ararat and the southern rim of the Black Sea.

The greatest source of confusion over the Chaldeans is probably the uneven survival of records from Babylon concerning their origin. Virtually every mention of Chaldean tribes in the era before and into the Neo-Babylonian Dynasty relates to the local tribes and their opposition to Assyria. It is a misleading impression that has detracted from the actual northern origin.

It would be best to regard "Chaldeans" as a term for people and "Hatti" as a term for land. When Assyrians fought the Kaldu, those were tribes in Asia Minor. When they fought the kings of Hatti, those were rulers of city-states in the same region. Chaldeans governed *parts* of the Hatti lands at various times, and Hittite allegiance to the Kaldu god does not necessarily imply ethnic uniformity.

---

11. Maspero VI 249
12. Brinkman 266
13. Wertime and Muhly 90.

GREEK REFERENCES TO HITTITES

The Greeks have preserved a few bits of information that provide interesting additions to our knowledge of the Hittites. As was mentioned in a previous chapter on Troy, Hittites may have been associated with the Amazons. Strabo noted that in the Iliad that the Amazons would not fight on Priam's side because of the fact that he had fought against them as an ally of the Phrygians. The Phrygians occupied the same area as the western Hittites and Hittite remains are thoroughly intermixed with Phrygian on those sites. The few examples of Hittite sculpture that occur in western Turkey probably had something to do with the Amazon legends, since they wore the typical short Hittite skirt. And "on the frieze of the Hellenistic Temple of Hecate at Lagina, Amazons are represented wearing helmets of the type worn by Hittite soldiers at Carchemish."[14]

There are at least two separate Greek sources of opinion on the idea of an empire based in Asia Minor. Strabo comes as close as possible to identifying the Chaldean Dynasty with a northern origin:

> In ancient times Greater Armenia ruled the whole of Asia, after it broke the empire of the Syrians (Assyria), but later, in the time of Astyages, it was deprived of that great authority by Cyrus and the Persians.[15]

This can be none other than the Neo-Babylonian Empire placed between the Assyrian and Persian Empires. The other Greek reference is less definitive but no less intriguing:

> The Greek legends tell us vaguely of some sort of Cilician empire which is said to have brought the eastern and central provinces of Asia Minor into subjection about ten centuries before our era.[16] Solinus, relying on the indirect evidence of Hecataeus of Miletus, tells us that Cilicia extended not only to countries afterward known as Cataonia, Pamphylia and Cappadocia; the conquests of the Assyrian kings must have greatly reduced its area. I am of opinion that the tradition preserved by Hecataeus referred both to the kingdom of Sapalulme and to that of the monarchs of this second epoch.[17]

---

14. CAH II 2, 418 FN.
15. Strabo 11.13.5.
16. Maspero VI 246.
17. Ibid. footnote.

Maspero here has assumed that the reference to Sapalulme must refer to an earlier Hittite Empire that the Assyrians reduced. No such assumption is required by the Synchronized Chronology.

We have no way of knowing whether Strabo had "Chaldeans" or "Hittites" in mind when referring to the rule by "Greater Armenia." He knew the region of Hatti by the name Cappadocia:

> . . . the Cauconians extended from Heracleia and the Mariandyni to the White Syrians, whom we call Cappadocians.[18] As for the Paphlagonians, they are bounded on the east by the Halys River "which" according to Herodotus "flows from the south between the Syrians and the Paphlagonians and empties into the Euxine Sea (Black Sea), as it is called." By "Syrians," however, he means the "Cappadocians," and in fact they are still today called "White Syrians," while those outside the Taurus are called "Syrians."[19]

THE CHALDEANS

The Neo-Babylonian Dynasty was not the first time Chaldeans had ruled Babylon. In the time of Sargon II (late 8th cent. BC), a Chaldean named Merodachbaladan was king of Babylon. Sargon not only conquered him, he did his best to rid the Sealands of Chaldeans (mainly the "Bit-Yakim" tribe who were ultimately exterminated by Assurbanipal). Sargon claimed:

> Merodachbaladan, king of Chaldea, who exercised the kingship over Babylon against the will of the gods . . . (illegible number) . . . people, together with their possessions, I snatched away . . . [In the land] of Hatti (Syria) I settled (them).[20]

The Assyrians were in constant conflict with, and ultimately were conquered by, the Chaldeans. At least some of the Chaldean tribes had settled in the vicinity of and also south of Babylon and were powerful enough to rule there. However, the Chaldeans that the Assyrians fought with the most were the Urartians.

THE URARTIANS

The Urartians were a more or less unified kingdom from at least the mid-ninth century to the end of the eighth. Assyrians recorded battles with Urartians

---

18. Strabo 12.3.5.
19. [complexion] Strabo 12.3.9
20. ARAB II 4.

(in well attested and dated records) from the time of Assurnasirpal (884-859 BC). The Urartians actually called themselves "Biani," from which the name of Lake Van is said to be derived. The "Kingdom of Van" was another name for the Urartians.

> Another title, however, has been proposed, that of "Khaldian," on the ground that in the inscriptions the people are called "the children of Khaldis," the supreme god. The name survived, it has been urged, among the Khalybes, who are also called "Chaldeans," and a medieval province of Khaldia extended along the coast of the Black Sea from Batun to Trebizond.[21]

The Assyrians routinely claimed victories against the Urartu but the frequency of their campaigns to that area suggests that the special Assyrian "code" is at work here. In fact, the Vannic fortress cities were virtually impregnable and the Assyrians mostly ravaged the unprotected countryside around the cities.

> Indeed while reading the history of that remote period and place, time tends to be so telescoped that the Assyrian invasions of Urartu seem to be much more frequent and permanent than they were in fact. How many times did Ashur invade the land of Khaldi? Five times during the course of over three hundred years, all of them raids, not conquests, for Assyrian garrisons were never established in Urartu.[22]

With the death of Shalmaneser in 824 BC Assyria began one of its episodes of weakness and Urartian power grew. By the reign of Sardure II (753-735 BC) the Urartians ruled a kingdom from north of Ararat to Cappadocia.

> Another 500-line text describes with pride his conquest of the rest of Commagene and Urartu's complete triumph over Assyria in Mannai. Between Isoglu and Kumu-han on the left bank of the Euphrates, an inscription gives details of Sarduri's conquest and occupation of Malatya.[23]

Malatya is one of the classic Syrian Hittite cities in the heart of Hatti land. The wealth of "Hittite" art in Malatya is actually Urartian or "Khaldian."

THE CIMMERIAN INVASION

The Urartu were the first in line of those peoples who were overrun by the Cimmerian invasion of the late 8th century. Moving down from the north, they

---

21. CAH III 170.
22. Chahin 194.
23. Chahin 77.

swept through Armenia and westward into Asia Minor. The Assyrians, under Sargon, took advantage of the situation by making inroads into southern Urartu, but soon enough the Cimmerians were causing trouble for Assyria also. The Phrygians never recovered from the Cimmerians but the invasion finally lost strength in Lydia. Urartia survived through the 7th century but their era of power was over.

The Urartu have more in common with the Hittites than just a chief deity Khaldi. Their art is virtually indistinguishable from Hittite and their languages have been speculated upon in the same manner. The Hurrian hypothesis for the origin of Hittite art was described as an act of desperation — "an explanation of the obscure by the yet more obscure."[24] It is no surprise that the Urartu are likewise linked to the Mitanni (who are considered to be Hurrians).

> Whence they came is not certainly known, but some features of their civilization are most easily accounted for by supposing that they migrated from a district of Asia Minor to the west of their new home. Their native language belongs to the group commonly called "Caucasian" and is believed by some to be akin to the tongue of the Mitanni people who disappeared from history in the thirteenth century BC.[25]

A leading Armenian scholar has the following to say about the origin of the people of Armenia:

> Hayk means Armenians in the native tongue. Hayk, the eponym of the mythical founder of the Armenian people, is said to have been the son of Togarmah (Torkom in Armenian), grandson of Japhet, son of Noah . . .
> Hayk (Armenians), Haay (Armenian), and Haya-stan (Armenia): these names together appear to originate from the name of the ancient kingdom of Hayasa (c. 1400 BC), situated on the eastern frontiers of the Hittite empire . . .
> Togarmah, the main city of Tabal, was on the western side of the Euphrates (Firat su), opposite Urartu and its dependencies. It was in that region of Tabal-Togarmah that the Armenians seem to have first settled. They appear to have been a tribe within the Phrygian community which crossed the Bosphorous into Asia during the tumultuous times of great ethnic movements and political change towards the end of the thirteenth century BC. They must have witnessed the destruction of the Hittite empire; indeed they probably took part in it, and occupied its lands.[26]

---

24. Vieyra 14.
25. CAH III 19.
26. Chahin 204.

This last interesting observation can only be based on an assumption and not fact. The three Phrygian occupational layers found in the excavation of Gordion, the capital city, were thoroughly intermixed with Hittite remains. Some creative explanations for this have not resolved the chronological difficulty of co-existence between Hittites remains of the 14th and 13th centuries with Phrygian remains of the 9th and 8th centuries. To make matters worse, the Phrygian layers are separated from the following Persian layers by several meters of "pure Hittite" strata. These are presumed to have been brought from elsewhere and spread over the site for leveling and preparation for Persian era construction. Not surprisingly, there have been no remains found from the 150 years separating the Phrygian from the Persian! Here we clearly see that the archaeology of the Late Hittite Empire should be placed immediately prior to the Persian Era. The layer of "pure Hittite" remains is the only one in which Hittite Royal Seals occur. *There is no more direct and clear indicator of the problem of conventional Hittite chronology than the stratigraphy of Gordion.*

THE TWO HITTITES

When scholars refer to the Hittites, they will distinguish between the Hittite empire of the 14th-13th centuries BC (and their ancestors) and the so-called Neo-Hittites of eastern Asia Minor in the 9th-7th centuries BC. Conventional Chronology sees the Neo-Hittites as successors of the empire following a "dark age" hiatus of several centuries. The Synchronized Chronology reverses this sequence with the Hittite Empire succeeding an earlier age of city-states sharing a common "Khaldi" or "Hattic" culture. In the *Hittite Empire* can be seen a stage of art at the end of a long history of evolution. The attempts by art historians to describe this evolution with the Empire period as the beginning has been a tortured exercise: the starting and ending points are the same.

This excursus into the origin and history of the people known as Hittites should emphasize some important points. They were a mixed culture with a dominant "Neshili" language people (probably from Kanesh/Kultepe) over several subservient peoples throughout Asia Minor. A special "Hattili" language was used for religious and palace purposes in much the same manner that Latin was used by European scholars long after it had ceased to be used by any major population.

The Khirbet Kerak pottery people, whose long evolution can be traced from the Caucasus in the Neolithic era to the Hittite royal tombs at Alaka Hujuk in the early 2nd Millennium, may be related to the "Hattic" language culture. The later influx of Phrygian-Armenians superimposed yet another layer on the Asia Minor layer cake.

UR OF THE CHALDEAS

The first step by Abraham's family from an original homeland in "Ur of the Chaldeas" was at Harran in the northern Euphrates Valley. The famous city of Ur in southern Mesopotamia was probably never a Chaldean city, especially in Patriarchal times. It is far more likely that another Ur (short for Urartu?) north of Harran was the Ur "of the Chaldeas." This makes the extreme detour in Abraham's migration unnecessary and places Chaldeans in the same region that later classical scholars (Strabo, et al.) placed them.

Those people that we call Hittites were Chaldeans. It is time to stop playing spelling games with derivatives of the Khaldi name. The false course of history caused by Egyptian dating makes (unintentionally backwards) quotations such as the following description of Urartu into a joke:

> . . . the remains of Urartian civilization as revealed by the excavations of Toprak Kaleh show very clearly the influence of the superior civilizations with which they came into contact. Among their Gods, called "Khaldi" gods — a term associated by some scholars with the (Chaldeans) who lived in Pontus — was Teisbas, the Hittite Teshub, and it is scarcely to be doubted that his cult was borrowed from the more ancient people.[27]

---

27. CAH III 19

15. CHALDEAN ART

Identifying the Hittites with the Chaldeans is of such importance to the Synchronized Chronology that one more chapter needs to be devoted to the cultural examination before exploring the historic side. You can look long and hard for books on the Art of the Chaldeans with disappointing results. Other than the few remains of Nebuchadnezzar's palace in Babylon, the Chaldeans are extremely difficult to detect in the archaeological record.

The historical records of the Neo-Babylonian or Chaldean Dynasty mirror this condition. Virtually the entire catalogue of chronicles of the Neo-Babylonian kings consists of six cuneiform tablets. Their contemporaries in Egypt, the Saitic 26th Dynasty, share the same scarcity of remains in both archaeological and written records. This is no coincidence. In spite of the abundant outside historical sources in Hebrew and Greek texts, both Egypt and Babylon for this time refuse to give up their secrets.

In the next chapter, a detailed comparison will be made of the Neo-Babylonian (Chaldean) kings Nabopolassar and Nebuchadnezzar as the alter egos of the Hittite kings Mursilis and Hattusilis III. In the present chapter, Cappadocian Hittite Art of the presumed 14th and 13th centuries BC will be compared with the art of "Neo-Hittite" sites in Eastern Anatolia from the 10th to 6th. Fundamental problems in the chronology of Hittite Art can be expected because of similarities in art forms separated by hundrseds of years of Conventional Chronology

This chapter is titled "Chaldean Art" rather than "Hittite Art." "Chaldeans" occupied the territories of the "Hittites" before, during and after the era assigned to the Hittites. Remember that "Hatti" is a geographic term and "Chaldean" is ethnic.

There appears to be an effort to rid the history of Anatolia and Northern Babylonia of any mention of Chaldea. I doubt that a conspiracy is at work, but there has been such a complete absence in more recent works that the phenomenon is definitely there. The quotations in the previous chapter concerning "Khaldis" as the supreme deity of the Hittites is taken from the 2nd Edition of CAH. The corresponding volume of the 3rd Edition has no word in its index that could even be derived from Chaldea; Chaldia, Khaldia, Khaldis, etc. The same is true of virtually all other recent works on the Hittites.

Thus the purpose of the chapter title is to emphasize that "Hittite Art" is encompassed *within* Chaldean Art. The Hittites may not figure prominently in the lives of the Hebrew Chroniclers, but the Chaldeans certainly do. The identity of the Hittites with the Chaldeans is one of the most important elements of the Synchronized Chronology. It will serve to enrich the history of the Hebrews and even the Greeks to place the records of the Hittite kings into the deeds of the Neo-Babylonian kings.

THE CONVENTIONAL ORDER

The conventional history of the Hittites is divided into two parts; the Hittite Empire (Old and New) of the middle and late 2nd Millennium BC (ending c. 1200 BCC), and then the "Neo-Hittites" of the 10th to 7th centuries BC. This division also applies to the two regions where Hittites are found; the Central Anatolian (or Cappadocian) Hittites of the "Empire" periods, and the eastern (or Syrian) Hittites of the "Neo-Hittite" period. In between these two eras lies a dark age absent of occupational remains yet, across which an artistic traditions spans.

The *Hittite Empire* is firmly fixed to the Egyptian 18th and 19th Dynasties. Correspondence from pharaohs of those two dynasties has been found in the Hittite archives of Boghazkoi in Central Anatolia. And the exploits of Egypt in the land of the Hittites are depicted on the monuments of Ramses II in Egypt. There is even a treaty between Egypt and Hatti that has been found in both countries.

The later "Neo-Hittites" are firmly fixed in time by many solid points of contact with Assyrian history. Their art likewise begins to show increasing numbers of similarities with Assyrian Art. Since several of the major Assyrian cities were excavated early in the second half of the nineteenth century, a great body of Assyrian Art was available for study with absolute dates fixed by inscription. When experts familiar with the Assyrian material first examined Hittite Art, a very different sequence was described compared to today's Conventional Chronology.

178

The study of Hittite Art has passed through 3 distinct phases to the present:

- Phase 1. The period before 1870 when the theory of the Hittite Empire was introduced.
- Phase 2. 1870 to 1906 when the Boghazkoi archives were deciphered.
- Phase 3. 1906 to present.

Scholars brought very different expectations in their examination of the evidence in each period. And the understanding of the history of Hittites in general has undergone a dramatic change over the years.

PHASE 1

The outdoor rock shrine of Yazilikaya, two miles from Boghazkoi, is an assemblage of relief carvings in the natural rock faces of two adjoining chambers. The back of the larger chamber shows the meeting of two long processions of figures. Those who studied these reliefs in the middle of the 19th century viewed them in the context of the History of Herodotus. The nearby Halys River suggested that the processions were the meetings of contemporary kings of perhaps Lydia and Persia. The headdresses were different for each side with tall Phrygian mitre caps on the left and Persian tiaras on the right. They might be either Alyattes and Cyaxares (Lydian and Medean) or Croesus and Cyrus (Lydian and Persian).

The reliefs were accompanied by a few of the hieroglyphic figures (as yet undeciphered) and certain artistic features such as clubs and battle axes that suggested a time frame for the reliefs.

> The Club and battle-axe appear for the first time on the Assyrian sculptures in the war pictures of the grandson of Sennancherib, who probably was the last king of Ninevah, and therefore the contemporary of Cyaxares.[1]

The eastern Anatolian sites had remains similar to those of the central region, and they frequently displayed the distinctive pictographic script. But here there was a broad range of execution and dates that suggested independent city-states evolving over the 10th to 6th centuries BC. The reliefs from Yazilikaya appeared to fit at the end of the artistic sequence.

---

1. Barth, Berlin 1859, trans. by V.4, 143. (I.e. 612 BC)

PHASE 2

In the 1870's the theory of the Hittite Empire was presented. The hieroglyphic script was the writing of the "Hittites," known from the inscriptions of Seti and Ramses II and therefore dating to the 14th-13th centuries BC. Experts were forced to choose sides in a debate pulled by the opposing evidence of artistic styles vs. chronological theory. In the one camp was the growing weight of evidence identifying the Egyptian "Kheta" with an empire west of the Assyrians in Asia Minor. In the other camp was the body of artistic evidence pointing to a later date.

> All those sculptures show clear signs of a much later time of origin; therefore their being creations of the Egyptian Kheta is excluded.
> In any case, there is neither here [in Asia Minor], nor in northern Syria, evidence that the so-called Hittite sculpture existed already in the tenth century B.C. This fact seems to me incompatible with the views of Sayce. For him, the greatest expansion of power of the Hittite Empire, and with it also the prime of Hittite art, lies almost a half a millennium before the time in which the extant monuments of ancient Commogene and Asia Minor were created. Therefore the art which has produced these and similar works does not have to be ascribed to the enigmatic Hittites of the second millennium B.C., but should be regarded as a remarkable sign of the then highly developed culture of the population of Asia Minor and Commogene in the time from 1000 to 600 B.C. [2]

PHASE 3

The second phase of Hittite Art theory came to an abrupt end in 1906 with the discovery and interpretation of the archives by Winckler at Boghazkoi. Among the tablets found there was a cuneiform version of the treaty between Ramses II and Hattusilis. No longer could there be any doubt about the age of the archives, the city and the sanctuary of Yazilikaya. They all dated to the last years of the Hittite Empire. The archives included copies of older texts carrying the history of the Hittites (or Hatti, Kheta) back several hundred more years.

Scholars who wrote so forcefully against an early date for the art were forced to change their entire opinion. Following Winckler's work at Boghazkoi, Puchstein, the same authority who wrote the forceful quote above, wrote in 1912:

---

2. (O. Puchstein, *Pseudohethitische Kunst*, Berlin, 1890, 13, 14, 22, trans. by V.4, 144)

The chief archaeological gain of this first excavation was, however, the realization, arrived at by Winckler from the clay tablets, that the old city layout at Boghazkoi had once been the capital of the Hatti Empire. How far it certainly reached back in time has been determined through the fragments of the letter exchanges carried on around 1300 B.C. between Ramses II and the Hittite king Hattusil.[3]

By the time the third phase was reached, the eastern (Syrian) Anatolian cities were clearly seen to overlap with the (Neo) Assyrian Empire. Yet the central Anatolian sites, dated by Egypt, had ended centuries before any datable remains in the east. Allowing for the known variations within the several Hittite art styles, the Cappadocian sites were intimately related to the east, but in a confusing evolution.

Three main sites (all within only 20 miles) represent the relief and sculptural art of the Cappadocian Hittites. As a modern work *Hittite Art* says:

> The sculpture of the period is rather inferior, and the other artistic remains are conspicuously rare. When mention is made of Boghaz-koy, Alaca Huyuk, the rock carvings of Yazilikaya and of a number of scattered finds here and there in Central Anatolia, nearly all has been said.[4]

In other words, the Empire is represented by only a small body of sculptural remains, all located within a small geographical area.

EAST AND WEST HITTITE COMPARED

One of the early experts of Hittite art, Hogarth, compared a thoroughly excavated Syrian city, Zinjirli, in the heart of the Neo-Hittite region, with Alaka Euyuk 20 miles north of Boghazkoi. Among the common features of Hittite Art, rows of panels sculpted in relief are a major element. Where natural outcrops are not available, slabs set by masons serve the purpose. In both locations there are comparable sets of sculpted panels. And each also has a variety of themes and qualities of execution. Hogarth's eye for the subtleties of artistic evolution is spelled out in his sequence of 5 artistic stages for relief sculpture at Zinjirli. The conclusions drawn from that analysis reflect a candor in the face of irreconcilable contradictions concerning the direction of influences. They deserve to be quoted at length.

---

3. O. Puchstein, *Boghaskoi, Die Bauwerke*, Leipzig, 1912, 2, trans. by V.4, 146.
4. Vieyra 24.

Such dating of the earliest extant sculptures at Zenjirli, which to all appearances are as early as any Hittite sculptures of Syria, raises the whole question of the parentage of Syrian Hittite civilization. From what source and in what age was this derived? Is it possible that a Syrian monumental art, whose first known work is of the eleventh century, owed its initial inspiration to a Cappadocian Hattic art, whose latest known work had reached, two centuries earlier, a stage of development far in advance of that in which Zenjirli began?[5]

Each gate into a Hittite city might have rows of sculpted slabs ("dados" or "orthostats") and Hogarth had determined that the South Gate to Zinjirli was the oldest (sometime after 1100 BC) and deserved to be compared to the "facade dados" at Alaka Euyuk.

> If the South Gate sculptures were to be affiliated to any known Cappadocian style, this could only be that of the Euyuk facade-dados, which belong probably to a period older again by two centuries than the latest Cappadocian style - that is, to the fifteenth century B.C. On that supposition some four hundred years must be supposed to have elapsed before the daughter art came to birth at Zenjirli, and some six centuries before the erection there of the oldest monument, whose age is approximately fixed.[6]

Actually, none of the Syrian cities have any Hittite remains dating before the 9th *century BC*. At least four hundred years without any datable remains anywhere in Anatolia is the problem only hinted at here. It is difficult to suppose that an artistic tradition could survive that hiatus and still provide inspiration. Hogarth continues:

> The Euyuk reliefs in question do offer, in fact, some analogies with certain Zenjirli reliefs of both the first and the second plastic styles; but they are analogies of motive, not execution...too many dissimilarities of style and treatment leap to the eye for a parental relationship to be credible...On the whole issue one can only conclude that the Cappadocian and the Syrian branches of Hittite art were derived independently of one another from some common stock, and that subsequently they developed in independence.

Since an alternate, older source of inspiration has not been found, the experts are faced with a dating gap. Neither end of that hiatus can be budged very far from fixed dates (as in the Greek Dark Age, both ends of the gap are

---

5. Hogarth 15
6. Hogarth 16

"fudged" whenever a solution to the problem is proposed). Either the gap is real or the Zinjirli reliefs are actually much older than believed, not that this would be preferable. He concludes,

> Alternately, should the earliest Zenjirli monuments be pushed back so as to approximate in time to such a pre-Euyuk style, and be presumed the fruit of prehistoric contact between Syria and the Cappadocian Hatti, then an immense chronological gulf will open between the first two classes of plastic monuments at Zenjirli and its third class, which is demonstrably of no earlier century than the ninth. To bridge that gulf Zenjirli offers nothing, deeply and carefully excavated though the best of its site has been.[7]

Welcome to Hittite Art!

The Script

When the first sculptured reliefs of the Hittites were found, they had a strange hieroglyphic or pictographic script associated with them. Sometimes the script completely covered portions of the sculpture, such as the sides of lions. Other cases have panels of script between the figures or even just a few hieroglyphs. Some have none at all. Being an unknown script in an unknown language, there was little chance of reading them. However, there was no doubt that these were the writing of the Hittites.

Very few inscriptions occurred in the Cappadocian areas, and none with the archives at Boghazkoi except on the seals stamped onto some tablets. In fact, the seals themselves represent an exquisite art form in miniature. Unlike the typical cylinder seals of Mesopotamia, the Hittite seals were mostly round and flat, rising to a cone in back for handling with a loop hanging on a cord. Some of the seals were bilingual with cuneiform on the rims. A certain number of hieroglyphs were deciphered from them.

A few of the hieroglyphs were found at Yazilikaya among the panels of the rock shrine. They were sufficient to identify the age of the panels to the kings of the Boghazkoi archives, all of the "Hittite Empire."

The real breakthrough in deciphering "Hieroglyphic Hittite" came with the discovery of several lengthy bilingual slabs at Kultepe. They were set up in typical Hittite row fashion and had easily read Phoenician translations. They

---

7. Hogarth 17

confirmed that the language of the hieroglyphs was yet another variety of Luwian, related to two of the languages found in the Boghazkoi archives.

The odd thing about the hieroglyphic inscriptions was the frequency of their occurrence in Syria compared to their rarity in Cappadocia where Babylonian cuneiform was used almost exclusively. If the culture of the Syrian Hittites was derived from Cappadocia, why wasn't cuneiform more common in Syria? Syria is closer to both Assyria and Babylon where cuneiform was used exclusively. And there is no evidence for the use of the hieroglyphs anywhere for at least 3-4 hundred years between the Cappadocian and Syrian inscriptions.

Some creative explanations have been offered for the rarity of the use of the hieroglyphic script in the heart of the empire. They emphasize the efficiency of cuneiform and the fact that Babylonian was the most frequently written language. Yet Syria is even closer to Babylon and resisted the "efficiency" of cuneiform. The clue is in the use of Babylonian.

As was mentioned earlier, the dynasties of Babylon are named for the homeland of the ruling kings. The Neo-Babylonian Empire was a dynasty of Chaldean kings. But the Assyrian records preserve many clear references to Chaldean tribes occupying regions of southern Mesopotamia from the time of the Assyrian king Assurnasirpal II, in 878 BC.[8] In spite of efforts to dismiss the relationship of Babylonian with Anatolian Chaldeans, placing the Cappadocian Hittites in their correct time powerfully supports the case. If the references to Ramses II in the Boghazkoi archives were not allowed to determine the date, the evolution of art styles would place them contemporary with the last stage of Assyrian art, near the end of the 7th century BC and early 6th.

The contemporary Chaldean king ruled "all of Hatti" as far as Lydia! Nebuchadnezzar spent much of his time as Babylonian king in "Hatti." In his palace at Babylon was found a large relief sculpture of the Hittite storm god dating to the ninth century BC from Aleppo. What has never been found at Babylon are the archives of the Neo-Babylonian kings. Even the traditional "Babylonian Chronicles" are represented by only 6 tablets.

The archives of the Chaldean kings were kept in Chaldea, at Boghazkoi, and were written in Babylonian cuneiform, the legal language of the Babylonian Empire. Hieroglyphic Hittite is typical of the Hittite city-states of Syria where the diverse expressions of a common culture withstood Assyrian domination until the late 8th century.

---

8. Frame 1992, 36.

MALATYA

Malatya, a city in the heart of the North Syrian Hittite area, was conquered by Sargon in 712 BC and occupied by the Assyrians. Archaeologically, that event has been clearly distinguished after careful study of the stratigraphy. When first examined, though, certain features were found to be so similar to Cappadocian, especially the Lion Gate, that a date of 14th or 13th century BC was proclaimed. Even after the evidence mounted in favor of associating the gate to the last occupation before Sargon, a number of experts in art history refused to accept so late a date.

> The lions guarding the gate show a number of peculiarities which link them with the art of Boghazkeuy; their manes are rendered by connected spirals...the small round marks between their eyes occur in the lions from Boghazkeuy.[9]

Frankfort believed that the lions could not possibly be later than the 12th century, and he was not alone. The difference in dating is almost five centuries. This contradiction has never been resolved and is simply ignored in modern general works.

The stratigraphy points to the true situation. Malatya was conquered and occupied by Sargon in 712, pushing those who refused to submit further west. Malatya had been ruled since 750 by Urartu, the "Children of Khaldu." In the reign of Sarduri II (753-735 BC) Urartu ruled a kingdom from north of Ararat to Cappadocia.

The carvings at Boghazkoi and Yazilikaya date from a few decades later under rulers who had recently moved their capitol to "Hattusa" from a city further to the east, probably Kanesh. Archaeologists dealing with Anatolia do not have the option of this simple solution, as long as Boghazkoi is anchored in the 14th-13th centuries by Ramses II.

PHRYGIA

On the opposite side of Anatolia from Syria lie cultures familiar to Greeks, among them the Phrygians. Their capital was at Gordion, famous for the dynasty of kings named Gordios and Midas. Phrygian ceramics reflect a tradition related to Aegean styles and therefore readily dated. We can expect that Hittite remains would be a problem here, and that is the case.

---

9. Frankfort 129, quoted in V.4, 166.

Gordion, as a Phrygian city, came to an end with the Cimmerian invasion in 687 BC. Although the invaders did not remain, the Phrygians did not recover and the city was vulnerable to take-over by neighbors, Lydians to the west and Chaldeans to the east. Recognizing the Chaldeans as the Hittites explains a glaring anomaly in the stratigraphy of Gordion.

According to conventional thinking the city was uninhabited between the destruction in 687 and the Persian occupation beginning with Cyrus in 548 BC. At least the strata that lies between these two dates is not considered an occupational level because it contains only Hittite remains of the Empire Age. It averages some twelve feet thick.

Since the a-priori assumption is that the Hittite Empire dates to the 14th-13th centuries BC, these remains at Gordion are believed to have been imported and spread over the site as a form of mass grading. Even the excavator R. S. Young admits that this would have been highly extravagant of labor.

Two additional problems are created by the theory of importation. First is the absence of an identifiable site from which the soil could have been taken. The other is the absence of a layer at Gordion that could be dated 687-548. Or perhaps it was carried off to make room for the Hittite "fill." To make things more confusing, Hittite remains occur throughout the Phrygian strata, but Hittite royal seals occur only in the "fill" layer.

A Synchronistic interpretation of Gordion would note that Phrygians coexisted with the Hittites (Chaldeans) and the "fill" layer simply represents the Chaldean Empire. Phrygians coexisted with the Hittites in other areas. Late Phrygian pottery was found in rooms at Boghazkoi, confusing the issue of just when the site was last occupied and destroyed. All of the architectural remains date to the Hittite Empire, yet some of the rooms were still occupied 700 BC! Likewise one of the sculptural groups in the gateway betrays a late and western influence:

> At Boghazkoi, in the gateway, was found a remarkable statue of the goddess Cybele wearing a high headdress and holding her nude breasts, but clad in a skirt . . . This remarkable group is attributed to the sixth century B.C.[10]

Redating the *Empire* to the end of the sequence rather than the start solves all of the problems with Hittite archaeology. While very early remains are found at Alaka Huyuk, they are not necessarily Hittite, there was a mixed population

---

10. CAH II 3rd, 2, 432.

throughout the Bronze and Iron ages. The remains of the Cappadocian Hittites are the remains of the Chaldean Empire.

Also solved is the problem of where the Chaldean remains are. When the Greeks traveled through eastern Anatolia, they were in the land of the Chaldeans. Before and during the Assyrian Empire, Khaldians or "Children of Khaldu" inhabited the same area. The land where we find their cities is called "Hatti." It was called Hatti by the Chaldean kings of the Neo-Babylonian Empire. It was called Hatti by the Egyptians in the inscriptions of Ramses II. And it was called Hatti in the Babylonian cuneiform tablets of Boghazkoi.

In later Greek and Roman times, the same region is the land of the Commagene kings whose sculpture bears "Hittite" elements. Even their royal seals continue to employ Hieroglyphic Hittite! For whatever reason, the stated existence of Chaldeans in this area by ancient authors has never (except by Velikovsky) triggered a recognition of the identity between Hittites and Chaldeans. For this reason, there are virtually no books on Chaldean Art, and plenty on Hittite.

THE CHALDEAN SECRET WRITING

One last clarification awaits this recognition. The word Chaldean was identified in the ancient world with an important priestly tradition:

> An on-going tradition for which Babylon was later to be remembered was that of its "astrologers". The Chaldean astrologers in Babylon lived in a special city-quarter and were distinguished from the tribe of the same name settled by the Persian Gulf.[11]

These Chaldeans were regarded with the sort of awe that was reserved for only a few priesthoods in the ancient world. Egypt and perhaps the Persian Magi were in that league (since the Hebrews never attained super power status, the legacy of the Levites was long term, not in their own time).

If the art of the Hittites is actually the art of the Chaldeans, then the sacred script of the Hittites is actually the sacred script of the Chaldeans. Imagine what this means. The mysterious hieroglyphic writing found all over Anatolia is the secret writing of the Chaldean priesthood. The language of the hieroglyphs was a variety of Luwian that was probably vestigial, preserved in original form and too sacred to alter. The Latin Mass of the Roman Catholic Church is a fair analogy. The hieroglyphic language may have been close enough to the common tongues

---

11. Wiseman 1983, 88.

of Anatolia to be understood if spoken. To keep sacred inscriptions from being read by the profane, the Chaldean priests could use their hieroglyphs.

Even into Roman times the hieroglyphs are found on coins from Commagene. It cannot be argued that the symbols were merely decorative because they spell out in Hittite the translation of the Greek! Perhaps they were still believed to convey some of that Chaldean magic.

A ROYAL "HITTITE" BURIAL IN CARCHEMISH

One last Chaldean Art example must be mentioned. Of all the challenges to Conventional Chronology, the miniature gold figurines from a burial in Carchemish are the most conspicuous:

> From a cremation burial within the city walls of Carchemish comes a set of small figurines (thirty-nine in all) of gold, lapis lazuli and steatite set in gold cloisons. It has been suggested with great probability that the burial belongs to the last period of Carchemish, and that it took place during the siege of the city by the Neo-Babylonian prince Nebuchadnezzar, in 604 B.C. The wealth of the material found together with the ashes, may also point to the burial being that of a prince of the House of Pisiris, the last native ruler of Carchemish, as suggested by Sir Leonard Wooley. The small figurines (the biggest measures 175 mm.) represent divinities of the Hittite pantheon and reproduce in miniature the figures of the divinities of Yazilikaya and Malatya. The extremely close relation between these representations sets a problem which is, at present, susceptible of two alternative explanations: the figures of Carchemish are either an instance of the unbroken artistic and religious tradition from the New Kingdom down to the very last days of the Hittite power in Carchemish, or they are an heirloom transmitted through generations from the days when Carchemish was ruled by princes of the Royal House of Hattusas.[12]

Are those really the only two alternatives? Perhaps they were the contemporary jewelry of the Royal House of Chaldea.

---

12. Vieyra 87-88, fig. 119.

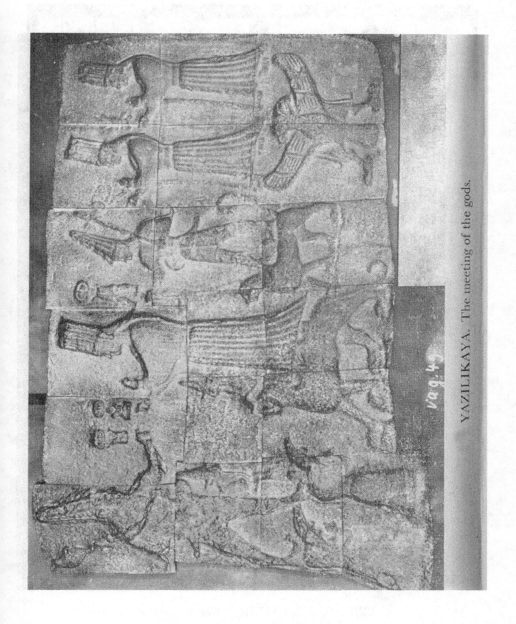

YAZILIKAYA. The meeting of the gods.

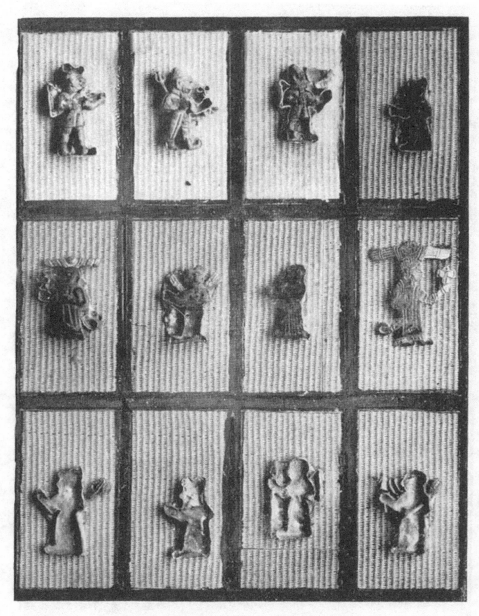

119. CARCHEMISH. Gold figurines.

16. The Battle of Carchemish

There are moments in history that focus all the currents of change into a single watershed event. The century between 650 and 550 BC witnessed so many important cultural landmarks that it is hard to pick out the most important. The Assyrian Empire came to an end. The Chaldean Empire rose to heights greater than Assyria's, but was then crushed and replaced by Persia. And in the midst of it all, the kingdom of Judah suffered greatly and perished.

Yet a single battle near the mid-point of this century determined the course of history for the Mediterranean for centuries. Just as Egypt was regaining its former strength and expanding that relatively benign form of Pax Aegyptica up through the Levant, a crushing defeat on the banks of the Euphrates reversed the hopes and futures of many.

What course might history have taken if Egypt had won the Battle of Carchemish? Perhaps Judah would have seen the death of Josiah as sufficient punishment for its unfaithfulness to the covenant, and continued in the religious revival he had begun. Egyptian dominance of the Levant had the effect of raising the standard of living for everyone. Egypt possessed the grain and papyrus to trade for the goods of the Phoenicians and their inland marketing partners. With wealth and power generated through trade, Egypt might have resisted even Persia. But we will never know because Egypt marched arrogantly and unprepared — into a trap.

We find references to the battle in both Hebrew and Greek sources. There is even a reference in one of the extant tablets of the Babylonian Chronicle. Scholars are not surprised that Egypt fails to mention the event, especially since there are no substantial inscriptions at all from the 26th Dynasty of Conventional Chronology. The true importance of the battle goes unrecognized, like the true stature of the 26th Dynasty pharaohs.

The capital cities of the 19th and 26th Dynasties are known by different names in Manetho: Tanis for the 19th and Sais for the 26th. Convention places them on opposite sides of the Delta. Since the 26th-Dynasty pharaohs are presumed to have had a Libyan connection, Sais was presumed be located in the west. The capital city for the 26th Dynasty, Sais, was identified 150 years ago by the German Egyptologist and linguist Lepsius on the west side of the Delta, on the Rosetta branch. But no ruins have ever been found there. Now, Ramses' capital, Tanis, lies on the branch of the Nile Delta that Herodotus calls the Saitic! And although Strabo differentiates between Tanis and Sais (as cities), he also places Tanis on the Saitic branch. Sais is probably Tell Nebesheh, a few miles from Tanis where ruins of the same age are found. One city was probably the capital, the other the royal residence.

Since the Synchronized Chronology identifies the 19th Dynasty with the 26th, our search for references to the Battle of Carchemish should be in the Dynasty of Seti, Ramses the Great and Merneptah. The similarities of the two dynasties are there from the start. In both the 19th and 26th Dynasties, the first great pharaoh Seti/Psamatich brought Egypt back to a position of international power by controlling important Phoenician coastal cities for trade and access inland to the Euphrates. The city of Riblah on the Orontes River was the military base for Psamatich and his successor Necho of the 26th Dynasty. From there the route to Carchemish, a crossroads of trade between Asia Minor and Babylonia, was controlled.

Of all the pharaohs in Egypt's long history, none has left more monuments than Ramses II. And featured most prominently on his monuments are lengthy descriptions and illustrated scenes from the "Battle of Kadesh." That battle pitched Ramses against the king of Kheta, and until the Boghazkoi archives were found, the victor was assumed to have been the Egyptians. The discovery of the Hittite records and careful study of the treaty between Kheta and Egypt, coupled with evidence of Egypt's diminished stature after the battle, led to a reevaluation of Ramses' boasts. In fact, he admits that his army deserted him during the surprise attack, and his glory was in single-handedly surviving the scene!

Demonstrating that the Battle of Kadesh depicted by Ramses II is the same as the Battle of Carchemish of Hebrew and Greek records is the topic of this chapter. But a more general comparison of the dynasties and their overall history will make the identity compelling.

PSAMATICH (SETI-PTAH-MAAT)

Seti was the first important pharaoh of the 19th Dynasty and left a great record of his reign on the walls of the Temple of Karnak. The impression given is that he marched up through Palestine in his first year and conquered all the way to "Naharin" (to the Euphrates). But since the same reliefs depict his Libyan battles, it is clear that numerous campaigns over several years are represented. Only his battle with the "Shasu," nomadic warriors from the Sinai-Egyptian border region, is dated (Year 1), the other panels are undated and the upper (third) tier of panels is missing almost completely.

Seti's campaigns to Syria went north along the coastal route but involved inland cities such as Beth Shan south of the Sea of Galilee. At some point he got word that the kings of Kheta were in Hamath and had taken Beth Shan and other Syrian cities. His Syrian campaign is depicted separately from his battles with the Hittites, so he must have first secured Phoenician ports and then the inland strongholds. A stele of Seti's was found at Tell Nebi Mend, a kilometer-long mound on the Orontes River near the modern village of Riblah. This mound is believed to be the remains of the fortress of "Kadesh" over which Seti's son fought his famous battle. Kadesh, in the Egyptian references, is on the river R-N-T, assumed to be the Orontes. But the river as we know it was named for a Bactrian general who built a bridge across it in the fourth century BC, so the name Orontes could not have been in use in dynastic times. This fact seems to have escaped the attention of scholars searching for the location of the famous "Kadesh." R-N-T is used (by Egyptians) in inscriptions indicating rivers that cannot be the Orontes. And if R-N-T does not refer to the Euphrates, then that river has no name, in Egyptian.

Thus, the mound (Tell Nebi Mend) is not "Kadesh." Rather, it appears more likely to be Riblah — military headquarters for Seti and then Necho (Ramses II) when he controlled the kings of Judah, and finally for Nebuchadnezzar after he defeated Necho. There is no other mound in the vicinity of the village of Riblah besides Tell Nebi Mend, and the village itself certainly is not the fortress. There is another city that much more closely fits the role of the battle city, and the clue is in the name.

The Egyptian name for the city of the famous battle "Kadesh" is one that we have met before and recognized as the generic term for a "Holy City." In this case it refers to Carchemish, the city "Kar" of the sun god "Chemosh," and perfectly fits Ramses' descriptions and illustrations of Kadesh, something that Tell Nebi Mend does not do.

What little that we know of Psamatich of the 26th Dynasty is consistent with his alter ego Seti of the 19th (Seti-Ptah-Maat). He passed on to his son

Necho a renewed Egyptian empire extending up the eastern coast of the Mediterranean and then inland to Carchemish.

Herodotus tells us (2.151) that Psamatich was one of the twelve regional kings of Egypt to govern by mutual consent after the last of the Ethiopian and Assyrian rulers. At a temple service the twelve were brought gold vessels for the libation by a priest who miscounted: one short. When it came to Psamatich's turn, he had no vessel, so he took his helmet and made the offering with it. He had unknowingly fulfilled a prophecy that he who poured the libation with a vessel of bronze would become sole king of Egypt. The other eleven recognized that no guile was involved here, but of course they refused to allow him to be crowned and instead ran him off. Psamatich consulted the oracle, who told him that revenge would come when bronze men emerged from the sea.

In fact, Ionian and Carian pirates who happened to be in the area caused a great stir among the Egyptians, who had never seen bronze armor before. Psamatich recognized in them the fulfillment of prophecy and made overtures to them. With their help, his Egyptian loyalists were able to take full control of Egypt. A new dynasty had taken hold with the help of Europeans, who were then allowed their own trading cities on the delta.

Scholars using Herodotus as their initial guide were confused to find reference to Europeans in the inscriptions of Seti and Ramses II, whom they had placed 700 years earlier. Ramses even employed them in his army. His father (with whom he probably shared a lengthy co-regency) does not mention them in that capacity, but he may also have used them. The similarities in the lives of Seti (Seti-Ptah-Maat) of the 19th and Psamatich of the 26th Dynasty cannot be taken too far because there is not enough material available for comparison. On the other hand, the next generation serves up a wealth of grist for the analyzing mill.

NECHO (RAMSES II)

The pharaohs had long wished to have a waterway between the Mediter-ranean Sea and the Indian Ocean. Herodotus tells us that Necho, the son of Psamatich, was the first to attempt the digging of a canal from the Nile to the Red Sea. He finally abandoned the project after the loss of 120,000 lives. The Persian "pharaoh" Darius was able to complete the canal. As with all his other accomplishments, Necho left no record of this gigantic exploit. Curiously, the route of the waterway bears the testimony of Ramses II along with Darius. This has led to the accusation that Herodotus was wrong here again in claiming Necho to be the first. Obviously, the canal had already been dug 700 years earlier! (The reader will find Herodotus to fare better in the Synchronized than the Conventional Chronology.)

Necho managed to (a) rule Egypt for a generation (16 years according to Manetho, 22 years in Herodotus, although a co-regency with Psamatich should be assumed). (b) He held an empire extending to the Euphrates at Carchemish, and (c) he sustained a decades-long military conflict with the most powerful ruler of the time, Nebuchadnezzar — all without leaving any evidence of his rule. Even if it is assumed that his capital, Sais (supposedly on the Rosetta Branch of the Nile), is lost under the sands of the Delta, it seems improbable that he left no other monuments anywhere. It is unthinkable that a native Egyptian pharaoh would dedicate no temples, build no mortuary structures or obelisks or even inscribe his exploits on an existing edifice such as Karnak. (The often-cited Apis bull dedication by a Neckau is not a reference to the pharaoh.[1]

If Necho were to write his history, it would be indistinguishable from the history left by Ramses II. We know now that Ramses' battle of Kadesh was largely a defeat, yet it figures prominently as a glorious accomplishment in his reliefs. Egyptians were not that different from Assyrians in using a secret code that disguised military defeats as victories. Ramses never returned to Kadesh. Necho never returned to Carchemish. And Egypt would never again have an Asian empire.

JUDAH

Judah was caught in the middle of this struggle between Egypt and Chaldea/Kheta. Ninevah under the Assyrian king Sin-shar-iskun was sacked in 612 BC by the combined forces of Chaldea, the Medes and the "Umman Manda" (a term that still causes confusion among scholars since it suggests Scythians but apparently seems to include Medes). Assyria as a power was finished. The successor to Sin-shar-iskun, Assur-uballit, escaped to Haran where he hoped to survive and regroup.

Egypt recognized the danger the sudden rise of Chaldea posed to its Asian territories. Psamatich apparently decided to overlook feelings of resentment stirred by recent Assyrian rule and went to their aid as an ally. It was at this time that Judah had its last great "righteous" king, Josiah.

Judah had reached its low point of faithfulness to the covenant under Manassah (696-642 BC). He not only permitted but also participated in the worship of foreign gods. He even allowed them into the temple, an act that at least some think led to the removal of the Ark from the Holy of Holies. While others believe it is buried under the temple mount, Graham Hancock[2] believes

---

1. See V.4,4
2. In *The Sign and the Seal.*

that the Ark was moved to the only other Hebrew temple existing at the time, at Elephantine in southern Egypt. When that temple was destroyed by native Egyptians (resentful that Persians had spared it the destruction wrought on their own monuments), he believes the Ark was again moved, to Ethiopia, where it remains to this day!

Josiah (640-609) began widespread religious reforms, ridding Judah of idolatry and destroying the places where it was practiced. While the Temple was being restored, a copy of the Mosaic Law was discovered hidden in the walls. It was probably suppressed under Manassah. Josiah was committed to the new regional power, Chaldea, and was thus inspired to commit an act that ended his life.

Necho, in his second year of rule of Egypt, assembled his armies and marched north to help Assur-uballit to take Harran from Chaldea. Josiah had an obligation (to Chaldea) to stop Egypt from giving aid to Assyria. He assembled the forces of Judah at Megiddo, along the route Necho would take, and defiantly obstructed their progress. Necho tried to dissuade him, since Josiah's land was not the target of Egypt's intents; finally, he resorted to force, taking down Josiah with a "dart." In one of his illustrations, Ramses II shows a Syrian prince mortally wounded by a spear. The Synchronized Chronology would wager that that depiction represents Josiah at Megiddo.

Egypt capitalized on the situation by installing a new king of its own choosing, Jehoahaz, and imposing heavy tribute. Jehoahaz was soon hauled off to Riblah to answer for insubordination and his brother Eliakim was appointed to replace him. Necho changed his name to Johoiakim.

In his fifth year Necho again assembled his armies and headed north. But this time the Chaldean king Nabopolassar had turned over the armies to his son Nebuchadnezzar, a much more formidable military strategist. Carchemish had already fallen before Necho arrived. The Babylonian Chronicle tells the story from the other side. It tells how Nebuchadnezzar:

> crossed the river to go against the Egyptian army which lay in Carchemish. . . . fought with each other and the Egyptian army withdrew before him. He accomplished their defeat and beat them into non-existence. As for the rest of the Egyptian army which had escaped from the defeat and no weapon had reached them, the Babylonian troops overtook and defeated them in the district of Hamath, so that not a single man escaped to his own country. At that time Nebuchadrezzar conquered the whole of Khatti-land.[3]

---

3. Wiseman, *Chronicles* pp. 25, 67-68.

Even the vaunted Babylonian Chronicle is prone to exaggeration, since the pharaoh and most of his forces did make it back to Egypt. While no Egyptian records exist under the name of Necho, the records left by Ramses II on the battle should be compared to those of another outside party, Jeremiah. What follows is a review of the battle by these sources that builds a more understandable whole.

THE BATTLE

The army of Ramses II was comprised of four divisions. "The division of Amon . . . the division of Re . . . the division of Ptah . . . the division of Sutekh."[4] Jeremiah also relates the four divisions of the pharaoh's army. In addition to Egyptians there are "Ethiopians and the Libyans, that handle the shield; and the Lydians, that handle and bend the bow."[5] Libya and Ethiopia were Egyptian territories; the Lydians were mercenaries sent by Gyges, king of Sardis (the Lydian capital).

Ramses employed Shardan troops just as his father Seti had. (Since the Lydian city of Sardis did not exist in the 13th century BC, "Shardan" is commonly assumed to mean men from Sardinia. The Synchronized Chronology has no such problem.) Thus Ramses II had the same four division army as Necho, including mercenaries from Sardis.

On the way to "Kadesh" Ramses encountered two Bedouin who had been sent by the Kheta king to mislead the pharaoh into believing his adversary was frightened and retreating far to the north. Emboldened by this crafty bit of disinformation, Ramses confidently advanced to Kadesh ahead of the rest of his army. Upon arriving, he captured two more Kheta scouts who, under the kind of pressure that prevails in such cases, admitted the truth. But it was too late. Ramses could only send for emergency reinforcements — the enemy troops were already crossing the river south of Kadesh. Ramses was caught unprepared and in the monuments he left behind, he claims to have almost single-handedly fought his way out. Only the timely arrival of reinforcements saved Egypt from a devastating rout.

The relief depictions as well as the written accounts of the battle all focus on Ramses in a battle against overwhelming odds. Lost in the grandiose self-adulation is fact that Egypt was defeated. Even though he enjoyed a very long reign, nothing Ramses did after this battle in his 5th year warranted as much recognition.

---

4. Gardiner *The Kadesh Inscriptions of Ramses II*, p8.
5. Jeremiah 46:9.

A few of the incidentals of the battle, as Ramses tells them, are confirmed by Jeremiah. When the king of Kheta crossed the river south of the city and attacked from a hidden position, the charge caught the Egyptian troops unprepared. "Then the infantry and chariotry of his majesty retreated before them, northward to the place where his majesty was."[6] Likewise, Jeremiah says of the Egyptian troops, "Let not the swift flee away, nor the mighty man escape; they shall stumble, and fall toward the north by the river Euphrates.[7] In both cases, an Egyptian army arriving from the south and encamping north of the city is surprised by the attackers and driven northward, away from Egypt.

Jeremiah also tells us that Nebuchadnezzar's forces were assisted by the "army of the Syrians."[8] Ramses faced the chief of Kheta "with an army of probably 20,000 men, the combined forces of the north Syrian princes, under the Hittite king, together with a large proportion of mercenaries from states in Asia Minor, adjacent to or subject of the Hittites."[9] Not only do the descriptions of the warring parties and their actions agree in both the Egyptian and Hebrew sources, but the illustrations of the city made by the Egyptian artists are a better fit to Carchemish than to Tell Nebi Mend.[10]

The argument over the location of "Kadesh" took many years and has almost unanimously recognized Tell Nebi Mend. It is the only site on the Orontes River resembling Ramses' illustrations. But since Strabo reminds us that the Orontes was named in the 4th century BC, doubts should have been raised. And even though the largest village nearby (5 miles away) is named Ribleh (which has no tell or mound), Tell Nebi Mend has not been recognized as Riblah (except by Velikovsky). Riblah was a military fortress from the time of Psamatich (Seti) through Necho (Ramses II) and then was captured and used by Nebuchadnezzar (Hattusis). The first archaeological campaign at Tell Nebi Mend was cut short by the death of its leader, but a portion of a steele of Seti I was found there and added support to the identification of the site with Kadesh of the Egyptian records. What has long been overlooked is the fact that the site does not match the topography of Kadesh in terms of both the waterways surrounding the city and the placement of troops anticipating the battle. Gardiner, the first to write extensively of the battle, was forced to dismiss the plain depiction of the battle formations indicated by the Egyptian record:

---

6. ARE III, 326.
7. Jeremiah 46:6.
8. Jeremiah 35:11.
9. ARE III 299.
10. see V.4.

But if the side of the Egyptian drawing where the pharaoh is, is north, then it represents him on the east side of the river. Or again, if, as the texts state, he should be on the west side of the river in the Egyptian drawing, then the drawing represents him as south of the city charging northward. In no way can any of the four ancient drawings of this battlefield be made to coincide with the data of the inscriptions.[11]

The reason, of course, is that the wrong site is being compared to the battle scenes. Other commentators have suggested that the Hittite army could not have been hidden behind the city assumed to be Kadesh of the Egyptian records, but the identity has been firm for so long that it is no longer ever questioned.

THE OTHER SIDE

The opposing side at the battle left records that must also be considered. The Hittite tablets from Boghazkoi are placed here alongside the Babylonian Chronicle. The histories they reveal are not separated by 600+ years; in fact, a more meaningful whole emerges by combining the sources.

The battle of Kadesh occurred while the *Hittite* army was commanded by the son of king Mursilis, Hattusis, before he became king. The battle of Carchemish occurred while the *Chaldean* army was commanded by the son of king Nabopolassar, Nebuchadnezzar, before he was king.

Mursilis had expanded the *Hittite Empire* in all directions, just as his father Suppiluliumas had done. Hattusis further enlarged the Empire to include "all of Hatti." Nabopolassar expanded the *Chaldean Empire* to include Babylonia. His son Nebuchadnezzar further enlarged it to include "all of Hatti."

The written "Deeds of Mursilis" are sufficiently complete to cover many of the important events of his reign. They deserve to be compared with what the Babylonian Chronicle records about Nabopolassar.

In his second year, Mursilis sent a military commander to his brother in Carchemish with orders to fight Assyria. In his seventh year, the alliance between Assyria and Egypt occurred. By his ninth year Carchemish was lost to Assyria, but then Mursilis says, "I moved toward Haran, my army reached Harran and I joined the army there." As Groetz reports, "Mursilis in his ninth year met his adversary, Assur-uballit, on the Euphrates line."[12]

Babylonian Chronicles Nos. B.M. 25127 and 21901 cover most of Nabopolassar's reign. In the early years he battled just the Assyrians. But by his 10th year

---

11. ARE III, Sec. 335.
12. Groetz *Annals* in V.4.

the Assyrians had allied with the Egyptians and begin to gain the upper hand. Over the next several years the Medes and Umman Manda add pressure at Assyria's rear and join with the Chaldeans to finally defeat Ninevah in 612 BC, the 14th year of Nabopolassar. The next Assyrian king, Assur-uballit, rules from Harran with the help of Egypt.

In his 16th year Nabopolassar moves on Harran with the help of the Umman Manda. Assur-uballit and the Egyptians abandon Harran and retreat to Syria. This would be the army of Psamatich and they may have gone either to Carchemish or Riblah, both controlled by Egypt.

The similarities of the events of the lives of Mursilis and Nabopolassar cannot be summarized better than by Velikovsky:

> In no other period of history were Assyria and Egypt allies in a war. The two cases dealt with here are separated by seven centuries of conventional history, but they are really one and the same.
>
> Mursilis' march along the Euphrates and his battles against the Assyrian troops, supported by Egyptian troops, and the military operations in Harran against Assuruballit are said to have occurred in the fourteenth century. The march of Nabopolassar along the Euphrates and his battles against the Assyrian troops, supported by the Egyptian army, and the military operations against Assuruballit in Harran are said to have taken place in the seventh century. Nabopolassar died in the twenty-second year of his reign. The last fragment of Mursilis' war annals is of his twenty-second regnal year.[13]

In order to drive the Egyptians out of Syria, Mursilis turned the army over to his son Hattusis, resulting in the victorious Battle of Kadesh. Likewise Nabopolassar drove the Egyptians out of Syria by turning over the army to his son Nebuchadnezzar, culminating in the victorious Battle of Carchemish.

The Battle of Carchemish was the first meeting between Necho and Nebuchadnezzar, but it would not be the last. Necho had only a few years experience as pharaoh and Nebuchadnezzar would soon take over as king of Chaldea. For the next 20 years or so, Palestine was the middle ground between powerful adversaries. A few years after the battle saw Nebuchadnezzar in control of all Syria and Palestine, including Judah. The emboldened Nebuchadnezzar marched toward Egypt and met Necho again in all-out battle. Necho was prepared this time, but both sides suffered major damage. Nebuchadnezzar had to return to Babylon to rebuild his army. Scripture also suggest that he suffered a mental breakdown. In "Ramses II and His Time," Velikovsky uses his psycho-

---

13. V.4 p. 98.

logical training in an interesting comparison of Nebuchadnezzar's psychosis with the character of Hattusis as revealed in his surviving autobiography found in Boghazkoi. Hattusis had a strongly religious youth, crediting divine support for his survival of early health problems. Velikovsky presents evidence that Hattusis suffered pangs of guilt for usurping the throne, and when his army failed to conquer Ramses/Necho the second time, he suffered a breakdown.[14]

Necho took advantage of the interlude to move back north. As Ramses, he left evidence at Beth Shan and even further north. But the reprieve from Chaldea was only temporary and by 597 Nebuchadnezzar was again moving into Judah, taking Jerusalem after a short siege and carrying off the best of the population to Babylon.

Jerusalem was still the crown jewel of the hill country of Palestine and worth pursuit by both Egypt and Chaldea. In what could only be an effort to fulfill prophecy (that Jerusalem would be destroyed by Nebuchadnezzar), the city once again rebelled. No doubt counting on Egypt to protect them, the city awaited the oncoming Chaldeans. Evidently Egypt did step forward, causing Nebuchadnezzar to retreat. But then Egypt backed off and Nebuchadnezzar moved in unopposed.

The Babylonian Chronicle does not tell us what had happened to cause Egypt to let down Jerusalem again. Of course there no 26th dynasty records at all, so the place to search is under Ramses.

After a generation of battle with the king of Kheta, Ramses II and Hattusis made a treaty of peace. Jerusalem would no longer be defended and the 18-month siege began. When the city finally fell, Nebuchadnezzar vented his wrath, carrying off the rest of the population to captivity in Babylon and then sending forces back to physically destroy the city.

For the rebellious king Zedekiah a special punishment was dealt out. He was taken to Riblah, where his children were killed in front of him and then he was blinded, doomed to die in prison with this one last vision for a memory. Those who were able to escape tried to go to Egypt. But even for them, we are told, "none of the remnant of Judah, which are gone into the land of Egypt to sojourn there, shall escape or remain."[15] The treaty tells us why:

> If a man flee from the land of Egypt, or two or three, and come to the great chief of Kheta, the great chief of Kheta shall seize upon them, and shall cause

---

14.- Nebuchadnezzar also doctored the records of dynastic succession. This important aspect of identifying Nebuchadnezzar with Hattusis is covered at length in *Ramses II and His Time* in the chapter on the "The Autobiography of Nebuchadnezzar."

15. Jeremiah 44:14.

them to be brought back to Usermare-Setepnere, the great ruler of Egypt. Now, as for the man who shall be brought (back) to Ramses-Meriamon, the great ruler of Egypt, let not his crime be set up against him; let not his house be injured, nor his wives, nor his children, [let] him [not be killed], and let no injury be done to his eyes, to his ears, to his mouth, nor his feet. Let not any crime be set up against him.[16]

By treaty, Ramses was obliged to extradite the refugees back to Khetesar. And knowing the way they might be treated if returned, the treaty includes a provision against mutilation. Once again the Synchronized Chronology provides minor incidents to fill in the details of the unified story.

HOPHRA (MERNEPTAH HOTPHIRMAE)

The comparison between the 19th and 26th Dynasties can be carried one more generation. Again there are no Egyptian texts from the successor to Necho, so the Greek and Hebrew sources must suffice. The son of Necho is called "Hophra" in Jeremiah and "Apries" in Herodotus (who interposed a brief reign of another son, Psammis, in between).

The 19th Dynasty successor to Ramses II is considered to be Merneptah Hotphirmae (the *t* is silent), whose numerous inscriptions deal almost exclusively with his Libyan campaigns:

> These sources enable us to see the already aged Merneptah facing the evil conditions on his Libyan frontier, inherited from the decades of neglect which concluded his great father's reign. The Libyans have for years past been pushing into and occupying the western Delta. They pressed in almost to the gates of Memphis, eastward to the district of Heliopolis, and southward to the two oases nearest the Fayum. Worse than this, they had made a coalition with the maritime peoples of the Mediterranean, who now poured into the Delta from Sardinia on the west to Asia Minor on the east. The mention of these peoples in these documents is the earliest appearance of Europeans in literature, and has always been the center of much study and interest.[17]
>
> That attack must have come from pretty far west, from Cyranaica or even beyond.[18]

The irony in Gardiner's last comment will become apparent soon.

---

16. ARE III 389.
17. ARE III 570.
18. Gardiner 272.

Merneptah's inscriptions date the Libyan war to his fifth year, with the battle itself lasting only six hours. Since we can probably expect no more honesty in the son's war annals than in the father's, we are left to wonder if there was more to this that was simply left out. The Libyans were assisted by a host of "Europeans" whose names so tantalize scholars: *Sherden* (men of Sardis), *Shekelesh* (Sicilians), *Ekwesh* (Acheans), *Luky* (Lycians) and *Teresh* (Etruscans or Therans). For the rest of the story, we turn to Herodotus, bearing in mind a prophetic declaration found in Jeremiah 44:30:

> Thus saith the Lord; Behold, I will give Pharaoh-hophra king of Egypt into the hand of his enemies.

According to Herodotus, the Greek colony of Cyranaica on the border of Libya had not grown at all from the time it was founded through the 56 years of the first two rulers. Its third ruler decided to invite new colonists and promised a distribution of land. This became the major Hellenic city of Cyrene.

> An immense collection of people came in Cyrene. Now, the Libyans who lived about there, and their king, whose name was Adicran, saw themselves being curtailed of a great part of their land and, indeed, robbed and insulted by the Cyrenaeans. So they sent to Egypt and surrendered themselves to the protection of Apries, king of Egypt. He gathered a large army of Egyptians and sent it against Cyrene. But the Cyrenaeans, advancing as far as Irasa and the spring called Thestes, fought the Egyptians and beat them in the battle. Indeed as the Egyptians had, prior to this, no experience of the Greeks and despised them, they were destroyed in such numbers that only a few came back to Egypt. The Egyptians were so angry at this result that they turned against Apries and revolted from him.[19]

According to Herodotus Apries sent his general, Amasis, to win back the rebels but they chose him instead to be their leader. Apries was so outraged over this that he cut the nose and ears off the messenger who brought him the news. The act of mutilation was too much even for the people of his capital and he had to fight his way out of the city to escape. When Amasis captured him, the people demanded revenge, strangling him in a mob. Amasis had him embalmed and buried. (A hole in the skull of Merneptah's mummy reflects a violent death.)

---

19. Herodotus 4.159.

THE ISRAEL STELE

The Synchronized Chronology has now reached a point that allows a comparison to Conventional Chronology that is overflowing with irony. Among the four documents left by Merneptah to glorify his Libyan victory is one that is seldom referred to by its formal title, the "Hymn on the Victory over the Libyans." Rather, it has come to be known as the "Israel Stele." The monument has attracted wide attention, because of the reference to Israel in the last section, "This is the earliest mention of Israel known to us in literature, not excluding the Hebrew Scriptures."[20]

The stele adds nothing new to the documentation of the Libyan war other than the joy of the people after the victory. It is the concluding "strophe" that generated interest:

> The kings are overthrown, saying: "Salam!"
> Not one holds up his head among the Nine Bows.
> Wasted is Tehenu,
> Kheta is pacified,
> Plundered is Pekanon, with every evil,
> Carried off is Askalon,
> Seized upon is Gezer,
> Yenoam is made as a thing not existing.
> Israel is desolate, his seed is not;
> Palestine has become a widow for Egypt.
> All lands are united, they are pacified;
> Everyone that is turbulent is bound by Merneptah,
> given life like Re, every day.[21]

With Merneptah placed 1224-1214 BC, this mention of Israel is a real eye-opener (not to mention the Hebrew word for "peace" in the first line). At least some scholars believed that the reference concerning Israel ("his seed is not") had to do with the killing of the firstborn. Others felt that a defeat during the Exodus was meant. But most think a campaign in Palestine fits the whole strophe better. The treaty with Kheta probably honored certain of Egypt's traditional protectorates, and a campaign in Palestine is suggested elsewhere for his third year, before the Libyan war.

---

20. ARE III 603.
21. ARE III 617.

In spite of the equivocal evidence, Merneptah has come to be known as the pharaoh of the Exodus. The Synchronized Chronology makes him a pharaoh of the Captivity! The segment of Hebrew history that lies between these dates demonstrates better than anything else the absolute confusion produced by the Conventional Chronology. The wandering, the Conquest, the time of the Judges, the United Kingdom, the Divided Kingdoms and finally the early years of the Captivity are all encompassed by the chronological error.

The 19th Dynasty pharaoh Merneptah Hotphi(r)mae has left what we recognize as the typical Egyptian documentation of the reign of the 26th Dynasty pharaoh Hophra. Left out are all the negatives, and what remains is elevated to exaggerated importance.

This is one case that begs to be recognized by scholars. Two pharaohs with the same name win early successes in Palestine and then battle a collection of "European" (Greek and Carian) seamen in Cyrene. The separate Egyptian, Hebrew and Greek sources complement and fill out the complete picture better than any one alone. Conventional Chronology requires that "Europeans" made identical colonial moves separated by some 650 years.

In conclusion, the three great pharaohs of the 19 Dynasty — Seti, Ramses II and Merneptah Hotphirmae, reveal themselves to be the alter-egos of the three pharaohs of the 26th— Psamatich, Necho and Hophra, as known from non-Egyptian sources. The 19th Dynasty capital Tanis lies on the branch of the Nile known to Herodotus and Strabo as the Saitic branch. Sais was the capital city of the 26th Dynasty at a time when Hebrew sources called it Tanis!

In these two dynasties, Egyptian pharaohs were allied with Assyrian kings named Assur-uballit in defense of Harran. In both cases the aging opponent put the army under a son's command. Khetesar and Nebuchadnezzar surprised the pharaoh's four army divisions, which included mercenaries from Sardis, and forced the Egyptians to retreat north. After a generation of conflict, the opponents reached a peace agreement that included reciprocal extradition. And, finally, the succeeding generation of pharaohs faced Europeans in Libya.

To this point, the Synchronized Chronology has covered some 1200 years of history, from the Middle Bronze Age settlements of Palestine to the Middle Kingdom Semitic settlements in the eastern Delta, to the famous 18th and 19th Dynasties (which are actually separated by the 22nd-25th), the chronology holds together. Generation after generation can be compared with rich reward, in contrast to the total absence of correspondence in the Conventional Chronology. But the story is not complete yet. The 20th dynasty, which follows the 19th in Manetho, must be placed in its proper place. In some ways the best has been left for last.

17. Ramses III and His Time

The Chaldean Dynasty barely outlasted Nebuchadnezzar's reign. The dynasty's alliance with the Medes could not survive the weak successors on the throne of Babylon, making the city a tempting target for the expanding Medean superpower. The rise of Cyrus to power (supernatural, according to Herodotus) led the Persians to revolt from the Medes and unite with them under his vigorous leadership.[1] Greeks continue to refer to them interchangeably as Medes or Persians . . .

The Chaldean capital in Boghazkoi was under similar pressure from the growing threat of Lydia. Croesus, the king of Lydia in Sardis, attacked and sacked Boghazkoi ("Pteria" in Herodotus) in 546 BC. Lydian dominance lasted only a few months because Cyrus was already moving into Asia Minor and met Croesus in a battle at Boghazkoi that, though it was not a decisive loss, forced the king to retreat to Sardis. In a bold tactical move, Cyrus secretly followed Croesus to Sardis and attacked him by surprise before the Lydians could regroup.

Cyrus captured Croesus and kept him as a companion and advisor on his further conquests (furnishing some of the better tales for Herodotus). Five years later, Cyrus took Babylon on the night of "the writing on the wall" described in the Book of Daniel, which credits the victory to Darius (who probably led the campaign).

Meanwhile, Egypt was enjoying forty years of peace under the Pharaoh Amasis, who took office in the uprising against Merneptah/Apries. Herodotus credits Amasis with promoting much building in Egypt, although little is left of

---

1. Herodotus 1.127-9

			Chronology to Chapters 17-18	
DATE	EGYPT	PERSIA	PALESTINE AND SYRIA	EVENTS
570	AMASIS		BABYLONIAN CAPTIVITY CONTINUES	
560		CYRUS		560 CROESUS KING OF LYDIA CYRUS KING OF PERSIA
550				546 CROESUS SACKS BOGHAZKOI 546 CYRUS CONQUERS LYDIA
540			EXILES RETURN TO JERUSALEM	
530	PSAMMETICH CAMBYSES	CAMBYSES		525 CAMBYSES CONQUERS EGYPT
520	DARIUS	DARIUS	ZERUBBABEL HAGGAI/ ZECHARIAH	
510			SECOND COMMON-WEALTH	510 DARIUS BUILDS CANAL TO GULF
500				
490	XERXES	XERXES		490 BATTLE OF MARATHON
480			ESTHER	
470				

Chronology to Chapters 17-18			
(continued)			
DATE	EGYPT	PERSIA PALESTINE & SYRIA	EVENTS
470		ARTAXERXES	INAROS' REBELLION AGAINST PERSIA AGE OF PERICLES
460			ARSAMES SATRAP OVER EGYPT
450	PSAMTEK APPOINTED SOUTHERN GOVERNOR		
440	NEKHT-HEBEF APPOINTED NORTHERN GOVERNOR	433 SECOND VISIT OF NEHEMIAH	
430	NEKHT-HOR-HEB APPOINTED GOVERNOR	DARIUS II	PELOPONNESIAN WAR
420	WENAMON'S JOURNEY	417 EZRA ARRIVES IN JERUSALEM	
410		ARTAXERXES II	
400	ACORIS		XENOPHON'S MARCH
390			
380	NECTANEBO I (RAMSES III)	PHARNABAZUS SATRAP	NECTANEBO SURVIVES PERSIA AND
370			AEGEAN MERCENARIES
360	TACHOS (RAMSES IV)	ARTAXERXES III	
350	NECTANEBO II (RAMSES VI)		
340		ALEXANDER THE GREAT INITIATES HELLENIC PERIOD OF HISTORY	ARTAXERXES III DEFEATS NECTANEBO II

it. Cyrus died in battle against Scythians and his son Cambyses (529-521) continued the expansion of the kingdom, this time toward Egypt. Amasis died before Cambyses got there and Psammetich took over for his brief tragic rule. Herodotus tells of the quick victory by Cambyses at the Nile and then at the capital, Memphis. Cambyses claimed that his mother was a daughter of Apries, married to his father Cyrus, making him a legitimate heir to the throne. This may explain why he systematically destroyed or defaced the name of Amasis, whom Cambyses considered a usurper, on all monuments and buildings where it occurred. It does not explain why he went on to despoil the rest of Egypt. Herodotus believed that insanity must play a part in the unspeakable atrocities he dealt upon Egypt.

Some consider that Herodotus exaggerated the details of those acts, since no native documents have verified them. However, a 21st-dynasty text known as *Ourmai's Lament*, if placed contemporary with the Persian dynasty, describes conditions strikingly similar to those detailed by Herodotus.

This chapter will attempt to show two corrections to historical chronology. First, the 21st dynasty did not follow the 20th, as normally believed, or even run concurrently with the 22nd and 23rd Libyan dynasties as suggested by James. Instead, the Synchronized Chronology places the priest-kings of the 21st dynasty as a native theocracy permitted (or even encouraged) by the Persian kings. The condition parallels the theocratic state of Judah in Jerusalem during the same period. The Egyptian priest-kings counted their line of successors right through the brief 28th-30th native dynasties and moved their power base to the western oases/oracle centers. They lasted there long enough for the last of the priest-kings to entertain Alexander as the liberator from Persian dominance.

The second object of this chapter will be to show that the 20th Dynasty is the same as the 30th. In the previous chapter, the 19th dynasty was shown to be the same as the 26th, sandwiched between the Assyrian and Persian eras. So where does that leave the 20th, which supposedly followed more or less uneventfully from the 19th? The principal figure of the 20th dynasty, Ramses III, left an entire temple complex (Medinet Habu) covered with details of his reign. Prominently featured were his land and sea battles against a coalition of northeastern soldiers and Aegean mercenaries, the famous "People of the Sea" (and "People of the Isles").

The events depicted by Ramses III will be compared with the reign of Nectanebo I of the 30th Dynasty as told by Diodorus Siculus. And the archaeological remains of Tell el Yahudiyeh near Heiropolis, as recorded by two famous scholars, will present the spectacle of two authorities, in the same volume, disagreeing by 800 years on the age of the material.

The Historical Scene

Cambyses supposedly held a grudge against Amasis for attempting to double cross him. Amasis was very much afraid of Cambyses, and when the Persian asked the pharaoh for his daughter, Amasis knew he had to come up with something. He could not bring himself to send his own daughter; so he sent a daughter of Apries instead, instructing her to pretend to be the royal daughter. Of course, she hated Amasis for having killed her father, so she immediately told Cambyses of the ruse.[2] This story may or may not be true, and the Persians have a different one; but it is meant to explain the passionate anger driving Cambyses. Indeed, his later irrational behavior, after defeating Egypt, indicates a severely disturbed individual.

The Persian defeat of Egypt by a powerful and battle-seasoned army was relatively quick and easy. The other African kingdoms were the next targets. Cambyses sent spies to Ethiopia with a pretext of delivering gifts. The Ethiopians saw through the strategy and sent back a huge unstrung bow and a taunting challenge for Cambyses or any of his men to use the bow. The Persians should feel lucky to avoid a conflict with such men as use these bows!

Cambyses, of course, took offense. Enraged at the insult, he launched a suicidal campaign to Ethiopia. Cambyses was so unprepared for the endeavor that the army was out of food before it even reaching the desert. Ultimately, they resorted to cannibalism, which finally got the leader's attention. At least this army made it back to Egypt. There were other disasters in parallel — the 50,000 troops Cambyses sent to the western oasis of Amon were apparently lost and died in a sandstorm. And his desire to attack Carthage was thwarted principally because his Phoenician seamen refused to participate in an attack on their brethren.

Herodotus portrays Cambyses in the classic role that runs throughout the work: a ruler obsessed with conquering other people. Once a king is no longer satisfied with prosperity for his own country, he is doomed to an ultimately tragic end. Cambyses was so extreme in his actions that Herodotus believed him to be insane. The scene of Cambyses punishing the defeated pharaoh deserves to be quoted extensively, not only for its portrayal of deliberate cruelty, but as a record to compare with *Ourmai's Lament*.

> On the tenth day after Cambyses captured the fort at Memphis, he set King Psammenitus (who had reigned just six months) in the outer part of the city to do him deliberate injury. He set him there with the other Egyptians and made

---

2. Herodotus 3.1

trial of the very soul of him. He did it thus: he put Psammenitus' daughter into slave's rags and sent her with a pitcher to draw water; he sent with her the daughters of noblemen, whom he had chosen out of the rest, all dressed like the princess herself. The girls passed by their fathers, screaming and crying; the fathers screamed and cried in answer as they saw their children so maltreated. Psammenitus looked fixedly at them first, took it all in, and then bowed himself to the ground. When the water-carriers were past, Cambyses sent Psammenitus' son, along with about two thousand Egyptians of the same age, with ropes tied around their necks and bits in their mouths. They were led along to pay for those Mytilenaeans who had been murdered when they came to Memphis with their ship. (The royal judges had rendered judgment that for each man lost on Cambyses' side, ten of the leading Egyptians should be killed.) Psammenitus saw these go by, noticed his own son leading the death procession, and, though all the other Egyptians around him lamented in terrible distress, he did just the same as he had done in the case of his daughter. When they were all gone by, it happened that a somewhat elderly man passed Psammenitus, son of Amasis, and those other Egyptians who were set in the outer part of the city. He had been one of the king's drinking companions, had lost all his estate, had indeed nothing but what a beggar might have, and he was begging from the army. When Psammenitus saw *him*, he burst into tears and called his old comrade by name and beat his own head.

As the story goes, he was most deeply touched by the sight of the old man struck down so unfairly after living a just life. This so impressed Cambyses that he had a change of heart and tried to stop the execution of the pharaoh's son, but it was too late.

A document from early in the 21st dynasty, the *Ourmai Papyrus*, describes conditions mirroring those rendered by Herodotus. Conventional Chronology would place the events described here in a presumably peaceful time, which is why scholars downplay and dismiss the clear wording. By the Synchronized Chronology this would be just after the Persian conquest of Egypt. Here is what survives of the papyrus (lacuna indicated by . . .):

> I was carried away unjustly, I am bereft of all, I am speechless [to protest], I am robbed, though I did nothing wrong; I am thrown out of my city, the property is seized, nothing is left [to me]. I am [defenseless] before the mighty wrongdoers . . . They are torn away from me; their wives are killed [before them]; their children are dispersed, some thrown into prison, others seized as prey. I am thrown out of my yesterday's domicile, compelled to roam in harsh wanderings. The land is engulfed by enemy's fire. South, north, west, and east belong to him . . . I suffered hunger . . . my grain that was given to me by soldiers.[3]

This passage is so similar to Herodotus that it could be about the same old man, even begging food from the army. Or did these events occur during the supposedly peaceful transition from the 20th to 21st dynasties of Conventional Chronology?

Herodotus continues with further evidence of the outrages committed by Cambyses:

> He stayed in Memphis and opened the ancient coffins and peered at the dead bodies. In the same spirit he came into the temple of Hephaestus and made great mockery of the image there . . . Cambyses also went into the shrine of the Cabiri, where it is unlawful for any but the priest to enter. These images he even burned, with much mockery.[4]

Again, a comparison with Ourmai:

> Bodies [of the dead] and bones [are] thrown out upon the ground, and who will cover them? . . . Their altars disappeared, and [so also] offerings, salt, natron, vegetables.[5]

Placing the 21st dynasty parallel with the Persian era solves another of the well-known inconsistencies of Egyptian archaeology. The tomb of Pseusennes of the 21st dynasty encroached into the tomb of Osorkon II of the 22nd dynasty. This would of course contradict the conventional understanding of the dynastic successions. "The overall picture of evidence certainly points to the 21st Dynasty Pseusennes I having constructed his tomb after the building work of the 22nd Dynasty Osorkon II."[6]

The Synchronized Chronology places the 21st dynasty not after the 20th but rather following the 26th (19th) and running concurrently with the 27th-31st dynasties. During the Persian 27th, at least after Cambyses, the Egyptian priest-kings served a theocracy apparently as acceptable to Persia as was the similar Hebrew theocracy in Jerusalem. Then with the native pharaohs of the 28th-30th dynasties the same high priests retained substantial power. They even continued through the 2nd Persian rule from the relative safety of the western oases.

Further evidence for the placement of the 21st dynasty during the Persian era will not be presented here. The interested reader, especially if familiar with

---

3. trans. in V.3, 113.
4. 3.37.
5. V.3, 114.
6. James 245.

The Third Intermediate Period in Egypt, by Kitchen, is invited to review the argument presented in *Peoples of the Sea*, where a compelling case is made for the latter 21st dynasty being immediately pre-Hellenic.

THE HARRIS PAPYRUS

It has been necessary to introduce the political scene of Egypt in the years prior to Ramses III in order to set the stage for another important Egyptian text. Probably the single most impressive written document surviving from ancient Egypt is the famous Harris Papyrus. The papyrus is 133 feet long with 117 columns of hieratic script serving as a testimonial to Ramses III of the 20th dynasty. In the Synchronized Chronology, the 20th is the same as the 30th and falls between the two periods of Persian dominance. Although 95% of the text is a repetitious catalogue of the pharaoh's generosity to the temples, the last 5% gives an interesting look at the historical conditions before and during his reign.

Keep in mind the conventional version of history, in which the 20th dynasty takes over from the 19th more or less peacefully. Even the direct evidence to the contrary, which will be quoted later, is dismissed as "a largely imaginary period of previous gloom." (Gardiner 281) Ramses' historical text deserves to be compared to the two previous records, Herodotus and the *Ourmai Papyrus*, in order to show that all three indicate a period of foreign rule before the 20th Dynasty.

The historical portion of the Harris Papyrus begins by describing an episode that would correspond to Cambyses' military victory. This is followed by a chaotic period that was calmed after Darius set up a system of administration.

> Hear ye, that I may inform you of my benefactions which I did while I was king of the people. The land of Egypt was overthrown from without, and every man was (thrown out) of his right; they had no chief mouth for many years formerly until other times. The land of Egypt was in the hands of chiefs and of rulers of towns; one slew his neighbor, great and small. Other times having come after it, with empty years, Yarsu, a certain Syrian was with them as chief. He set the whole land tributary before him together; he united his companions and plundered their possessions. They made the gods like men, and no offerings were presented in the temples.[7]

Cambyses had the kind of ill-fated demise for which Herodotus excels in providing the poignant details. He is followed by Darius (the Great), who did

---

7. ARE IV, 398.

little to help the Egyptians, but at least did not oppress them. In Jerusalem, work on the new temple was supported by Darius after a copy of the original decree of Cyrus was found in Persia. The alien population that was settled throughout Palestine by Assyrian and Babylonian conquerors was opposing the "second commonwealth" of the Hebrews. The decree overcame that resistance and enabled the rebuilding of Jerusalem.

Darius established a system of administrators under satraps, responsible for delivering tribute to Persia. He also wished to bring the Greek mainland under tribute, but efforts to that end were postponed. It was attempted under his successor, Xerxes. In the Greeks, Persia had met their military match. Not only was the endeavor a failure, but Persia created resentment among Greeks that led ultimately to the advent and adventures of Alexander.

The conditions described in the Harris Papyrus show a shift into a time of servitude under a Syrian satrap by the name of "Yarsu," whose aggressive collection of tribute amounts to "plunder." During the 53-year period from Artaxerxes, the successor to Xerxes, in 465 until the latter time of Darius II (c. 410), the satrap of Egypt was a Babylonian named Arsames.

Arsames is a well-known figure whose activities and personality were highlighted by the find in Egypt of a collection of leather scrolls (or letters) dealing with the size and quality of tribute and responsibilities for enlarging the "estate" of Arsames. They show a glaring contempt for the native Egyptians who served as regional governors. The letters are written in Aramaic (Syrian), from Babylon. In the Harris Papyrus, the Arsu (Yarsu) who collects tribute and plunders the people is referred to as a Syrian.

In a letter to Nekht-hor, Arsames writes:

> Do you show yourself active and take strict care of your staff and property that my estate may suffer no sort of loss; also seek out enough staff of craftsmen of various races from elsewhere and bring them into my court and mark them with my brand and make them over to my estate, just as the previous pekidia (governors) used to do. Thus let it be known to thee; if my staff [of serfs] or other property suffer any sort of loss and you [plural] do not seek out others from elsewhere and add them to my estate, you will be called strictly to account, and reprimanded.[8]

The span of time between the end of the 26th (19th) dynasty and the 30th (20th) began with Cambyses' reign of manic terror and developed into the ruthless exploitation by satraps like Arsames. Compare again the description from the Harris Papyrus:

---

8. G. R. Driver, *Aramaic Documents of the Fifth Century* B.C. Oxford, 1954.

The land of Egypt was overthrown from without, . . . Other times having come after it, with empty years, Yarsu, a certain Syrian was with them as chief. He set the whole land tributary before him together; he united his companions and plundered their possessions.[9]

Keep in mind the attitude that this is "a largely imaginary period of previous gloom . . . In this strange passage the glorious achievements of Dynasty XVIII and XIX are ignored."[10] Since the plain language cannot be made to agree with the presumed history of the 20th dynasty, it is dismissed as fictitious.

This brief and selective review of the first Persian era in Egypt is meant to set the scene for the true history of the following native Egyptian rule. The 30th dynasty is another like the 26th, for which no monuments, no temples or any other buildings remain (except for very minor items credited to individuals who will be shown to belong to the 21st dynasty). And, like the 26th, the history must be found in outside sources. We are well past the time of Herodotus (actually, the early 4th century BC) so we must go to later Greek historians for the story.

It must be emphasized that the entire chronology depends on this last synchronism. The 20th dynasty cannot remain in the 12th century BC if the 19th dynasty is moved to the 7th. The basis for asserting this last major synchronism will be the compelling evidence for placing the 20th dynasty in the 4th century BC (being identical with the 30th Manethonian dynasty).

The evidence presented in this chapter and the next will be both historical and archaeological. Written records separated by 800 years in Conventional Chronology will be shown to describe the same events, in the same order, among the same parties down to a level of detail seldom reached even in later eras of history. And dating estimates for archaeological material from an important Egyptian site differ by the same 800 years.

Diodorus Siculus[11] records a series of interactions among the major players of the time, Egypt, Persia, Asia Minor and the Aegean. At the center of the action is the last great pharaoh of the last native dynasty, Nectanebo I. His formidable exploits have no record in the Egypt of Conventional Chronology. They will be compared with the extensive record left by the 20th dynasty pharaoh known as Ramses III.

---

9. ARE IV, 398.

10. Gardiner 281.

11. A writer born in Agyrium, Sicily, c. 90 BC, he traveled throughout Asia and Europe and compiled a "Historical Library."

THE EGYPTIAN RECORD

"Medinet Habu," the mortuary temple of Ramses III in the west Theban necropolis, is literally covered with historic reliefs. For a temple supposedly built in the 12th century BC, it is in amazingly good condition, somehow escaping the destructions visited upon other Egyptian monuments by Assurbanipal in 663 and Cambyses in 525. In fact, the near identity between Medinet Habu and Ptolomaic temples must be seen to be appreciated. Conventionally they are separated by some 900 years, but in appearance and in reality only a couple of generations.

The historical records from the earliest part of Ramses' reign are inscribed toward the back of the temple, with later events progressing towards the front, probably indicating that the reliefs were added as the temple was built over time. As is the case for all Egyptian "historical" art, the reliefs are extremely precise in details of physique, dress and armaments. This is of great importance for the chronological comparison.

Just as Ramses II devoted considerable space to recording his Battle of Kadesh, Ramses III covered large portions of his temple with reliefs of his three major military campaigns, in years 5, 8 and 11. The events depicted for years 5 and 8 are of most interest. Although the actual historical order is so confused as to be unusable, the events speak for themselves in terms of players and outcomes. Year 5 is the first Libyan war, and Year 8 covers his famous land and sea battles with the "Sea Peoples." What makes these reliefs so special are the various peoples depicted and named.

The Harris Papyrus repeats a summary of the reliefs but does not clarify some of the problems in interpreting them. Breasted explains:

> Perhaps, under the influence of the Kadesh poem, it has now become impossible to narrate a war or a victory of the Pharaoh in any other than poetic style. The record must be a poem. This would not be an unmixed misfortune, if the poem were intelligible; but the style is such as to render not merely whole lines, but entire strophes and whole passages, utterly unintelligible. This is due to two facts: first, total lack of order or progress in the narrative; second, the figurative character of the language. The first fault renders the reader's impressions fragmentary and confused in the highest degree.[12]

A contributing factor in the confusion created by the reliefs is the changing roles played by the various "Sea Peoples," without any explanation. In the Libyan war of year 5, the Egyptian army is supported by people that in year 8 are

---

12. ARE IV, 21.

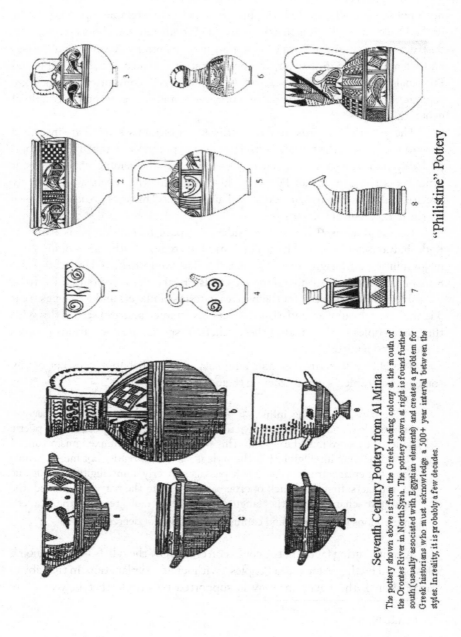

"Philistine" Pottery

Seventh Century Pottery from Al Mina

The pottery shown above is from the Greek trading colony at the mouth of the Orontes River in North Syria. The pottery shown at right is found further south (usually associated with Egyptian elements) and creates a problem for Greek historians who must acknowledge a 500+ year interval between the styles. In reality, it is probably a few decades.

enemies. Not only did "Sea Peoples" fight alongside Egyptians against Libyans, they were also joined by certain troops wearing the "feathered headdress," the P-R-S-TT. The entire conventional picture of the end of the Bronze Age is built around these P-R-S-TT.

Supposedly, the breakdown of Mycenaean civilization unleashed the forces of roving brigands that eventually united for the purpose of conquering Egypt, but settled on Palestine instead. In the Conventional Chronology the people in the "feathered" headdress (not actually feathers, but the term has stuck) give their name to Palestine: the Philistines. (Since R and L are the same letter in Egyptian, P-R-S-TT could also be P-L-S-TT, although choices have to be made, and, for example, we are accustomed to saying Ramses, not Lamses).

Placed conventionally in the generations following the Trojan War, the destruction of civilization from Greece through Asia Minor and into Syria and Palestine is blamed on the "Sea Peoples." The Dorian invasion in Greece is often regarded as a triggering factor, or at least an element in the overall picture. By the time they reached Egypt, they were a well-organized army. This would be quite a feat for roving brigands, if it actually occurred.

An example of the problems encountered by the theory of an Aegean origin for the "feathered" headdress people is illustrated by the reliefs. The P-R-S-TT are accompanied by their women and children in ox carts, something that was never shown to have happened before. "The oxen are the humped zebu which were used in Anatolia and Mesopotamia, but not in Palestine or the Aegean, though they may have reached Cypress," we are told.[13] The use of these ox carts is a well-known feature of the army of the "real" P-R-S-TT. This is just a minor point, but it is just as enriching to Synchronized Chronology as it is confusing for Conventional.

Identifying the P-R-S-TT as Philistines has naturally led to an archaeological search for them in Palestine. Expecting to find late and post Mycenaean evidence, the scholars were not disappointed. There is even a characteristic pottery decoration (a bird looking backwards) that has become an index for them. To my eye, Philistine pottery looks so much like East Greek "bird bowls" that they must be closely related. They are colonial Greek and have nothing to do with the true Philistines of the 11th century.

The real significance of the Synchronized Chronology can be illustrated by three books, readily available in even modest libraries, that have almost identical titles: *The Sea Peoples*, by Nancy Sandars, *The People of the Sea*, by Moshe and Trude Dothan, and *The Peoples of the Sea*, by Velikovsky. Sandars examines the archaeological picture of the various people that could be behind the Philistine invasion.

---

13. Sandars 121.

Her range of inquiry extends to northern Greece and even further into Europe looking for evidence. The Dothans examine the sites in Palestine associated with either "archaeological" Philistines or biblical Philistines. Each is a tortuous attempt to fit the Bible and archaeology to the historical record of Ramses III. The Synchronized Chronology offered by Velikovsky presents a comfortable alternative. The roles and identities of all the parties, and the historical context of the events, are readily accessible in the History of Diodorus.

WHO ARE THE P-R-S-TT?

If the Rosetta Stone had not been found, the "Canopus Decree," another trilingual inscription, could have served the same purpose for deciphering Egyptian hieroglyphics. The decree was issued in 239 BC in the city of Canopus by an enclave of priests. It concerns mostly temple issues, but also promulgates an unsuccessful calendar reform. Within the text is a reference to Persia, "And the sacred images which had been carried off from the country by the Persians, the King, having made an expedition outside Egypt, brought them back safely unto Egypt, and restored them to the temples wherefrom they had been carried off. . ."[14]

Whether or not this unlikely event actually took place, the real importance is the reference to Persia, *and the way it is spelled*, P-R-S-TT, just as it appears on Ramses' temple. (Other cities named in the decree have a similar double T ending, for perhaps aesthetic purposes). Did the Hellenic pharaohs know Persians by the same name as the Philistines, 900 year earlier?

Reproductions of the famous "feathered" headdress of the P-R-S-TT are used whenever Philistines are portrayed, as in catechisms, documentaries, and especially Hollywood movies. Other than the Trojan helmets made famous in Trojan War depictions, the "Philistine" feathered headdress is the most frequently used pre-Roman helmet. It even appears in the confused setting of a movie about Akhnaton.

The helmet is clearly not made of feathers, because when Egyptians depict feathers on headwear, there is no mistaking them. Some type of fabric is more likely, or, much less likely, bronze. The following reference to the appearance and origin of the headdress is certainly unintentionally ironic:

> The question of the headdress must remain open, but either feathers or folded material appear the more likely candidates. The conventional represen-

---

14. V.3, 35.

From the Medinet Habu reliefs of Rames III. An oxcart with women and children is caught in the battle. The Persian helmet should be compared with the Royal Guard depicted on Persepolis.

Persian guard from bas-reliefs at the palace of Darius at Persepolis.

tation at Persepolis in the 5th century BC of the linen headdress of the Persian Imperial Guard is a fair comparison in a similar medium.[15]

Indeed the "feathered headdress" on Medinet Habu is one of the most distinctive in the ancient repertoire. It is not just a "fair comparison" to the Persian, it is *identical!* Should not "similar medium" rather be "identical medium," i.e. military headdress?

Another distinctive headdress is the "Armenian," which is also found at both Medinet Habu and Persepolis.[16] Note that an Armenian contingent is awkward for the conventional picture. But an obvious and agreeable role for Armenian conscripts in the Persian army is found in the 4th century.

Identifying the P-R-S-TT of Ramses' inscriptions as 4th-century Persians places them firmly in well-known history. The detailed comparisons place extreme demands on the Synchronized Chronology to prove itself. This is the last major link in the historical reconstruction and it is of critical importance throughout the Middle East, where artifacts of Ramses III create unsolvable problems for archaeologists.

TELL EL YAHUDIYEH

It is hard to imagine a stranger book than the *Seventh Memoir of the Egypt Exploration Fund.* In one volume, two of the most eminent Egyptologists of all times separately review the results of their excavations at the Tell and its nearby cemeteries. In the preface to the work one of the authors, Edouard Naville, says:

> During the winter of 1887 I had the valuable help of Mr. Griffith, who in the present work deals chiefly with the archaeological side of the excavations. The reader will notice that our opinions disagree as to the age to which some of the objects discovered in the necropolis of Tell el Yahoodieh should be attributed. Each of us is alone responsible for the views he states on this point, which we submit to the judgment of the reader.

Mr. Griffith added in his review of the troubling conflicts, "Light will be thrown on the question someday."[17]

In no other context than the Synchronized Chronology can the opinions of the two writers be made to agree. The difference is some 800 years and represents the final anchor point of this reconstruction. And it is not just the

---

15. Sandars 137.
16. Ibid.
17. Op. cit., p. 41.

Necropolis that presented conflicting data. The most important structure on the mound itself also added to the confusion.

The site is almost certainly "the house of Ra north of On (Heliopolis),"[18] mentioned in the Harris Papyrus. Structures and artifacts from three eras were found, Middle Kingdom and Hyksos, Ramesside, and Late Greek and Roman. Most prominent among the building remains was the pavilion of Ramses III. He apparently had a special connection with the city, since it is mentioned three times in the Harris Papyrus.

Griffith discusses the nature of the evidence and the dilemma created:

> Arriving at the XXth dynasty we reach perhaps the most interesting point in the history of the city. Setnekht has left no trace, but of his son Ramses III, a variety of memorials have been found. Chief amongst them is the building which lay at the west end of the temple. It was on a small scale, but beautifully decorated with choice materials. The floor was of oriental alabaster; the roof was supported by columns resting on bases of alabaster and red granite; the limestone walls were covered with patterns in mosaic, and their uniformity was broken by semi-circular stands rising in steps, each of which was ornamented with rosettes and other devices in variegated enamel.
>
> The Ramesside date of these remains has been contested by E. Brugsch, who assigns the enamels to the Ptolemaic period. Hayter Lewis also supposes that they are in part Ptolemaic restorations. *The question involves a great difficulty.* The potters' marks include, besides less definite cyphers, several hieroglyphics and the following which may be interpreted as Greek letters, AEIΛMOCTX. The rosettes are abundant, and bear all varieties of marks. Good examples of the other tiles being rarer, there is some doubt about them; but I have found a "T" endorsed on a captive's head, and on one of a similar series a label is attached to the girdle, bearing the name of Ramses III.[19]

Mr. Naville expresses similar thoughts, "There is a curious fact about the discs which have been found in such a large number; some of them are inscribed on the back with Greek letters *A, E, Λ, X*, while others bear Egyptian signs. The Greek letters show that strangers were at some time employed in the work."[20]

The archaeologist who had earlier examined the tiles was more specific in his declarations concerning their age. "The Greek letters, and especially *alpha*, found on the fragments and disks leave no room for doubt that the work was executed during the last centuries of the Egyptian Empire and probably in the time of the Ptolemies; but the matter becomes more difficult if we ask who the

---

18. P. 12.
19. p. 41, italics added.
20. P. 6.

author of this work was."[21] Perhaps Naville says it best: "This work strikingly reminds us of Persian art, both modern and ancient."[22]

In their discussions of the tiles, these authors were desperately close to the truth. Coupled with the evidence that they went on to describe from the cemetery, it is a wonder that they failed to recognize — or admit — that conflicting data from both areas pointed to the same solution.

THE NECROPOLIS

Within sight of the mound was an area well suited for a necropolis. Loose surface rocks of basalt provided material for mounds or "tumuli." The burials themselves were in large clay coffins bearing the crudely modeled features of the head and arms at one end on the upper surface. Because of their identification with Ramses III, these distinctive coffins have become a chronological indicator wherever they have been found, especially in Palestine. Needless to say, the consequences of this dating are dramatic.

It is with respect to these coffins that Naville and Griffith openly disagree. First, Mr. Griffith:

> The coffins were numerous, lying parallel to each other in rows. We found that the plunderers in ancient times had been busy amongst them, and all the coffins of adults had been opened and pillaged. On the other hand, the graves of children were intact — the thieves knew well that they contained no valuables. In one of these, two pottery scarabs were found which bear the name of Ramses III, and thus give most satisfactory evidence for the precise date of the Tumuli.[23]

The scarab was not the only indication of dating, since much pottery was placed alongside the coffins. Griffith concludes regarding the necropolis:

> The general result of the excavations in the tumuli is to show that they belong to the XXth dynasty, at least as the central period. Out of the first seven tumuli, there is nothing certainly later or earlier than this, while the finding of scarabs of Ramses III and VI, in agreement with the fact that the most striking type amongst the pottery, "the false amphora," is found in the paintings of the tomb of Ramses III, fixes the date. At the same period the royal hall was built in the city. . . .[24]

---

21. Brugsch trans. in V.3.
22. p. 6.
23. P. 41.
24. P. 48.

Anthropoid coffin from Tell el Yahudiyeh necropolis near the Nile Delta

Anthropoid coffins from Dier el-Balah near Gaza

When these coffins were first found in Palestine they were thought to be coffins of the Sea People. They are now considered evidence of Egyptian presence at those sites. However, already in 1892 Naville had noted that the Tell el-Yahudiyeh samples were very late, Greek or even Roman in age.

226

Mr. Naville refused to let the scarabs influence his opinion on the age of the coffins. "In assigning a date to the coffin there is no more unsafe criterion than the amulets, especially the scarabs."[25] He was quite emphatic in his evaluation of the coffins:

> A curious fact in connection with these tombs is the discovery of so-called Cypriot pottery. Mr. Petrie had already found similar specimens at Nebesheh, in tombs which he attributes to the Saite epoch [*i.e. 26th dyn.*].[26] The hieroglyphics written on these coffins are so carelessly painted as to make it difficult to assign a date to the tombs, although the Greek and Roman period is indicated by the general style. I could readily believe them to be contemporaneous with some of the Jewish burials, which, from the style of the writing on the tablets, must be attributed either to the late Ptolemies or to the early Romans.[27]

Naville's cautions have been completely disregarded. Today, the coffins are considered to be a benchmark for the time of the Philistine entrance into Palestine. Sandars says, "At one time clay coffins with anthropomorphic lids were taken as evidence of Sea Peoples, specifically 'Philistine.'"[28] Today they are considered to indicate an Egyptian presence during that era.

A hundred years after Naville expressed reservations about the dating, the problem has not gone away; it is simply ignored. Perhaps only a handful of modern scholars are even aware that such concerns were ever expressed. The missing element is the challenge to the date of Ramses III, something that was just as unthinkable 100 years ago as it is today.

---

25. p. 17.
26. P. 17.
27. Ibid.
28. Sandars *caption on p. 73.*

18. THE PEOPLE OF THE SEA

The majority of historical reliefs on Medinet Habu concern the Libyan War of Year 5, the land and sea attacks of Year 8, the second Libyan War of Year 11, and the Amorite wars of uncertain date (and doubtful authenticity). Given the most space are the celebrated land and sea wars of Year 8.

The time frame against which the Egyptian reliefs are set helps to understand the roles of the participants. The beginning of the 4th century was a time of great political chaos. Artaxerxes (404-358) was challenged early in his reign by an alliance led by Cyrus the Younger. Fortunately for history, Xenophon was one of the leaders of the Greek contingent and lived to write of the adventures of 10,000 Greeks who escaped after the death of Cyrus near Babylon. His *Anabasis* ("Going Up") follows this group as they travel north to the safety of the Black Sea.

The peace following the Peloponnesian War was not to last long and soon Persia was backing Athens against Sparta in their campaign to liberate Ionia from Persia. (Next, Ionia had to revolt against Sparta.) The satraps had to deal with rebellions all over the Empire. Cyprus, which had been helping Athens, was initially loyal to Persia, but took advantage of the unsettled times to declare independence. Egypt likewise revolted under Amyrteos, the only representative of the 28th dynasty. Persia fixed its sights on Cyprus, the recovery of which it viewed as absolutely necessary to preparations for re-taking Egypt.

The unstable Egyptian situation was caused by the replacement of Amyrteos by one Nephrites, who was in turn usurped by Acoris, possibly with Persian help. During this same era, Carthage was invading Italy and Sicily was attacking the Greek settlement of Croton in southern Italy.

In Year 5 of his reign, Ramses III participated in a war against Libya. In the extensive reliefs devoted to this campaign, the Egyptians fight alongside troops with the "feathered" headdress and others with a helmet sporting small horns and a disk or sphere mounted between them.

Just as Ramses II counted as part of his own reign his co-regency during the later part of his father's reign, so also Ramses III took over the years of his illegitimate predecessor. As Nectanebo, he probably did serve as an important military figure who could legitimately depict himself engaged in the campaign. Diodorus did not record a battle with Libya in the early years of Nectanebo (or before, in the reign of Acoris), because it amounted to the suppression of a more or less internal Egyptian revolt. Only when affairs of Egypt make international impact do they appear in Diodorus. In this case, with Cyprus's revolt against Persia, Egypt is also emboldened to rebel. The Libyan War would date to the time of Acoris preceding that event, when Egypt was still under Persian rule and Persian troops would have been a natural contingent of Egyptian forces, as would Aegean mercenaries.

The important thing to remember about the Libyan War is the alliance of Egypt with both the P-R-S-TT and the horned-helmet armies. These parties play differing roles in the next two encounters.

THE BATTLES

With the historical stage now set, the reader is invited to compare extensive and detailed quotes from Book 15 of Diodorus with the written and illustrated record of Ramses III (see the illustrations at the end of this chapter). The Persian military was under the command of Pharnabazus, whose forces include both regular army conscripts from throughout the Persian Empire and Aegean mercenaries. The regular army wore Persian uniforms. The mercenaries wore their native battle dress.

> When Mystichides was archon in Athens, the Romans elected in place of consuls three military tribunes, Marcus Furius, Gaius, and Aemilius. This year Ataxerxes, the King of the Persians, made war upon Evagoras, the king of Cyprus. He busied himself for a long time with the preparations for the war and gathered a large armament, both naval and land; his land force consisted of three hundred thousand men including cavalry, and he equipped more than three hundred triremes.[1] Evagoras made an alliance with Acoris, the king of the Egyptians, who was an enemy of the Persians, and received a strong force from him, and from Hecatomnus, the lord of Caria, who was secretly co-operating

---

1. Diodorus 15.2.1.

with him, he got a large sum of money to support his mercenary troops. Likewise he drew on such others to join in the war with Persia as were at odds with the Persians, either secretly or openly.[2]

Evagoras at first held an advantage in ships and supplies, but Persia was determined and, after a surprising naval victory, gained the upper hand and soon laid siege to Salamis. Evagoras was able to withstand the Persians long enough to sue for a face-saving peace that allowed him rule over Salamis alone. Meanwhile Persia was determined to re-take Egypt.

Ramses tells us briefly of the extent of the united forces and their intention to take on Egypt. The "Peleset" (P-R-S-TT) are named first among the forces.

> The countries — , the Northerners in their isles were disturbed, taken away in the fray — at one time. Not one stood before their hands, from Kheta, Kode, Carchemish, Arvad, Alasa (Cyprus), they were wasted. They set up a camp in one place in Amor. They desolated his people and his land like that which is not. They came with fire prepared before them, forward to Egypt. Their main support was Peleset, Thekel, Shekelesh, Denyen, and Weshesh, These lands were united, and they laid their hands upon the land as far as the Circle of the Earth. Their hearts were confident, full of their plans.[3]

Diodorus gives us the details:

> While these things were going on, Acoris, the king of the Egyptians (actually Nectanebo would have been king at this time), being on unfriendly terms with the Persian King, collected a large mercenary force; for by offering high pay to those who enrolled and doing favors to many of them, he quickly induced many of the Greeks to take service with him for the campaign. But having no capable general, he sent for Chabrias the Athenian, a man distinguished both for his prudence as general and his shrewdness in the art of war, who had also won great repute for personal prowess. Now Chabrias, without first securing the permission of the Athenian people, accepted the appointment and took command of the forces in Egypt and with great dispatch made preparations to fight the Persians. But Pharnabazus, who had been appointed by the King general of the Persian armies, prepared large supplies of war material, and also sent ambassadors to Athens, first to denounce Chabrias, who by becoming general of the Egyptians was alienating, so he said, the King's affection from the people of Athens, and, secondly, to urge them to give him Iphicrates as general. The Athenians, being eager to gain the favour of the Persian King and to incline Pharnabazus to themselves, quickly recalled

---

2. Diodorus 15.2.3.
3. ARE IV, 64.

Chabrias from Egypt and dispatched Iphicrates as general to act in alliance with the Persians.[4]

This passage explains the most curious element of the Year 8 reliefs at Medinet Habu. For the land war, the Egyptians are allied with mercenaries who wear the horned helmet with the disk. The enemy all wear the "feathered" headdress of the P-R-S-TT, but are actually troops from a variety of countries all wearing a common uniform. Fighting with Egypt were Aegean mercenaries under Chabrias. Then Pharnabazus exerted pressure on Athens to withdraw from Egypt or risk losing the support of Persia in their conflicts with Sparta.

Pharnabazus, the leader of the Persian forces, was Satrap of the Persian province "Tyaiy Drayahya" or "Those [or the people] of the Sea." The capital of the province was in the Phrygian region of Asia Minor and the troops mustered under his command were from all parts of the province and served as regular forces in Persian military attire.

After the recall of Chabrias, a large contingent of Greek mercenaries under the command of Iphicrates was added to the Persian forces. Iphicrates had developed a reputation for being a brilliant innovator. During the Corinthian War (-391), he armed troops with lighter armor and new offensive weapons for greater speed and mobility and won a renowned victory over a division of heavily armored Spartan hoplites. If you look carefully, many of the Greek troops on Ramses' reliefs employ Iphicrates' new weapons: swords up to three times their former length, spears half again as long, and smaller, round shields.

Iphicrates was also bold in his military tactics but in his role with Pharnabazus, he was doomed to frustration. Diodorus tells the story of the Persian confederation and the attempt to invade Egypt by sea.

> When Socratides was archon at Athens, the Romans elected four military tribunes with consular power, Quintus Servilius, Servius Cornelius, and Spurius Papirius. During their term of office King Atarxerxes sent an expedition against the Egyptians, who had revolted from Persia. The leaders of the army were Pharnabazus, commanding the barbarian contingent, and Iphicrates the Athenian, commanding the mercenaries who numbered twenty thousand. Iphicrates, who had been summoned for the campaign by the King, was given the assignment because of his strategic skill. After Pharnabazus had wasted several years making preparations, Iphicrates, perceiving that though in talk he was clever, he was sluggish in action, frankly told him that he marveled that anyone so quick in speech could be so dilatory in action. Pharnabazus replied that it was because he was master of his words but the

---

4. 15.29.1-4.

King was master of his actions. When the Persian army had assembled at the city of Ace, it numbered two hundred thousand barbarians under the command of Pharnabazus and twenty thousand Greek mercenaries led by Iphicrates. The triremes numbered three hundred, and thirty-oared vessels two hundred. The number of those conveying food and other supplies was great. At the beginning of the summer the King's generals broke camp with the entire army, and accompanied the fleet sailing along the coast proceeded to Egypt. When they came near the Nile they found that the Egyptians had manifestly completed their preparations for the war. For Pharnabazus marched slowly and had given plenty of time for the enemy to prepare. Indeed it is the usual custom for the Persian commanders, not being independent in the general conduct of war, to refer all matters to the King and await his replies concerning every detail.[5] The Egyptian king Nectanebos learned the size of the Persian armies, but was emboldened, chiefly by the strength of the country, for Egypt is extremely difficult of approach, and secondly by the fact that all points of invasion from land or sea had been carefully blocked. For the Nile empties in the Egyptian Sea by seven mouths, and at each mouth a city had been established along with great towers on each bank of the stream and a wooden bridge commanding its entrance. He especially fortified the Pelusiac mouth because it is the first to be encountered by those approaching from Syria and seemed to be the most likely route of the enemy approach. He dug channels connecting with this, fortified the entrances for ships at the most suitable points, and inundated the approaches by land while blocking the sea approaches by embankments. Accordingly it was not easy either for the ships to sail in, or for the cavalry to draw near, or for the infantry to approach. Accordingly they voyaged on the open sea so that the ships should not be sighted by the enemy, and sailed in by the mouth known as Mendesian, which had a beach stretching over a considerable space. Landing here with three thousand horse and infantry, and a sharp battle ensued, but many men from their ships came to increase the number of the Persians, until finally the Egyptians were surrounded, many slain, and not a few captured alive; and the rest were driven in confusion into the city. Iphicrates' men dashed in with the defenders inside the walls, took possession of the fortress, razed it, and enslaved the inhabitants.[6] After this, discord set in amongst the commanders, causing the failure of the enterprise. For Iphicrates, learning from the captives that Memphis, the most strategically situated of the Egyptian cities, was undefended, advised sailing immediately up to Memphis before the Egyptian forces arrived there, but Pharnabazus thought they should await the entire Persian force; for in this way the campaign against Memphis would be less dangerous. When Iphicrates demanded that he be given the mercenaries that were on hand and promised if he had them to capture the city, Pharnabazus became suspicious of his boldness and his courage for fear lest he

---

5. 15.41.1-5.
6. 15.42.1-5.

take possession of Egypt for himself. Accordingly when Pharnabazus would not yield, Iphicrates protested that if they let slip the exact moment of opportunity, they would make the whole campaign a failure. Some generals indeed bore a grudge against him and were attempting to fasten unfair charges upon him. Meanwhile the Egyptians, having had plenty of time to recuperate, first sent an adequate garrison into Memphis, and then, proceeding with all their forces against the ravaged stronghold at the Mendesian mouth of the Nile and being now at a great advantage owing to the strength of their position, fought constant engagements with the enemy. With ever-increasing strength they slew many Persians and gained confidence against them. As the campaign about this stronghold dragged on, and the Etesian winds had already set in, the Nile, which was filling up and flooding the whole region with the abundance of its waters, made Egypt daily more secure. The Persian commanders, as this state of affairs constantly operated against them, decided to withdraw from Egypt.[7]

With the benefit of hindsight, Ramses is able to put a spin on the actual course of battle that implies he planned it as a trap:

> Now it happened through this god, the lord of gods, that I was prepared and armed to trap them like wild fowl. He furnished my strength and caused my plans to prosper. I went forth, directing these marvelous things. I equipped my frontier in Zahi, prepared before them. The chiefs, the captains of infantry, the nobles, I caused to equip the harbor-mouths, like a strong wall, with warships, galleys, and barges, . . .[8] Those who reached my boundary, their seed is not; their heart and their soul are finished forever and ever. As for those who had assembled before them on the sea, the full flame was in their front before the harbor-mouths, and a wall of metal upon the shore surrounded them. They were dragged, overturned, and laid low upon the beach; slain and made heaps from stern to bow of their galleys, while all their things were cast upon the water.[9] The countries which came from their isles in the midst of the sea, they advanced to Egypt, their hearts relying upon their arms. The net was made ready for them, to ensnare them. Entering stealthily into the harbor-mouths, they fell into it. Caught in their place, they were dispatched, and their bodies stripped.[10]

In this final naval battle, the pharaoh's forces are all Egyptians because the soldiers with the horned helmets have *changed sides* and are now fighting with the

---

7. 15.43.1-4.
8. ARE IV, 65.
9. ARE IV, 66.
10. ARE IV, 77.

P-R-S-TT. Only their helmets are a little different this time — there is no disk between the horns. These are Greek mercenaries, but not the same Greek mercenaries who had previously fought with the Egyptians.

As Diodorus explains, Pharnabazus had pressured Athens to recall Chabrias and the collection of mercenaries he had assembled. The mercenaries brought by Iphicrates were different Greeks and their helmets reflected this difference. Fifty years later the only Greek helmet whose appearance we know with certainty was Alexander's, and it had two horns. Ramses III shows us what Greek mercenaries looked like in the early 4th century.

Note also that "the full flame was in their front before the harbor-mouths." The attackers were using fire ships to hurl incendiaries. Egyptians were in a defensive position "and a wall of metal upon the shore surrounded them." They had anticipated this tactic. Fire ships were introduced by Assyria and are uncomfortable in a supposed 12th-century time frame.

WHERE IS THE EGYPTIAN RECORD?

For some reason, scholars do not seem to be disturbed that the significant events described by Diodorus for Nectanebo remain unrecorded in Egypt (by Conventional Chronology). There is actually an Egyptian whose name is close enough to Nectanebo (Necht-nebef) that he had been accepted as that pharaoh. However, even though all of Necht-nebef's inscriptions are vainglorious, he failed to record his war of victory over the King of Persia!

In fact, the names of Necht-nebef (and also Necht-hor-heb, assumed to be Nectanebo II) occur in the same collection of letters to Arsames, the Persian satrap in Babylon mentioned in the previous chapter. Both were Egyptian administrators under Arsames and, as the highest ranking natives, assumed as grandiose a title, and style, as they could get away with, including putting their names in cartouches. But neither claims to have confronted Artaxerxes II in battle; they were appointed to their positions in 445 and 424, respectively, under *Artaxerxes I*.

Adequately covering the evidence on Necht-nebef and Necht-hor-heb is beyond the scope of this summary work (it is addressed in *Peoples of the Sea*). However, there are many archaeological remains for these two Egyptian leaders and they were identified as Nectanebo I and Nectanebo II of the 30th dynasty simply because they are the closest sounding names, *not on the basis of any evidence*.

This reconstruction of ancient history has presented many cases of parallel events, separated by hundreds of years of conventional history, where large and small details correspond. But nowhere else does the identity approach that of Ramses III and Nectanebo I.

We are very fortunate to have Diodorus' account of the wars of Nectanebo. And Ramses III clearly states who his main opponent is: the P-R-S-TT, the exact same name as used for Persia in the Ptolomaic *Canopus Decree*. Ramses even depicts his P-R-S-TT wearing the same distinctive "feathered headdress" as is worn by the Persian guard reliefs found at Persepolis. Diodorus describes the international scene in great detail so as to make the course of events more understandable. Ramses condenses events into hieroglyphic artwork and reliefs. Taking into consideration these different approaches to recording an event, the agreement is complete.

Ramses identified specifics in the makeup of the invading forces, something Diodorus doesn't bother with. Besides the P-R-S-TT, there are Tjkr, Skls, Trs, Wss Srds, and Dnn. Keeping in mind that the name of the province for which Pharnabazus was satrap was "Those [people] of the Sea" (in Asia Minor), these *could* be the translated names: Tjkr as the *Teucrians* of Western Asia Minor, Skls as *Sagassos*, Trs as *Tarsus*, Wss as *Issos*, Srdn as *Sardis* and Dnn (people of the isles) as *Athenian* (rather than Danaans). Ramses does not name the commander of the Greeks who were recalled and then reassigned to the other side, but he clearly illustrates that shift with a change of the emblematic helmets.

Illustrations of the three battle scenes are found at the end of this chapter. In the first one you can see Egyptians allied with *both* P-R-S-TT and Greek mercenaries as they fight against Libyans. The Libyans have pointed beards, neck-length cropped hair and what appear to be braided locks hanging in front of the ears. At this time Acoris is actually pharaoh and Nectanebo is a military commander. When Nectanebo became pharaoh, as we mentioned above, he appropriated the years of Acoris, whom he considered "illigitimate."

In the second panel there are Greeks fighting with Egyptians against P-R-S-TT. Masses of dead and dying P-R-S-TT cover the lower registers. Near the oxcart on the upper right side of the illustration can be seen troops with horned helmets and a disk between the horns. Aegean mercenaries had a history of service with Egypt going back to the 19th/26th Dynasty.

In the third and final panel, the sea battle, the Egyptians on the left attack P-R-S-TT on the upper and lower right and mercenaries in the middle register. Their horned helmets have no disk. This last battle fuels the theories of Aegean "Sea Peoples" sweeping down the eastern Mediterranean to lay siege to Egypt. The graphic reality of the other two panels is simply ignored. It cannot be integrated into the theory

The recognition that Ramses III was dated wrongly was almost forced on Naville and Griffith in 1887 while they were excavating Tell el Yahudiyeh, but they resisted the evidence. Ramses' pavilion was decorated with what everyone agreed looked like Persian tiles stamped with 4th century Greek letters on the back. Artistic and epigraphic evidence agreed on a 4th century date. Griffith says of the nearby necropolis, "The general result of the excavation in the tumuli is to show that they belong to the XXth Dynasty."[11]

Yet Naville was insistent that the coffins were late, fourth century at the earliest. That they could come so close to recognizing that both were right is a testament to the strength of the a-priori idea that Ramses III must be 12th century BC. The evidence was telling them otherwise.

11. 48.

4. The Egyptians, supported by the Pereset and the Peoples of the Sea, assault the Libyans. Observe the head-gear, the small shields of the Peoples of the Sea. *From Medinet-Habu, Vol. II, Courtesy of the University of Chicago Press.*

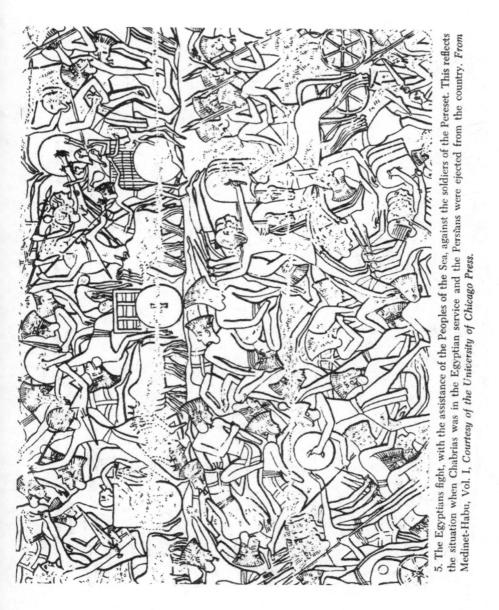

5. The Egyptians fight, with the assistance of the Peoples of the Sea, against the soldiers of the Pereset. This reflects the situation when Chabrias was in the Egyptian service and the Persians were ejected from the country. *From Medinet-Habu, Vol. I, Courtesy of the University of Chicago Press.*

7. The Egyptian fleet of Ramses III destroying the fleet of the Pereset. The Peoples of the Sea are, at this stage, allies of the Pereset. The helmets of the Peoples of the Sea have horns but not the disks between the horns. *From Medinet-Habu*, Vol. I, *Courtesy of the University of Chicago Press.*

19. SUMMARY

If any single issue raised by the Synchronized Chronology were argued in a vacuum, the strength and tradition supporting the Conventional Chronology would overwhelm it. But when viewed as a whole, it can be seen to extend and reinforce the synchronisms in all directions. Arguing the placement of Ramses II into the role of Necho is compelling when it is seen how his whole dynasty, the 19th, fits the role of the 26th. But the case is strengthened even more when the 20th dynasty fits logically and consistently into the role of the 30th.

This reconstruction covers more than 1500 years of real history, from the first movement of Hebrews into Palestine and Egypt in the early Middle Bronze Age to the end of the last native Egyptian pharaohs at the arrival of Alexander. The origin of the Conventional Chronology was examined and found to be a fragile artifice indeed, based on numerous independent assumptions, any one of which can bring down the whole.

The commitment to undertake this book was not made without considerable reservation. Experts will recognize the limitations of my research and I can only acknowledge that it is beyond my abilities to master 1500 years of history and archaeology for the entire Near East. And the nature of my writing strategy — of reviewing a broad swath of material related to a given topic and then composing the chapter, in chronological succession — held the possibility of stumbling onto a mine that could bring down the whole edifice at any point. It nearly happened at the midpoint of this project.

I had hoped to avoid the involvement of Assyria in this work as much as possible. For whatever reason, the details and chronological structure of the early Assyrian kingdom seemed uninteresting and remote to the problem of biblical chronology. Assyria is also closely interrelated with Babylon, and thus

241

entails yet another field of study. And indeed, what started out as a review of Assyria turned into a yearlong detour from Greece, Egypt and Israel.

One day I received an Internet message stating that the "Kassite" chronology of Babylon was incompatible with the Synchronized Chronology. As my research progressed, I began to realize that the Kassite problem and the reconstruction of the early Assyrian king lists both mask the very real problem that is the "Post-Kassite" period of Babylon. At some point the hiatus in archaeological remains for the Post-Kassite period throughout Mesopotamia and Elam must be addressed; but not here. Nor will this book attempt a re-evaluation of the Assyrian king lists; but both of these subjects need to be examined.

Chapter 3 of this work takes a look back into the Middle Bronze Age and sees evidence for the Hebrew sojourn in Egypt at Tell el-Dab'a. A Western Semitic population had occupied the site for a long time before leaving and being replaced by the Hyksos. Identifying the change in occupation with the Exodus is an obvious extension of the Synchronized Chronology, and this was written before *Pharaohs and Kings* appeared in the U.S. In that work, Rohl gives the briefest credit to Velikovsky for the idea and then dismisses the rest of *Ages in Chaos*. I do not wish to minimize the importance of Rohl's work, especially in furthering the challenge to Egyptian Chronology begun by Peter James. But I will leave it to the reader to decide which replacement of Conventional Chronology completes the reconstruction most satisfyingly.

In the attempt to present the Synchronized Chronology in a single volume, I have presented evidence in each chapter selected from a much larger pool of available material. By condensing and focusing the case, I hope to promote further investigation and open-minded study of the conundrums presented. Individual chapters could easily be expanded into complete works, and some of the better evidence simply required too much supporting explanation (of background, context and interrelationship) to warrant inclusion. Wherever possible the most well known and available reference works have been cited. Those who are familiar with those works may be surprised to see them used for a purpose unintended by their authors. But as mentioned above, the perspective offered by the Synchronized Chronology triggers significance that previously went unrecognized.

The whole case for the Synchronized Chronology hinges on the duplication of two pairs of dynasties from the lists of Manetho. Even those who have used the lists in their current order acknowledge the huge problems involved. For example, there are no names given for the 20th dynasty. How, then, did Ramses III wind up there even before hieroglyphs were deciphered? Why are there no remains for the 26th Dynasty at a time when Greek and Hebrew sources document the existence of powerful pharaohs?

The answer, of course, is that Manetho preserves king lists in just the way the Egyptians always did. The native pharaohs following the Hyksos are presented as a distinct whole, purged of embarrassing entries (such as Akhnaton) and non-natives. Appended to that list is the sequence of non-native pharaohs and the one assembled at Alexandria with Hellenized names. This is one of the realities of the Synchronized Chronology that looms ever larger and more obvious with time.

The other obstacle to overhauling a chronology based on Egypt is the idea that a "Sothic" dating system ever existed. No evidence that it was ever known in Egypt has been discovered. And any argument for use of the Sothic period benchmarked at the date given by Censorinus of 139 AD must explain why it escaped the attention of Claudius Ptolomy, the most renowned astronomical author of ancient times, whose books date from that time.

Eliminating the duplicated dynasties from Egypt is the only means of addressing irreconcilable problems of Greek and Hebrew history. Bringing the 18th dynasty from the 16th-14th centuries down to the 11th-9th corrects the parallel problems that plague the study of other cultures where the dating has been dependent on the Egyptian chronology. Those problems are recognized as having a common origin. The imaginary episode of the Greek Dark Age must be seen as having been caused by the same error that denies the Hebrews a Bronze Age Empire, and crediting it to none other than the Canaanites.

A review of the synchronisms of this proposed chronology begins all the way back in the time of Abraham, which should be placed about at the end of MB I or early MB IIA. The movement of Amorites in MB I shows in a new occupational assemblage in Palestine. There are many burials, but few domestic structures, suggesting a lifestyle emphasizing tents, just like that which has been declared for the early Assyrian kings. Egyptian texts indicate a social structure of chieftains in peaceful coexistence, in agreement with Genesis.

Abraham built an altar outside Shechem and Jacob purchased the "field" when he built his altar there. The "Temenos" or sacred area of Shechem was outside the limits of the MB IIA city. If this is not the place of Jacob's altar, it is at least not in disagreement. By MB IIC, the sacred area was within the city walls and was occupied by a large "Migdol" temple tower. The destruction of this temple and the following occupational gap are in perfect agreement with the story of Abimelech, in Judges, Chapter 9. By contrast, the temple that was built on the same site in Late Bronze Age times and that, by Conventional Chronology, would be Abimelech's target, does not fit. The structure is much smaller.

Placing the Exodus contemporary with the events leading to the takeover of Egypt by the Hyksos is the next important synchronism. It calls for comparison of the non-native populations of Egypt before and after that date. Beitak's work at Tel el-Dab'a reveals a long-standing Semitic population growing into a large community. The end of those people involved mass graves, destruction and abandonment followed by a re-occupation by Hyksos. David Rohl presents a convincing case for Tell el-Dab'a being a Hebrew community, in complete agreement with the Synchronized Chronology.

The Hebrews first encounter, following the Exodus, was with the Amalekites heading the other way. They dominated the region from southern Judah to Egypt, throughout the time of the Judges. They prevented the Hebrews from entering the Promised Land from the south. An eastern detour around Moab was required in order to approach Canaan from north of the Amalekites. The Amalekites are the same Arabs who were called Amu by the Egyptians and are known to history as the Hyksos. The archaeological record of the Hyksos extended from Lower Egypt into Palestine south of Judah.

Cities throughout Palestine are fortified for the first time toward the end of MB IIA. This was the time of the conquest and early Judges and corresponds to the Hyksos era. Conventional Chronology credits the high culture and artistic levels of Palestine in MB IIB-C to Canaanites; in fact, this review shows it was the Hebrews.

True alphabetic writing can be traced back to the earliest form, known as "Proto-Sinaitic," found in the vicinity of the El Khadem turquoise mines in the Sinai. By Conventional Chronology it is impossible to identify this with the Hebrews, but the Synchronized Chronology reveals that they are at least likely to be the source.

During the long period of the Judges (MB IIB-C), the Old Testament shows a remarkable absence of Egyptian involvement in Palestine. Instead, there is the ever present threat of Amalekites and Philistines. Conventional Chronology places the era of the Judges alongside the 19th and 20th dynasties. The extensive international engagements of the pharaohs of those dynasties, as understood by the conventional reading of the historical record, cannot be reconciled with the apparent silence in scripture.

The Theban kings who founded the mighty 18th dynasty finally drove the Hyksos out of Egypt. Meanwhile, Saul was defeating the Amalekites from Havilah to the "Brook of Egypt" (the Wadi El Arish), which was the location of the Hyksos capital, Avaris (or Auaris). The 18th dynasty affords large quantities of written material to compare with the Chronicles of the Kings of the Old Testament. For generation after generation throughout the Theban dynasty, interactions with the Hebrew kings are depicted on both sides in remarkable agreement. David and Solomon remained on good terms with the early pharaohs of the dynasty, and Solomon even had an Egyptian princess for a wife. The only female to reign in Egypt, Queen Hatshepsut, portrays her visit to "God's Land" as the most prominent event of her reign. She can only be Queen Sheba (a personal name), whom Josephus says was queen of Egypt and Ethiopia.

Hatshepsut's young successor, Thutmose III, is depicted on her reliefs in a religious offering after returning from the trip with his aunt (?). He was actually filled with resentment for her, considered her illegitimate, and defaced her monuments after her reign. He also counted the years of her reign as part of his own. More importantly, he had seen the riches of "God's Land" and returned as a conqueror. We know him in scripture as Shishak. The treasures he removed from the temple at Jerusalem are depicted on a wall of the temple at Karnak.

The Conventional Chronology has the Libyan pharaoh Shoshenq I playing that role. The Libyan dynasty has to be stretched back about 100 years to make the fit, against all the archaeological evidence. And none of the cities he claims to have subdued in Palestine are in Judah — a strange situation for the argument that Shoshenq is Shishak. This is the only synchronism offered by the Conventional Chronology for hundreds of years of history for Egypt and Israel as neighbors, and it is clearly wrong.

The next Theban Pharaoh, Amenhotep II, led his last and disastrous campaign into southern Palestine fairly early in his reign. The Amenhoteps were the Ethiopian connection of the 18th dynasty and this pharaoh would be Zerah the Ethiopian, whose huge forces were defeated by King Asa of Jerusalem at Moresheth Gath. The Egyptian records place the battle at "the arm (ford) of Arseth," not far from Egypt. In Hebrew it is the *waters* (Mor) of *Reshet*. Another generation reveals yet another synchronism to enrich the history of both countries.

Jehosaphat, a king who inspired greatness in Jerusalem, succeeded Asa. Meanwhile, Israel had a bloody turnover of leaders with Omri finally taking power. Although his reign was short, and his mention in scripture brief, his name was to be attached to Israel by Assyria, where it was referred to as the *House of Omri*.

By great good fortune, this era has a wealth of historical material provided by Egypt: the Tell el-Amarna Letters. This diplomatic archive preserves a large collection of letters from Ahab, son of Omri, and several from Jehosaphat, not to mention letters from three of Jehosephat's military commanders. Letters from other important figures in the Old Testament, such as Ben Hadad and Hazael, are likewise included. With the exception of kings' personal names (which we don't know for many Hebrew kings), the cast of characters and events in common between the letters and scripture is astonishing.

The letters illuminate the complicated relationship of Israel with Damascus and Moab. The siege, drought and famine dominate many letters.

Even the resulting battle of the "breadbasket" area of Rammoth Gilead figures in the tablets. And finally, the exile of Ahab to Phoenicia resolves one of the long standing conflicts in scripture — whether Ahab died at the battle. He didn't, but there were rumors that he did.

Likewise, the growing threat to the Jerusalem of Jehosaphat from the renegade tribes of the east (Habiru in the tablets) has a surprise ending that is not preserved in the letters. The prayers of the city are rewarded when the threatening tribes destroy each other!

The letters provide as much insight into the politics behind Chronicles and Kings as the scriptures provide into the international scene at the close of the 18th dynasty. Akhnaton was far too deeply immersed in his vain religious obsession to care that he was losing everything gained by generations of Amenhoteps and Thutmsosids. The tragic (or, rather, pathetic) life and family of this pharaoh is highlighted in the most interesting way by the trilogy of Greek plays about Oedipus. The details of the closing years of the 18th dynasty can be greatly enhanced by the study of the plays.

Restoring the 18th dynasty to its proper time solves another of the nagging problems to Conventional Chronology, the enormous artistic and cultural differences between the 18th and 19th dynasties. These differences confound the notion that the dynasties were successive. Manetho's native king list is responsible for this. The 18th dynasty actually fell to Libya, undoubtedly as the culmination of a situation that was brewing during the reign of Akhnaton. Osorkons and Shoshenqs ruled Egypt for the next 140 or so years.

Assyria was beginning its rise to international power already in the time of Ahab and Jehosaphat. Shalmaneser III needed access to the Mediterranean and that brought him into contact with Israel. The coalition of Aramean city-states faced down Shalmaneser at first, but Assyria could not be withstood forever. The consequences of Shalmaneser's impact on Phoenicia are incompletely preserved in Assyrian records, but they are dramatically told in the Amarna letters. The desperate requests for help from Egypt went unanswered, so the king of Tyre loaded up his ships with all his people and left, to (almost certainly) Carthage.

At about the same time, the lexicographer-king of Ugarit, *Nikdem*, was expelled along with Ionians and other foreigners. Placed not in the 14th but rather the 9th century BC this raises the possibility that his city of refuge was Thebes, in Greece. Nikdem would be *Cadmus*, the Phoenician who adapted the Hebrew alphabet to Greek. In the Synchronized Chronology the time, place of origin, destination, profession and even name provide a compelling identity.

Among the texts found at Ugarit were some in alphabetic Phoenician (Hebrew) written in cuneiform, creating another dilemma for 14th century dating — but not for 9th. Many of those texts use the language and idioms of contemporary 9th century BC scripture.

Moving the 18th dynasty to its correct time has profound effects on the archaeology throughout the Mediterranean and Near East. So many sites are directly or indirectly (through Mycenaean pottery) dated by the 18th dynasty that a widespread cross-linking of regions has evolved. And in every one of these areas a problematic "Dark Age" exists.

Italy in the west has the Villanovan (Etruscan) culture arriving (c. 750 BC) at various sites and leaving their remains stratified directly above Apennine culture layers dated by Mycenaean remains to 1300 BC and before. There is even a little Mycenaean mixed into the early Villanovan. Reinforcing the dilemma is the absence of any sterile layers in between. Italy is one of the clearest examples of the fiction that is the Dark Age.

Troy is one of the sites excavated with glorious abandon by the famous Schliemann before modern techniques were developed. Fortunately, enough of the site remained undisturbed, leaving an untainted record for more modern recovery. Being strongly dated by good Mycenaean pottery, the Dark Age problem of Troy is profound. The latest Mycenaean level, VIIb, contains anomalous early Geometric pottery, of the 8th century at the earliest. The Geometric pottery is typical of the following level VIII. There is at least one residence that was occupied across the transition between these two levels. By Conventional Chronology no possible explanation can be made for this, and none has.

Greek scholars of the 19th and early 20th century refused to accept a gap between Mycenaean and Archaic Greece. It was forced on them by the juggernaut of Egyptian Chronology. An entire field of study on the Dark Age arose. From the start it was realized that the gap was glaringly large, so efforts to minimize the problem were made. The beginning and end were artificially brought closer together. First, the beginning was stretched to include a "Sub-Mycenaean" period that could rationally be brought into the time of Ramses III and his battles against the "Sea Peoples." It allows viewing the Dorian invasion/ Mycenaean breakdown in an international context (i.e. Pelasgian = Philistine).

The problems with this popular theory are many. There is an absence of evidence linking Ramses III to any Mycenaean context. A Dorian invasion actually occurred, but in the 8th century BC. And the Aegean Sea Peoples were actually mercenaries for the Persians, not for the Philistines. It is amazing how such an elaborate theory can evolve with so little support from actual Greek evidence.

The Dorian invasion was a major factor in Greek history. Traditionally dated two generations after the Trojan War, the invasion did occur, but not in the 12th century. Archaeological and linguistic evidence agree. Greeks themselves knew of no Dark Age separating their history from Mycenaea. Scholars have determined that the Greeks' own estimates for early events were greatly exaggerated. The further back, the greater the error. So why is the traditional Greek date for the Trojan War never questioned?

The Trojan War can no more be pushed back to 1200 BC than Pheidon can be placed 895 (as preserved on the Parian Marble, the oldest surviving Greek inscription of the 5th century BC). Since all evidence would place Pheidon c. 600 BC, where does that leave the Greek estimate for the Trojan War? Conveniently, the greatly exaggerated date is accepted because it agrees with the prevailing view of Egypt. *No one dares raise an objection to the Greek estimate.* Where else could they place it?

Dark Age Studies have another problem with the waves of colonization triggered by the Dorian takeover of the Peloponnesians. The colonies show an uncomfortably short transition from Mycenaean to Geometric remains. The situation illuminated by Italy is mirrored all along the Aegean coast of Anatolia.

Back in Greece, the Dorians of Argos showed their strength and confidence by constructing their famous temple, the Heraeum, in the manner of their Mycenaean ancestors. With no rehearsal, they managed to build using stones weighing as much as boxcars. It so typified Mycenaean works that it was originally mis-dated by 500 years. The Conventional Chronology of Dark Age Studies must assume that the building tradition survived those 500 years without anyone practicing it in the interim.

At least the Greek Dark Age has not denied Greeks their history, as is the case for the Hebrews. All of the archaeological remains of the Hebrews from the time of the Egyptian sojourn to the rise of Assyria are credited to Canaanites. Even a site such as Samaria, excavated with exquisite care, has resulted in levels of rude disagreement unmatched anywhere else in the world. The archaeologist's (Kenyon's) methods were universally lauded and were even used to train new generations of students. Yet her results were attacked and her competence called into question. This is nothing out of the ordinary for biblical archaeology (if I can still use that term), where passions run high. Hopefully, the reexamination of Egyptian Chronology initiated by James and Rohl will lead to a new era in biblical archaeology.

The Synchronized Chronology offers a solution to the multiple problems of Hittite archaeology. The monumental remains of the "Hittite Empire" stand alone, in a sort of time warp, representing both the beginning and end of the evolutionary sequence. Artistically, they fit the very end of the Assyrian sequence. Chronologically they are forced back to the 14th and 13th century by the cross dating to Ramses II. Thus, they are caught in limbo. Almost a century has passed since this logical absurdity began. Except for Velikovsky, it has remained unchallenged. Peter James cannot fix the problem by reducing the gap by two or three hundred years; another three hundred years remain unaccounted for!

The Hittite Empire, dated to the end of the Assyrian Empire (where it belongs), reveals itself as the Chaldean Empire. The mystery of the missing records of the Neo-Babylonian Empire is also solved. They were kept in the Chaldean capital, Boghazkoi. The region known as the Hatti Lands was homeland of the Chaldeans before, during and after the time of the Hittites. The Chaldean Empire can be recognized as the end stage of "Hittite" evolution.

The famous "Battle of Kadesh" fought by Ramses II against Hattusilis agrees in great detail with the Battle of Carchemish between the Pharaoh Necho and Nebuchadnezzar. The 19th (Tanitic) dynasty takes its rightful place as the 26th (Saitic) dynasty. The missing records, monuments and city of the imaginary Saitic dynasty cease to be a problem. Seti, Ramses II and Merneptah are the alter egos of Psammetich, Necho and Apries.

The 19th/26th dynasty was not succeeded by the 20th; it fell to Cambyses the Persian. When the Hebrews were allowed to return to Jerusalem from Babylon, they were permitted a theocratic form of government. Egypt, likewise, was allowed to have native High Priests pretending to be real pharaohs. This was the enigmatic 21st dynasty. The last of the priest kings salvaged the remains of many great pharaohs of the past, and hid them in a place near Thebes were they lay until found in modern times.

Egypt had one last great native pharaoh who withstood the combined attack of Persia, its allies and mercenaries. But Nectanebo of the 30th dynasty suffered the same fate as Necho of the 26th. His records and monuments are credited to a ghost-like forerunner, Ramses III.

The Synchronized Chronology covers over 1500 years of history between Egypt and Israel using the chronology of the Old Testament, with a little help from Greece. Virtually every generation finds compelling agreement. The Conventional Chronology offers "Shoshenq as Shishak," a connection contradicted by every bit of actual evidence. Which version deserves the title of "history"?

BIBLIOGRAPHY

Abbreviations

ARE	*Ancient Records of Egypt.* Breasted, James Henry
CAH	*Cambridge Ancient History* 2nd. Ed.
ARAB	*Ancient Records of Assyria and Babylonia*, Luckinbill, Daniel David.
AJ	*Antiquities of the Jews.* Josephus
V.1	*Ages in Chaos*, Velikovsky, Immanuel
V.2	*Oedipus and Akhnaton*, Velikovsky, Immanuel
V.3	*Peoples of the Sea*, Velikovsky, Immanuel
V.4	*Ramses II and His Time*, Velikovsky, Immanuel

Adams, William Y. (1977). *Nubia Corridor to Africa.* Princeton, N. J.: Princeton University Press.

Akurgal, Ekrem. (1973). *Ancient Civilizations and Ruins of Turkey.* Ankara: Turk Tarih Kurumu Basimevi.

Albright, William Foxwell, (reprinted 1971). *The Archaeology of Palestine.* Glouchester, Mass.: Peter Smith Publishers, Inc.

Andrews, A. (reprint 1963). *The Greek Tyrants.* New York: Harper & Row, Publishers.

Atlas of Ancient & Classical Geography. (reprint 1925). Everyman's Library. New York: E. P. Dutton & Co.

Bean, George E. (1966). *Aegean Turkey an Archaeological Guide.* New York: Frederick A. Praeger.

Beaulieu, Paul-Alain. (1989). *The Reign of Nabonidus King of Babylon 556-539 B.C.* New Haven: Yale University Press.

Bernal, Martin. (1987). *Black Athena Vol. I.* New Brunswick, New Jersey: Rutgers University Press.

Biblical Archaeology. (1974). (Ed. Shalom M. Paul and William G. Dever). New York: Quadrangle/The New York Times Book Co.

Bierbrier, Morris. (1984). *The Tomb-Builders of the Pharoahs.* New York: Charles Scribner's Sons.

Bietak, Manfred. (1966). *Avaris, the Capital of the Hyksos.* London: British Museum Press.

Bimson, John J. (1981). *Redating the Exodus and Conquest.* Sheffield: The Almond Press.

Biran, Avraham. (1994). *Biblical Dan.* Jerusalem: Israel Exploration Society.

Blegen, Carl W. (reprint 1995). *Troy and the Trojans.* New York: Barnes and Noble Books.

Boardman, John. (1964). *The Greeks Overseas.* Baltimore, Maryland: Penguin Books.

Breasted, James Henry, PhD. (1951). *A History of Egypt.* New York: Charles Scribner's Sons.

Breasted, James Henry, PhD. (1988). *Ancient Records of Egypt.* (4 Vols) London. Histories and Mysteries of Man.

Brinkman, J. A. (1968). *A Political History of Post-Kassite Babylonia.* Roma: Pontificum Institutum Biblicum.

Brinkman, J. A. (1984). *Prelude to Empire, Babylonian Society and Politics, 747-626 B.C.* Philadelphia: Occasional Publications of the Babylonian Fund, 7.

Bryce, Trevor. (1998). *The Kingdom of the Hittites.* New York. Oxford University Press.

The Cambridge History of Iran. (1985). Cambridge University Press.

Chahin, M. (1987). *The Kindgom of Armenia.* New York: Dorset Press.

Childe, V. Gordon. (reprint 1987). *The Aryans.* New York: Dorset Press.

The Coming of the Age of Iron. Wertime, T. A. and Muhly, J. D. (Eds.). New Haven: Yale University Press

Davies, Graham I. (1986). *Megiddo.* Grand Rapids, Michigan: William B. Eerdmans Publishing.

Desborough, V. R. d'A. (1972) *The Greek Dark Ages.* N. Y.: St. Martins Press.

Dever, William G. (2001) *What Did the Hebrew Writers Know and When Did They Know It.* Cambridge, U.K. / Grand Rapids, Michigan: William B. Eerdmans Publishing.

Diodorus, *The History.* (Jones, Horace Leonard, trans.) Loeb Classical Library. Harvard University Press.

Dornemann, Rudolph H. (1981). *Excavations at Ras Shamra and Their Place in the Current Archaeological Picture of Ancient Syria.* Young, Gordon Douglas. (Ed.) (1981). *Ugarit in Retrospective.* Winona Lake, Indiana: Eisenbrauns.

Drews, Robert. (1988). *The Coming of the Greeks.* Princeton, New Jersey: Princeton University Press.

Drews, Robert. (1993). *The End of the Bronze Age.* Princeton, New Jersey: Princeton University Press.

Ehrich, Robert W. (Ed. 1965). *Chronologies in Old World Archaeology.* Chicago: The University of Chicago Press.

Finley, M. I. (reprint 1979). *The World of Odysseus.* Penguin Books.

Fornara, Charles W. (Ed. & trans.). (reprint 1983). *Archaic Times to the end of the Peloponnesian War (Translated Documents of Greece and Rome).* Cambridge: Cambridge University Press.

Forrest, W. G. (1968). *A History of Sparta 950-192 B.C.* New York: W. W. Norton & Company.

Forsdyke, John. (1964). *Greece Before Homer.* New York: W. W. Norton & Company, Inc.

Frame, Grant. (1992). *Babylonia 689-627 B.C. A Political History.* Istanbul: Nederlands Historisch-Archaeologish Institute.

Frame, Grant. (1995). *Rulers of Babylonia From the Second Dynasty of Isin to the End of Assyrian Domination (1157-612 BC).* University of Toronto Press

Galil, Gershon. (1996). *The Chronology of the Kings of Israel and Judah.* New York: E. J. Brill.

Gardiner, Sir Alan. (1961). *Egypt of the Pharaohs.* London: Oxford University Press.

Glueck, Nelson. (1959). *Rivers in the Desert.* New York: Farrar, Straus and Cudahy.

Grant, Michael. (1980). *The Etruscans.* New York: Charles Scribner's Sons.

Gurney, O. R. (reprint 1966). *The Hittites.*. Baltimore, Maryland: Penguin Books.

Harden, Donald. (1963). *The Phoenicians.* New York: Frederick A. Praeger.

Harper, Robert Francis. (1904). *Assyrian and Babylonian Literature.* New York: D. Appleton and Company.

Heaton, E. W. (1968). *The Hebrew Kingdoms.* London: Oxford University Press.

Herodotus. (trans. David Green 1987). *The History.* Chicago: The University of Chicago Press.

Hogarth, David George. (1924). *Kings of the Hittites (The Schweich Lectures).* London: British Academy.

Hopper, R. J. (1976). *The Early Greeks.* New York: Barnes & Noble Books.

Hyde, Walter Woodburn. (1947). *Ancient Greek Mariners.* New York: Oxford University Press.

James, Peter. (1993). *Centuries of Darkness.* New Brunswick, New Jersey: Rutgers University Press.

Karageorghis, Vassos. (1982). *Cyprus from the Stone Age to the Romans.* London: Thames and Hudson.

Katzenstein, H. Jacob. (1997). *The History of Tyre.* Ben Gurion Universiry of the Negev Press

Kelly, Thomas. (1976). *A History of Argos to 500 B.C.* Minneapolis: University of Minnesota Press.

Kenyon, Kathleen M. (1957). *Digging Up Jericho.* New York: Frederick A. Praeger.

Kenyon, Kathleen (1971). *Royal Cities of the Old Testament.* New York: Schocken Books.

Kitchen, K. A. (1962). *Suppiluliuma and the Amarna Pharoahs.* Liverpool University Press.

Luckinbill, Daniel David. (reprint 1989). *Ancient Records of Assyria and Babylonia.* London: Histories & Mysteries of Man Ltd.

Macqueen, James G. (1965). *Babylon.* New York: Frederick A. Praeger.

Manetho. (trans. W. G. Waddell). (reprint 1971). Cambridge, Massachusetts: Harvard University Press. Loeb Classical Library.

Maspero, G. (1902) (trans. Amelia B. Edwards.). *Manual of Egyptian Archaeology.* Covent Garden, W.C: H. Grevel and Co.

Maspero, G. *History of Egypt, Chaldea, Syria, Babylonia and Assyria.* London: The Grolier Society.

Mazar, Amahai. (1990). *Archaeology of the Land of the Bible 10,000-586 B.C.E.* New York: Doubleday.

Mercer, Samuel A. B. (Ed.). (1939). *The Tell El-Amarna Letters.* Toronto: The Macmillan Company of Canada Limited.

Merrill, Eugene H. (1966). *An Historical Survey of the Old Testament.* Phillipsburg, New Jersey: Prespyterian and Reformed Publishing Company.

Moran, William. (Ed. & Trans.). (1992). *The Amarna Letters.* Baltimore: The Johns Hopkins University Press.

Olmstead. A. T. (reprint 1959). *History of the Persian Empire.* Chicago: The University of Chicago Press.

Osborne, Robin. (1996). *Greece in the Making, 1200-479 BC.* London and New York: Routledge.

Page, Denys. (1963). *History and the Homeric Iliad.* Berkeley and Los Angeles. Universiry of California Press.

Petrie, W. A. Flanders. (1898). *Syria and Egypt >From the Tell El Amarna Letters.* London: Methuen & Co.

Pfeiffer, Charles F. (revised 1979). *Baker's Bible Atlas.* Grand Rapids, Michigan: Baker Book House.

Pitard, Wayne T. (1987). *Ancient Damascus.* Winona Lake, Indiana: Eisenbrauns.

Raschke, Wendy J. (1988). *The Archaeology of the Olympics.* The University of Wisconsin Press.

Redford, Donald B. (1992). *Egypt, Canaan, and Israel in Ancient Times.* Princeton, New Jersey: Princeton University Press.

Robinson, George Livingston. (1930). *The Sarcophagus of an Ancient Civilization. Petra, Edom and the Edomites.* New York: the MacMillan Company.

Roebuck, Carl. (reprint 1984). *Ionian Trade and Colonization.* Chicago: Ares Publishers, Inc.

Rohl, David M. (1995). *Pharaohs and Kings a Biblical Quest.* New York: Crown Publishers, Inc.

Rowley, H. H. (1950). *From Joseph to Joshua.* London: Oxford University Press.

Saggs, H. W. F. (1984). *The Might That Was Assyria.* London: Sidgwick & Jackson.

Sandars, N. K. (1978). *The Sea Peoples.* London: Thames and Hudson.

Schaeffer, Claude F. A. (1939). *The Cuneiform Texts of Ras Shamra-Ugarit.* London: Oxford University Press.

Sealey, Raphael. (1976). *A History of the Greek City States ca. 700-338 B.C.* Berkeley: University of California Press.

Seventh Memoir of the Egypt Exploration Fund. (1890). Naville, Edouard. *Mound of the Jew and the City of Onias.* Griffith, F. Ll. *The Antiquities of Tell el Yahudiyeh.* London: Messrs. Kegan Paul, Trench, Trubner & Co.

Shanks, Hershel. (Ed.) *Recent Archaeology in the Land of Israel.* Wash., D. C.: Biblical Archaeology Society.

Sparks, Brian A. (reprint 1994). *Greek Pottery an Introduction.* Manchester: Manchester University Press.

Starr, Chester G. (1977). *The Economic and Social Growth of Early Greece.* New York: Oxford University Press.

Starr, Chester G. (reprint 1991). *The Origins of Greek Civilization.* New York: W. W. Norton & Company.

Strabo. *The Geography.* (Jones, Horace Leonard, trans.) Loeb Classical Library. Harvard University Press.

Tappy, Ron E. (1992). *The Archaeology of Israelite Samaria.* Atlanta, Georgia: Scholars Press.

Taylor, Isaac. (1910). *The Origin of the Aryans.* New York: Charles Scribner's Sons.

Thomson, George. (1949). *The Prehistoric Aegean.* New York: International Publishers.

Tubb, Jonathan N. (Ed.). (1985). *Palestine in the Bronze and Iron Ages, Papers in Honour of Olga Tufnell.* London: Institute of Archaeology.

Velikovsky, Immanuel (1952) *Ages in Chaos,* Doubleday & Company, Inc. Garden City, NY.

Velikovsky, Immanuel (1960) *Oedipus and Akhnaton,* Doubleday & Company, Inc. Garden City, NY.

Velikovsky, Immanuel (1977) *Peoples of the Sea,* Doubleday & Company, Inc. Garden City, NY.

Velikovsky, Immanuel (1978) *Ramses II and His Time,* Doubleday & Company, Inc. Garden City, NY.

Vieyra, Maurice. (1955). *Hittite Art 2300-750 B.C.* London: Alec Tiranti Ltd.

Whiston, William. (trans. 1960). *Josephus Complete Works.* Grand Rapids, Michigan: Kregel Publications.

Wiseman, D. J. (1956). *Chronicles of the Chaldean Kings (626-556 B.C.) in the British Museum.* London: British Museum Publications, Ltd.

Wiseman, D. J. (1983). *Nebuchadrezzar and Babylon.* New York: Oxford University Press.

Wright, G. Ernest. (1965). *Schechem.* New York: McGraw-Hill.

Wolf, Herbert Martin. (1967). *The Apology of Hattusis Compared With Other Political Self-justifications of the Ancient Near East.* Brandeis University.

Woodhead, A. G. (1962). *The Greeks in the West.* New York: Frederick A. Praeger.

Wooley, Sir Leonard. (1953). *A Forgotten Kingdon.* Baltimore, Maryland: Penguin Books.

Yadin, Yigael. (1975). *Hazor.* New York: Random House.